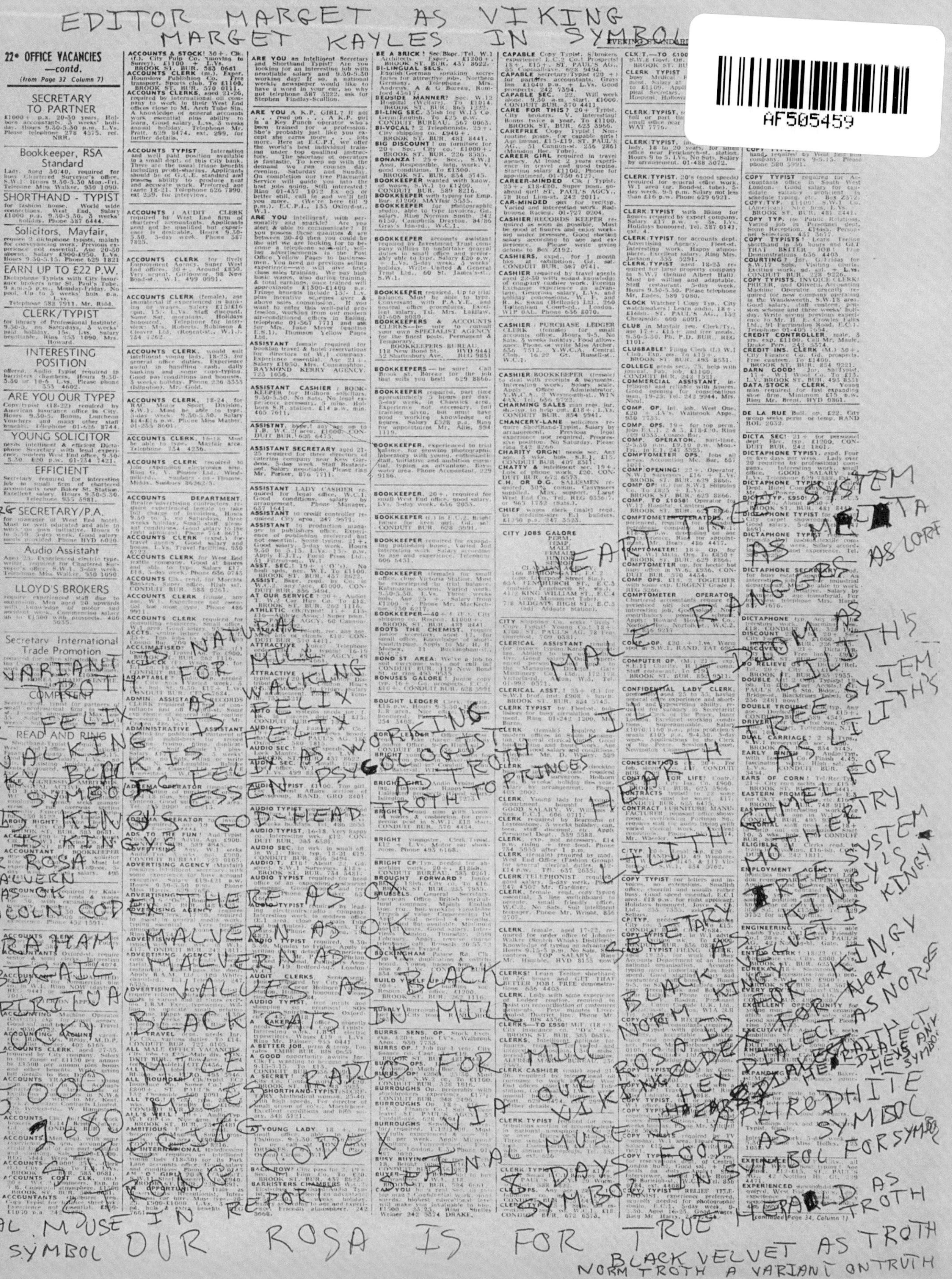

22• OFFICE VACANCIES
—contd.
(from Page 32 Column 7)

EVENING STANDARD

Luke Fowler

Kunsthalle Zürich, Zurich
Serpentine Gallery, London

jrp|ringier

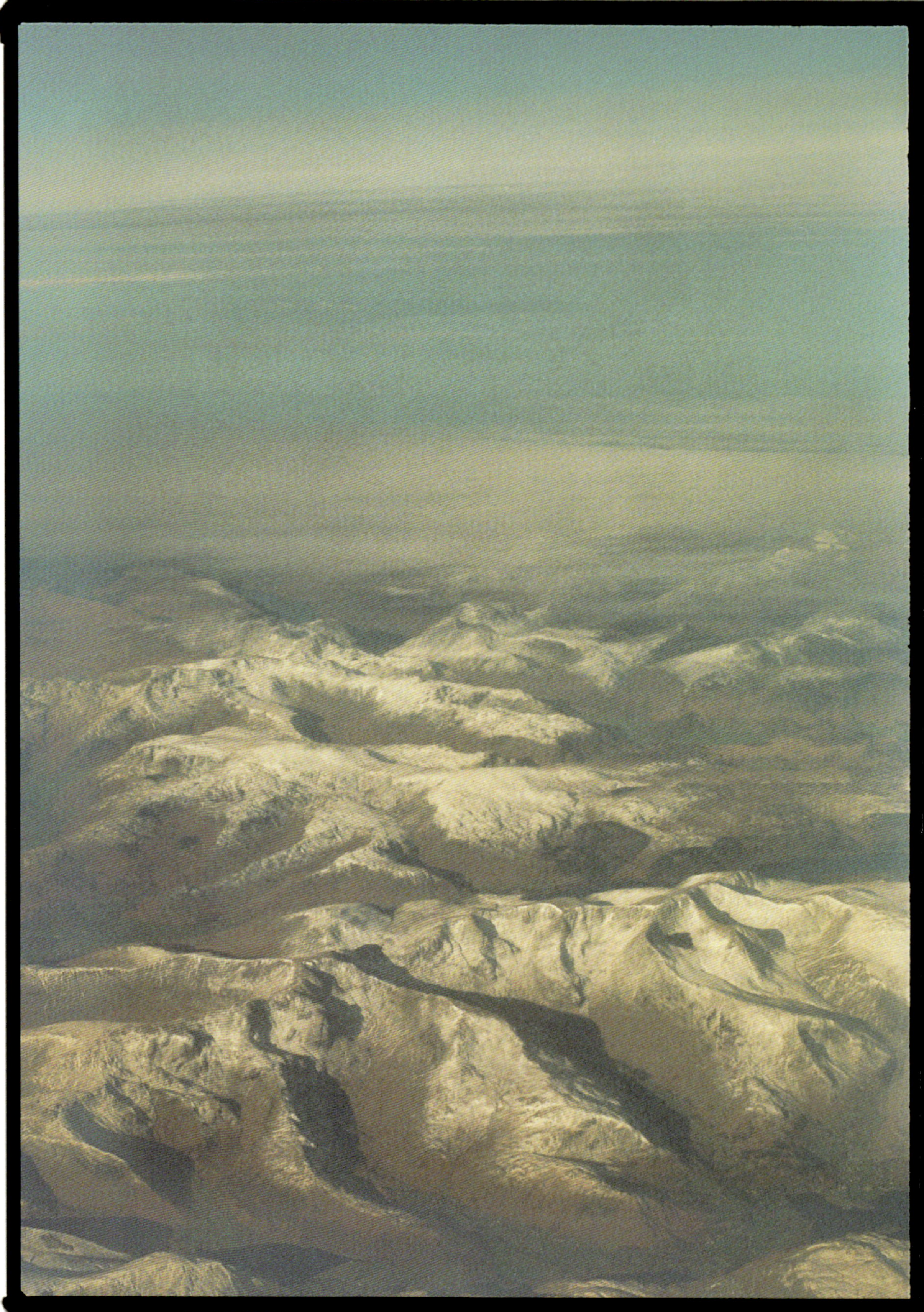

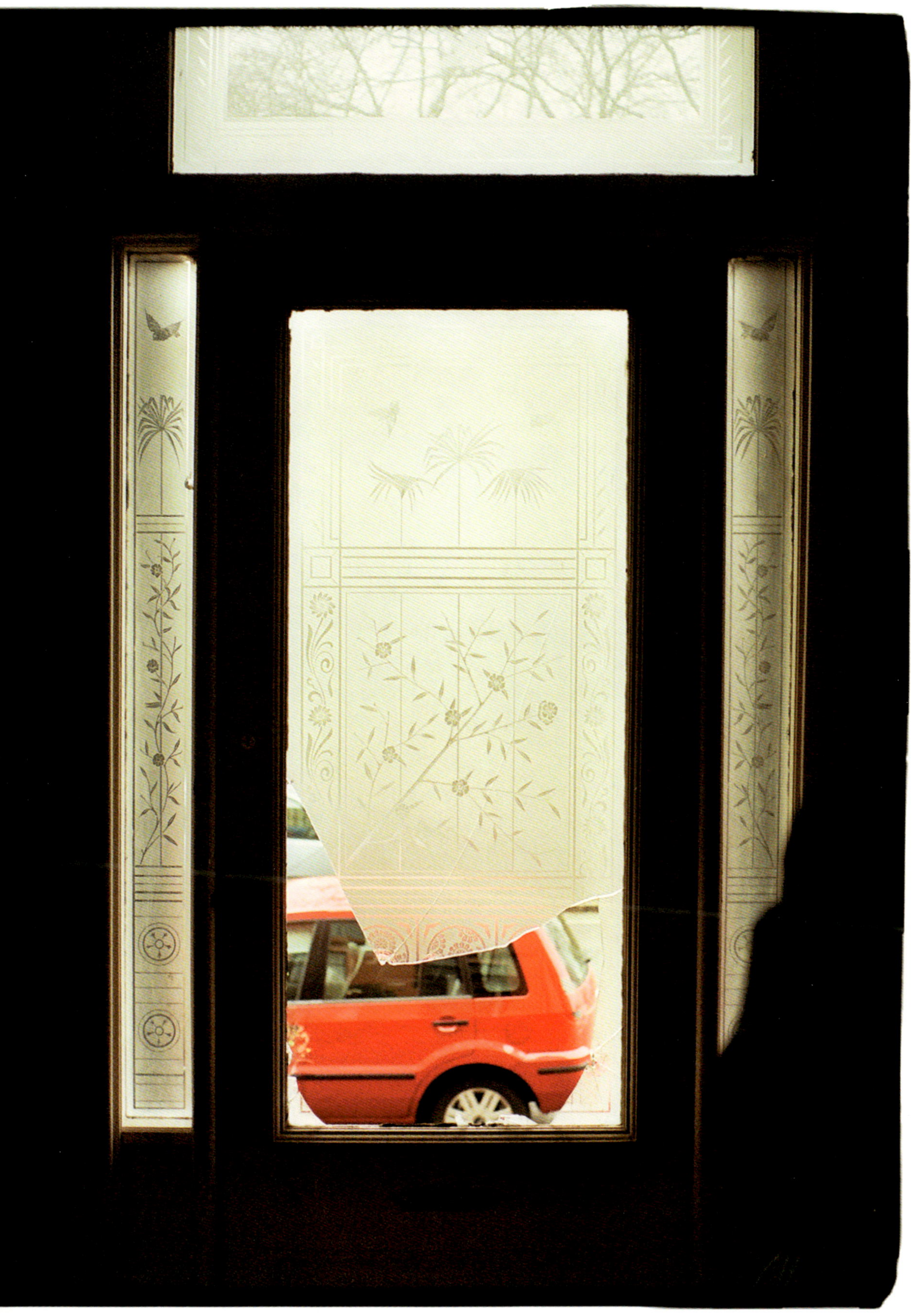

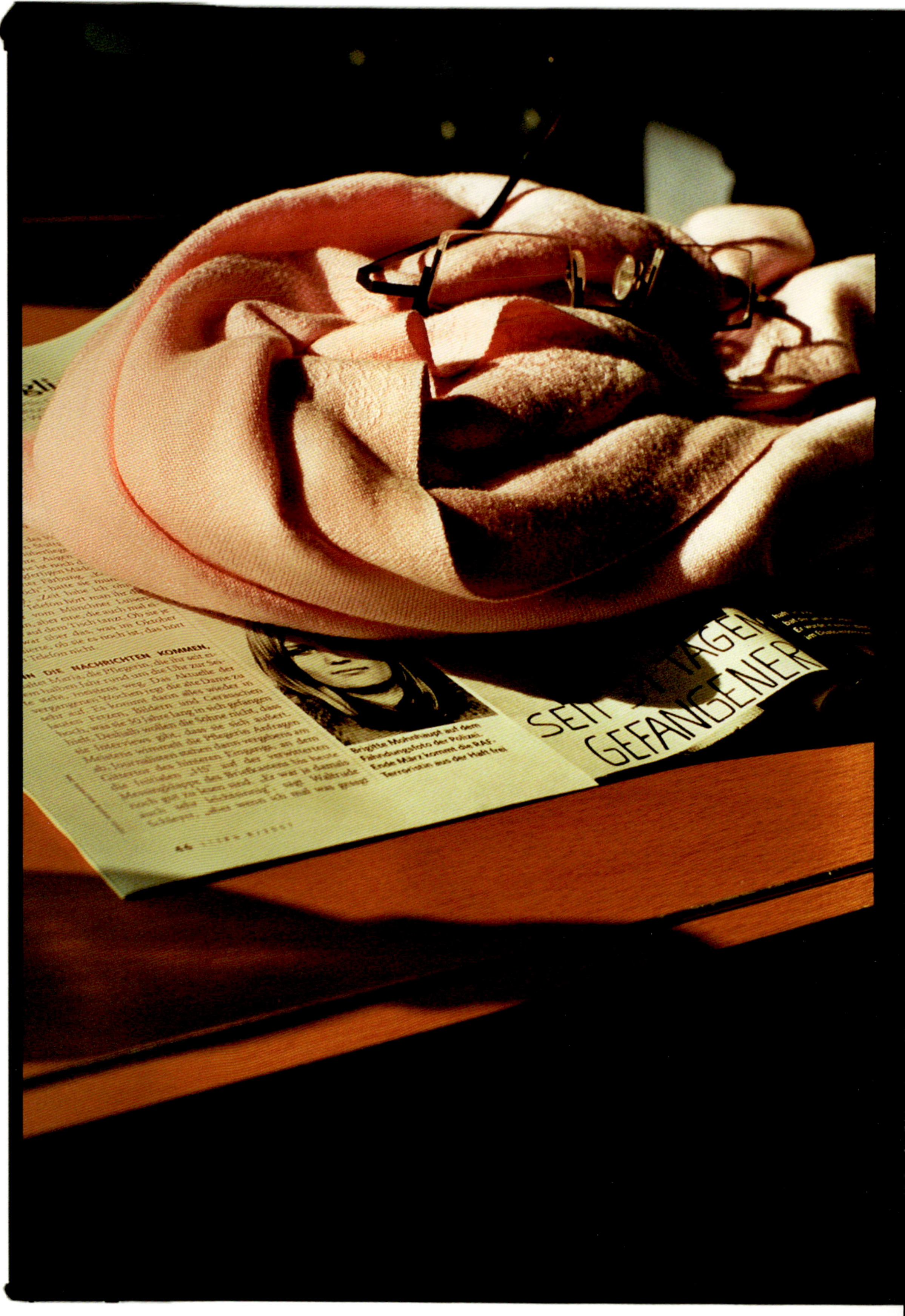

GEFANGENEN

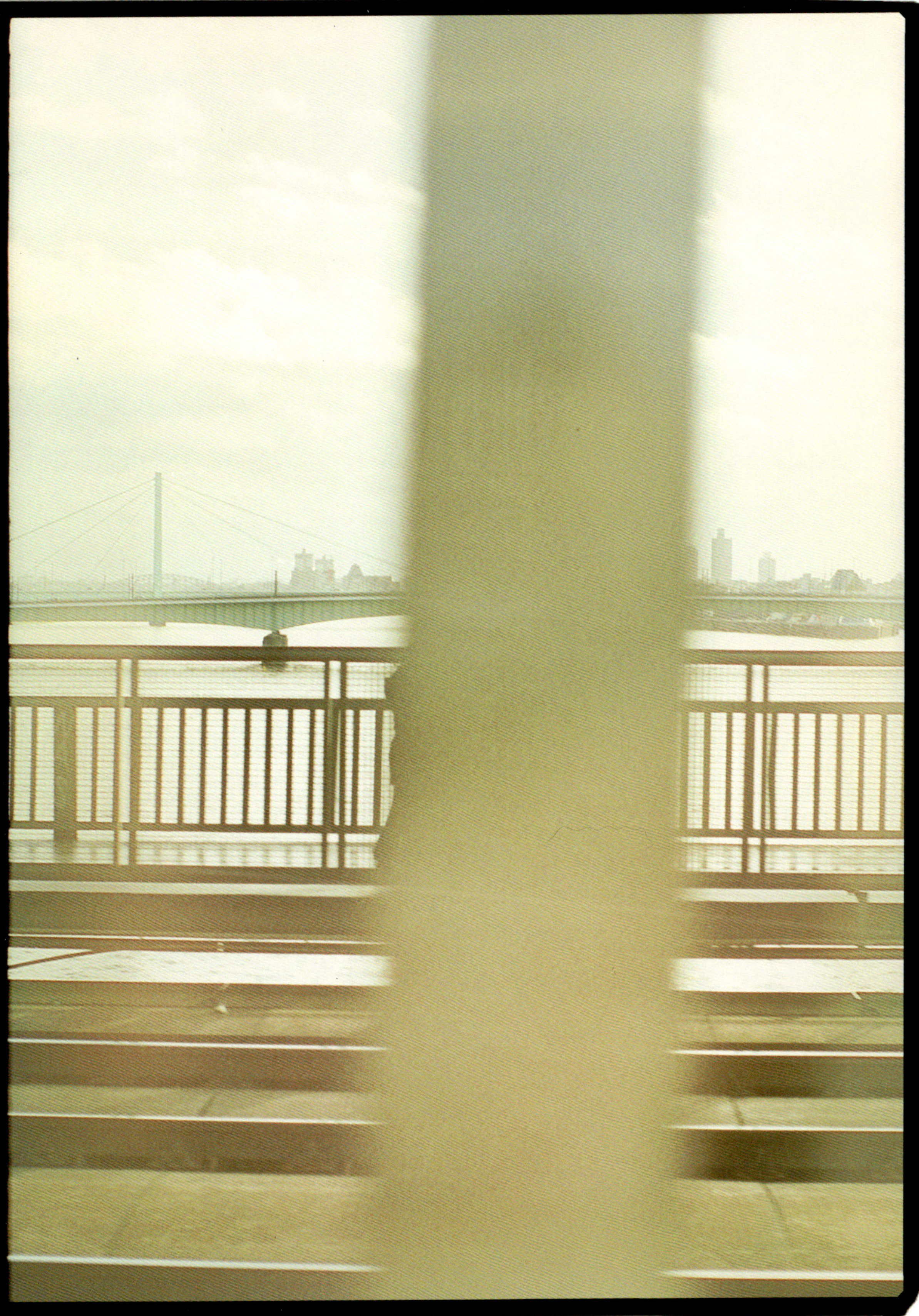

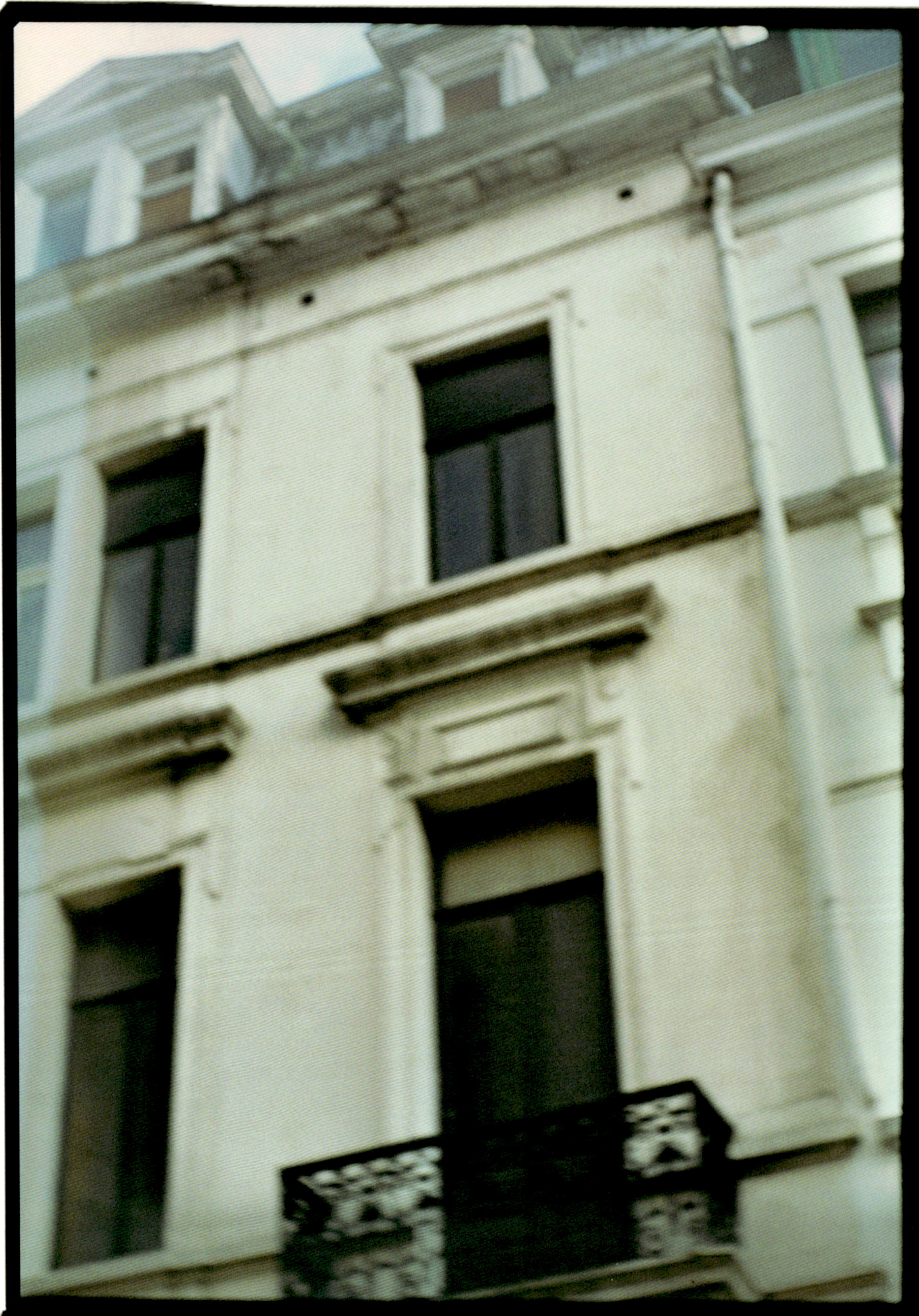

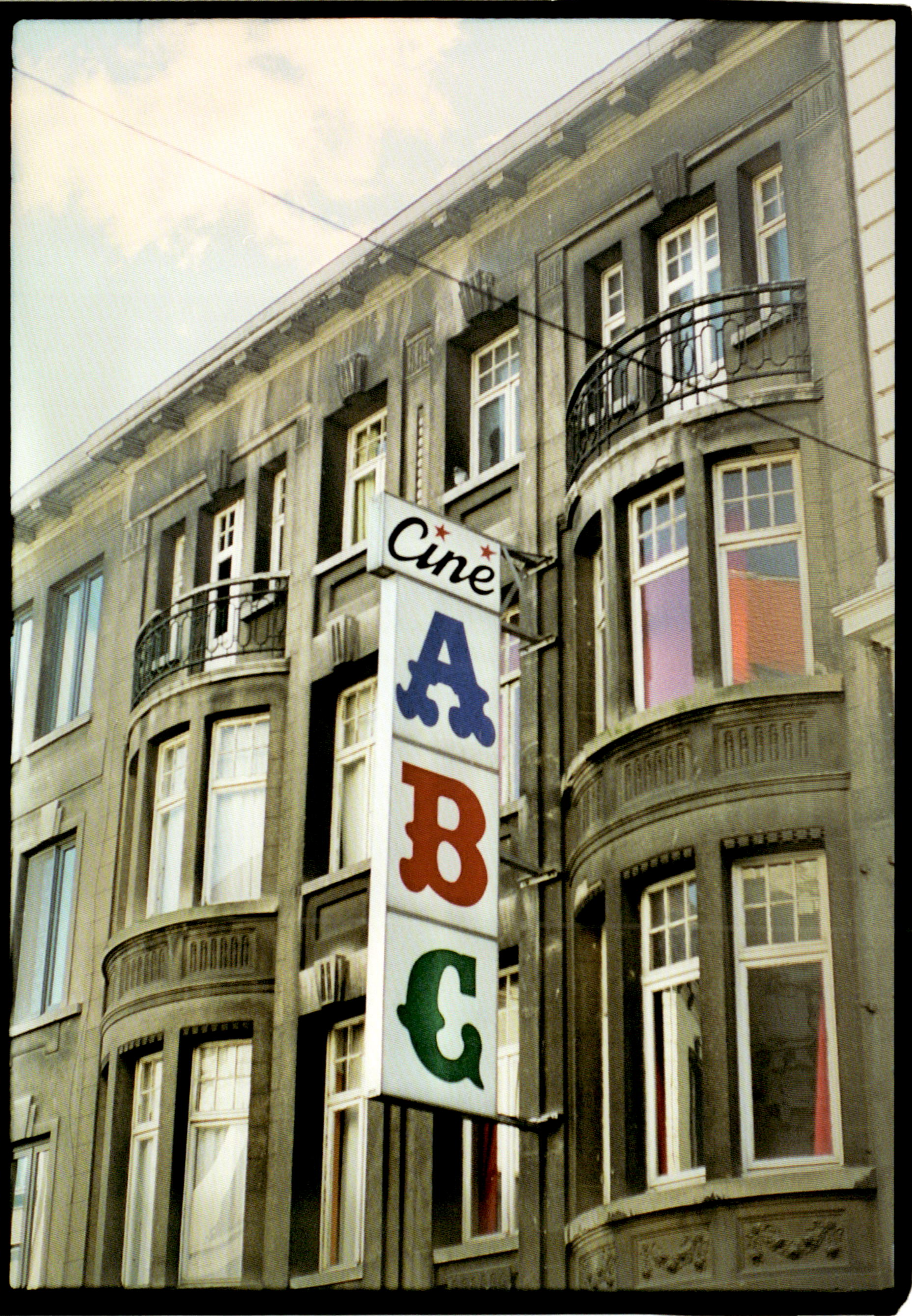
Cine
A
B
C

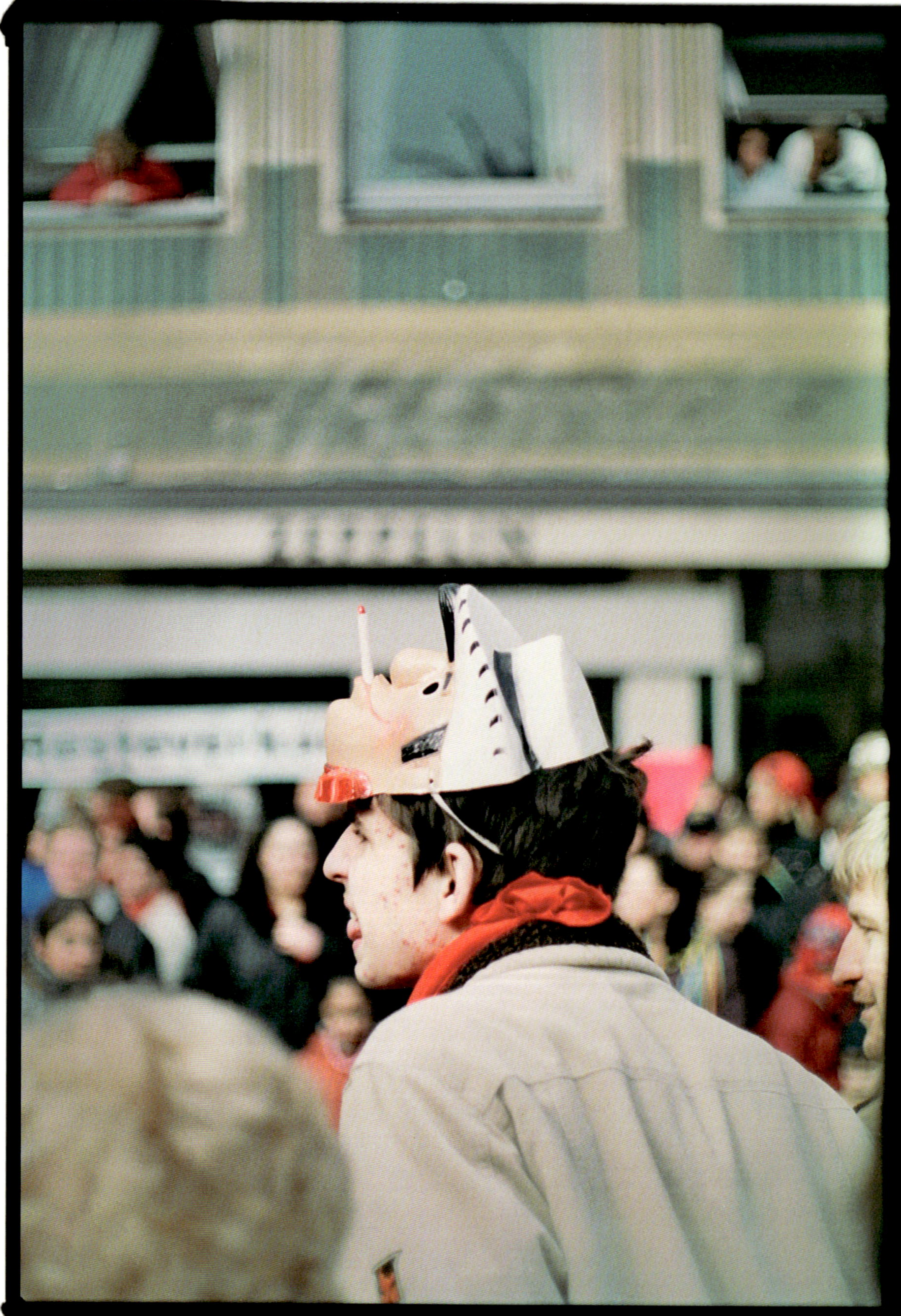

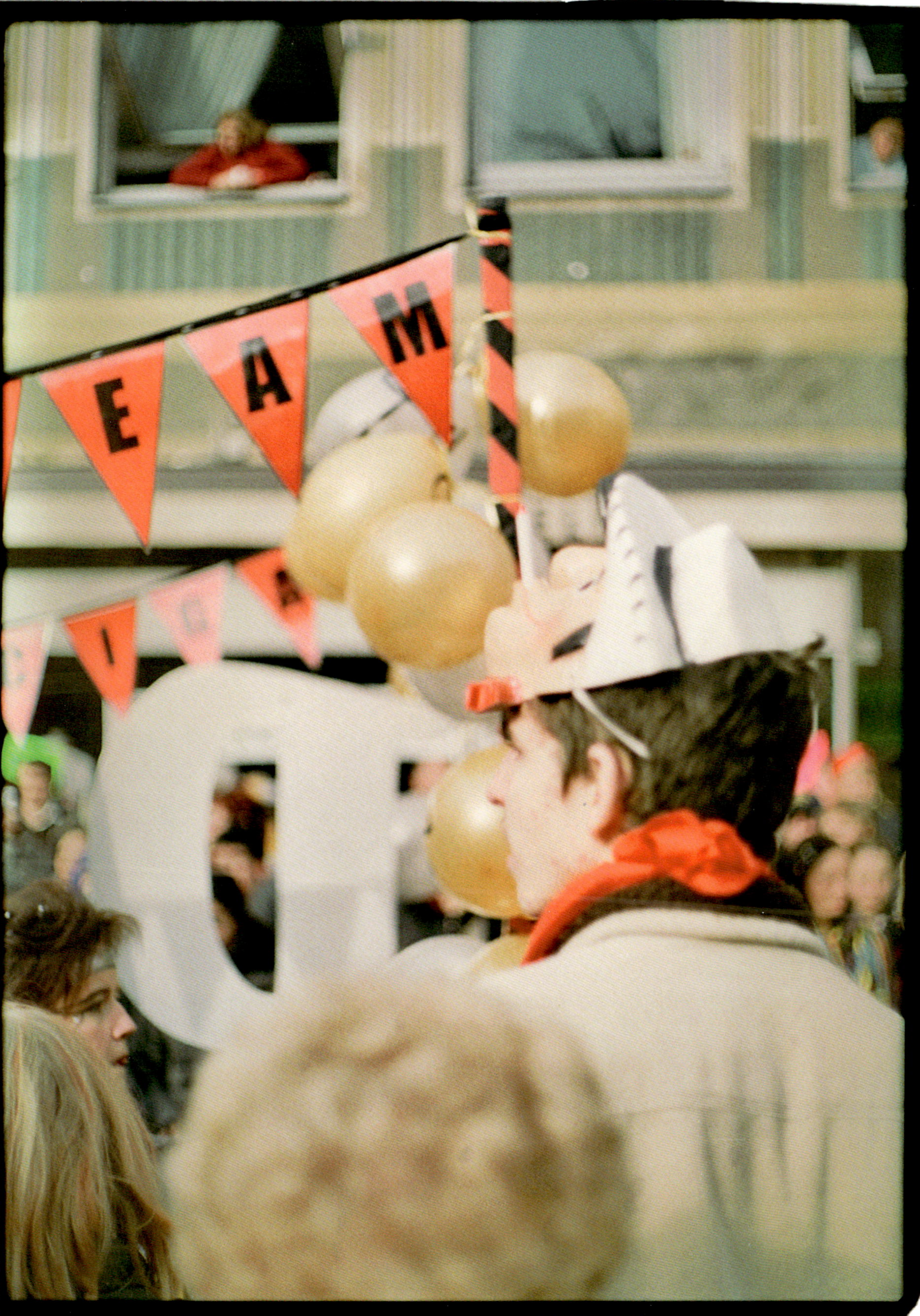
E A M

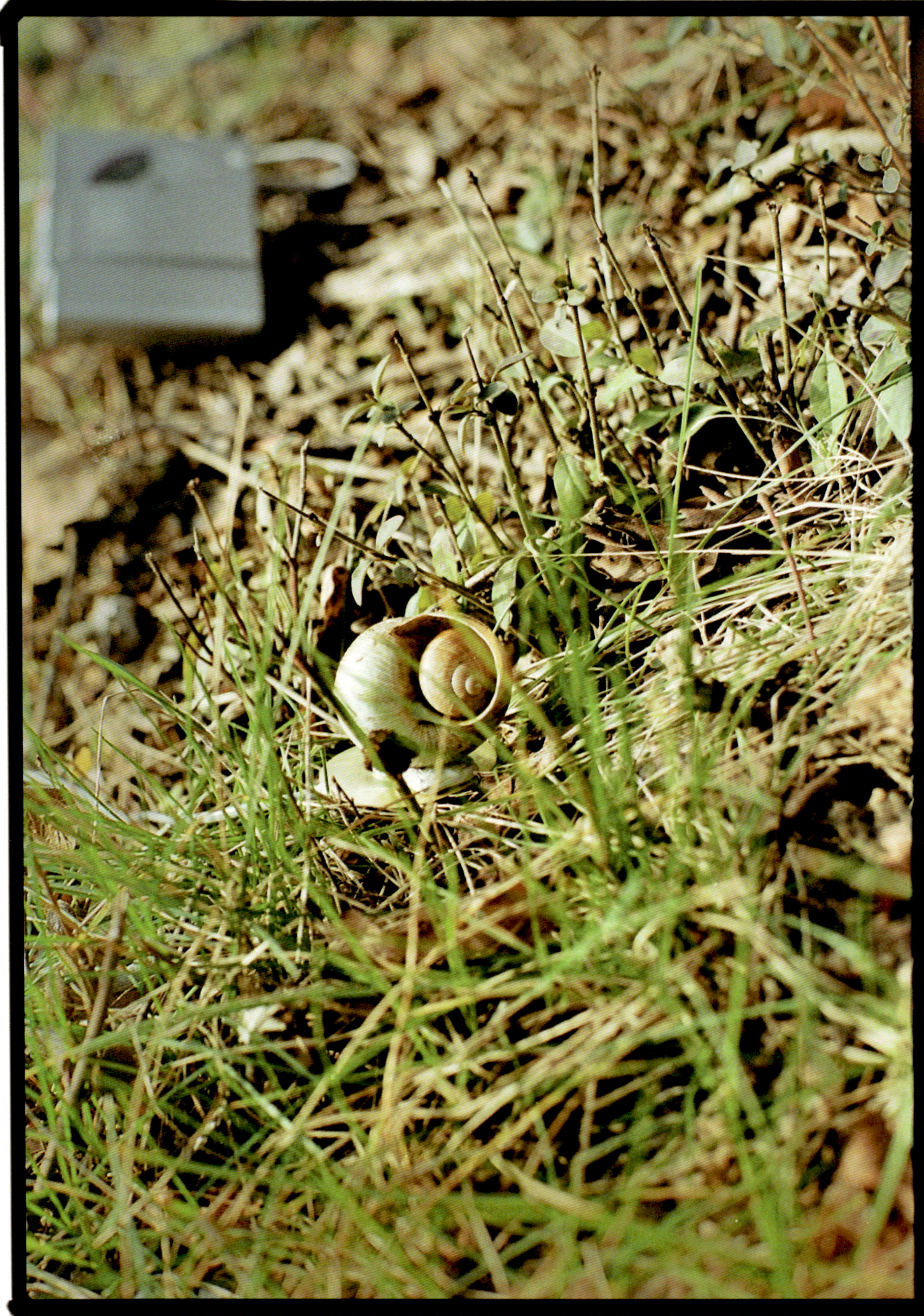

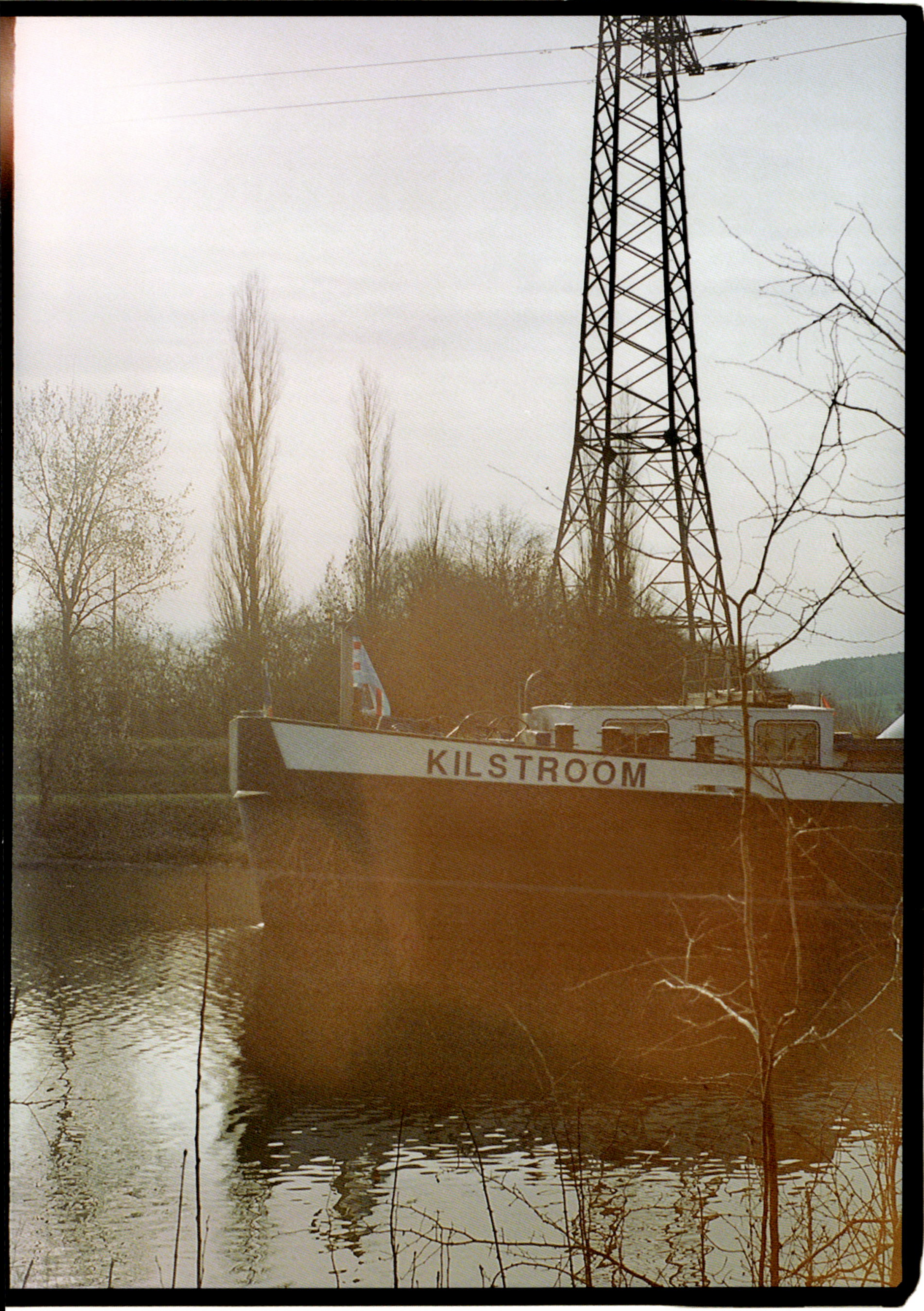
KILSTROOM

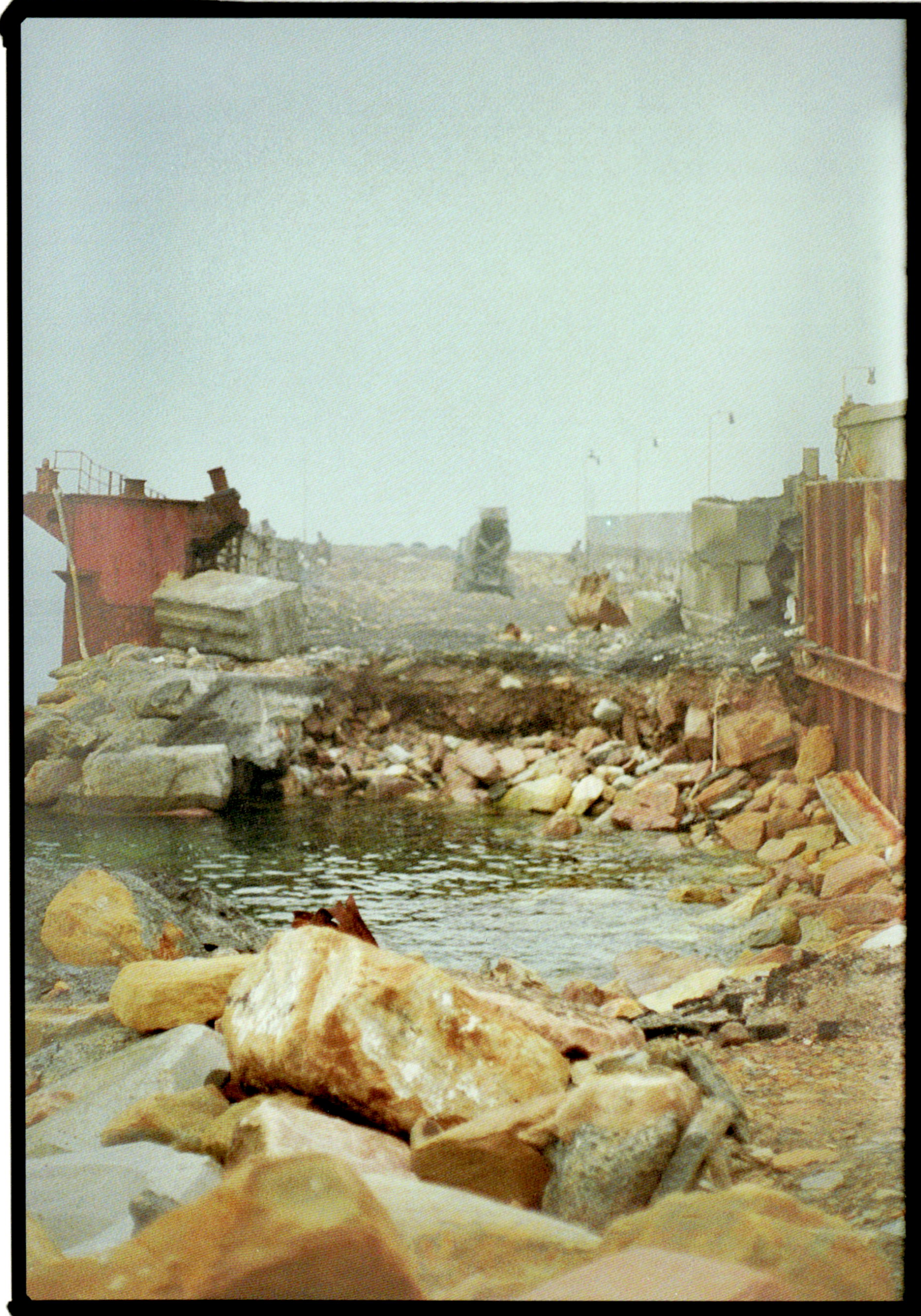

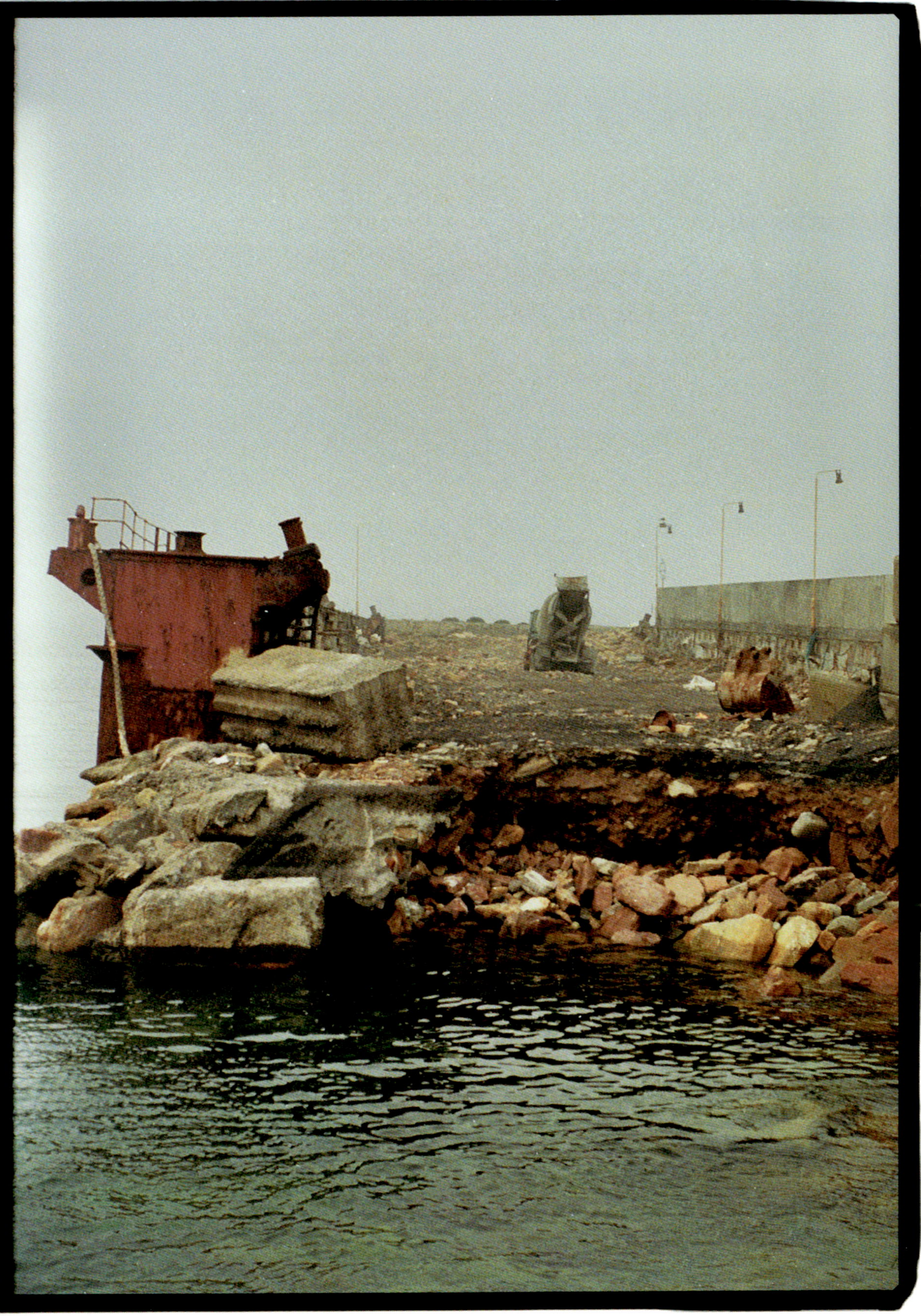

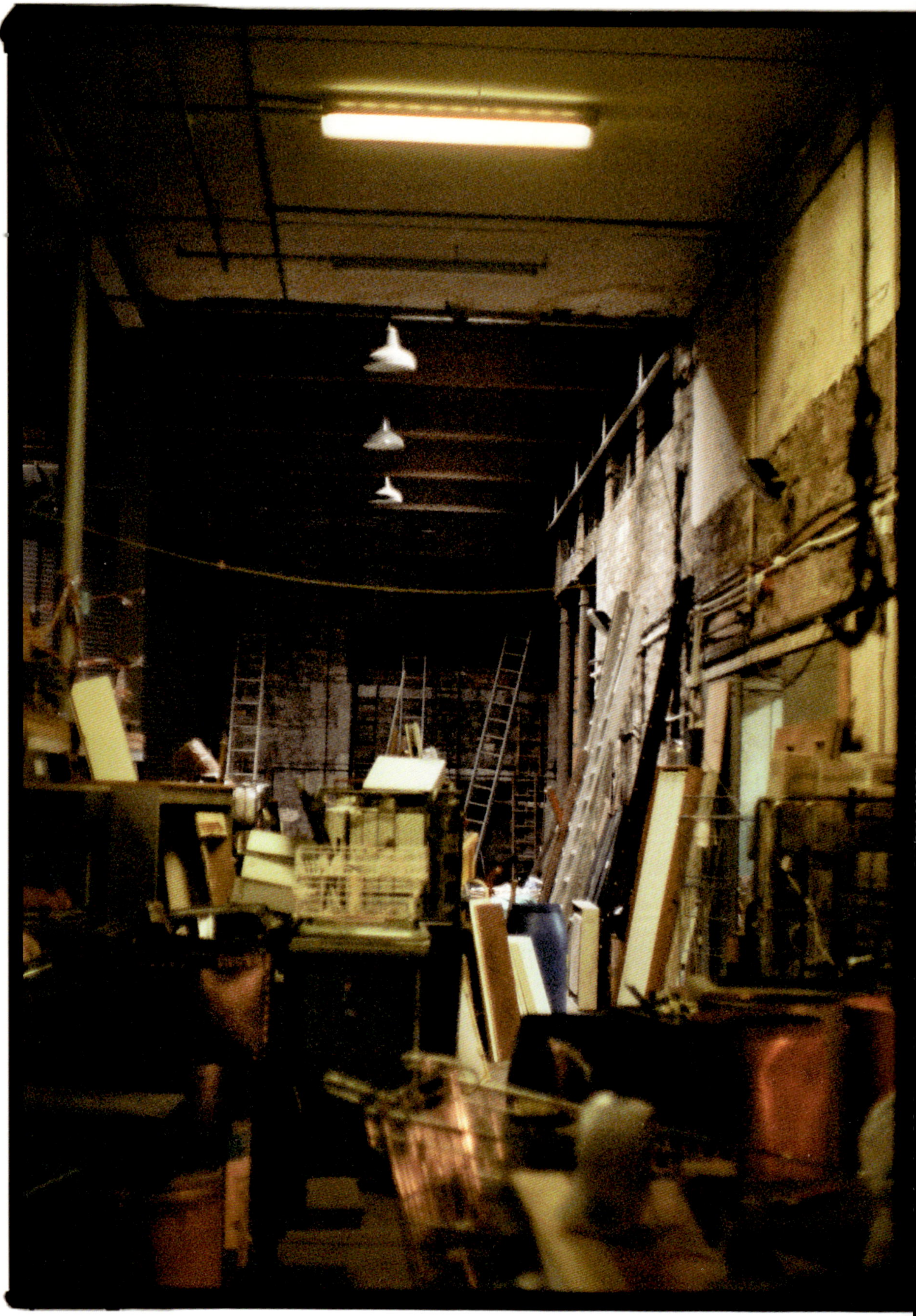

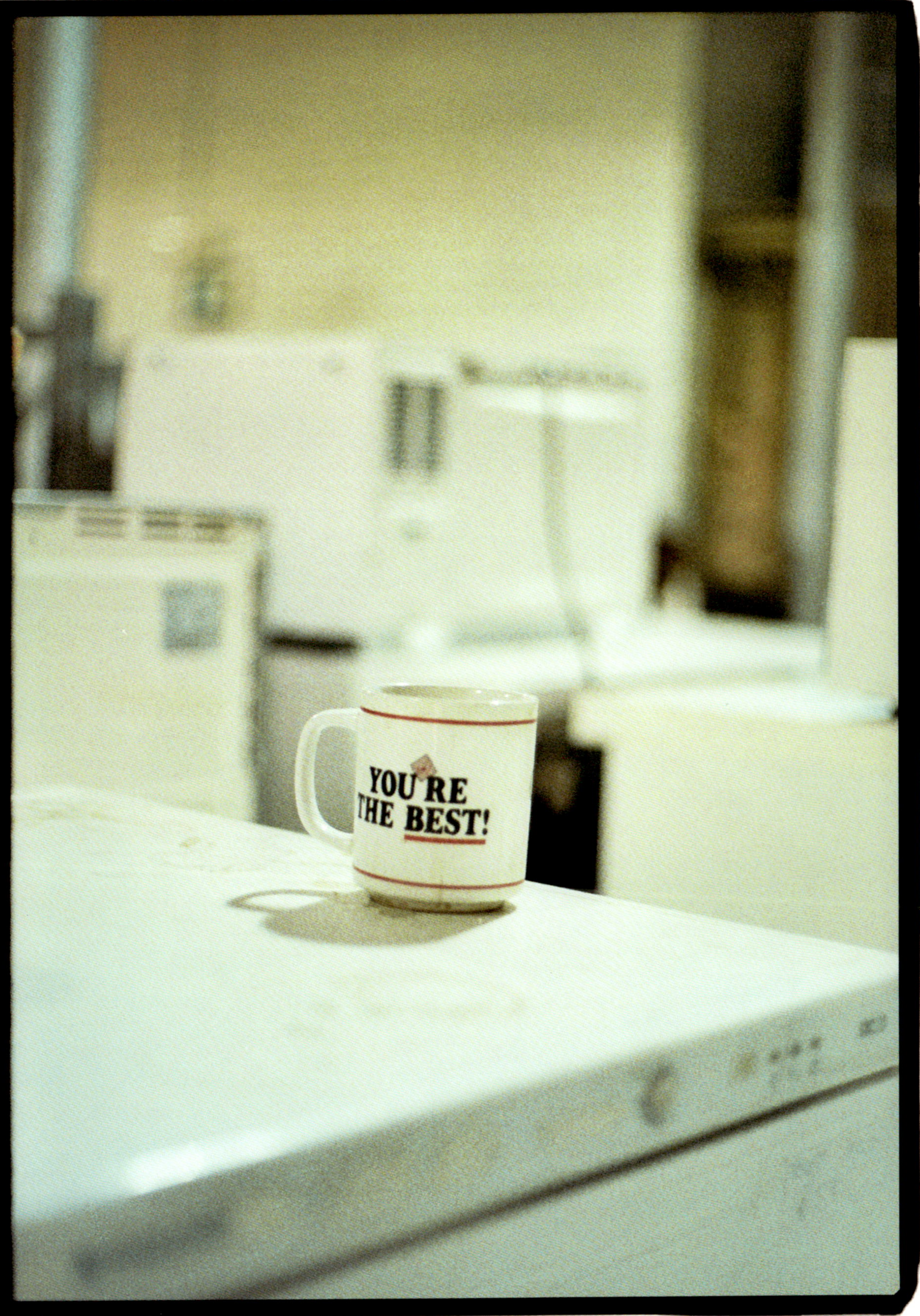
YOU'RE
THE BEST!

P. 2–3
Cairngorms and Large Glass, 2007
C-Print
30 × 45 cm

P. 4–5
Deutsche Bahn, 2006
C-Print
30 × 45 cm

P. 6–7
Cine ABC, Ghent, 2007
C-Print
30 × 45 cm

P. 8–9
Faschingsumzug, Bamberg 1/3, 2007
C-Print
30 × 45 cm

P. 10–11
Location Recording, Bamberg, 2007
C-Print
30 × 45 cm

P. 12–13
Location Recording, Caithness, 2007
C-Print
30 × 45 cm

P. 14–15
Recycling Centre, Dundee, 2007
C-Print
30 × 45 cm

Table of Contents   Inhaltsverzeichnis

Introduction

Luke Fowler's films explore the limits and conventions of documentary filmmaking, offering a critical response to the idea that the form can offer the viewer a single objective truth. Innovatively combining new and archival footage, interviews and photography with densely layered sound, Fowler constructs impressionistic portraits of vanguard thinkers and counter-cultural figures, presenting us with a chance to rethink our relationship to history and to the radical possibilities of film.

These highly constructed yet improvisational cinematic collages break down traditional approaches to biographical filmmaking. They transform the footage into multidimensional portraits, often retrieving forgotten or hidden histories. Fowler's meticulously researched subjects – including radical composer Cornelius Cardew, maverick psychologist Ronald D. Laing, postpunk musician Xentos 'Fray Bentos' Jones, and outsider and conservationist Bogman Palmjaguar – are all figures who challenge socio-cultural norms. Intuitively applying the logic, aesthetics and politics of his subjects to the film he is making about them, Fowler creates atmospheric, sampled histories that reverberate with the vitality of the people he studies. Bringing together film, photographs and archive documents, he takes us on a journey where there is no fixed or single truth, questioning our relationship to the past and our memories of it.

Collaboration is a key part of Fowler's creative process, and he moves fluidly between the roles of artist, curator, historian, filmmaker and musician. As a part of the experimental music scene, he is a member of several bands, and runs the multimedia platform SHADAZZ, whose activities include the production of LPs in collaboration with other musicians and artists. These projects often fold into his filmmaking practice, especially since sound and music are such an essential part of his films and installations, and musicians are so often the focus of his work.

The works in the Luke Fowler exhibitions at the Kunsthalle Zürich and the Serpentine Gallery have been selected to represent the breadth of Fowler's practice, including film, music, photography and installation.

His exhibition at the Kunsthalle Zürich (30 August to 2 November 2008) was the artist's first comprehensive institutional show to date, and was an important presentation in the Kunsthalle's programme of emerging artists. The exhibition coincided with the presentation of *Derek Jarman: Brutal Beauty*, curated by Isaac Julien, which was another collaborative project between the two organisations. At the Serpentine Gallery the Luke Fowler exhibition runs from 7 May to 14 June 2009, and continues the tradition of featuring the work of artists who are still in the early stages of their careers, as well as the series of exhibitions focusing on avant-garde film. The exhibition is the first solo exhibition of Fowler's work to be held in a public institution in the UK.

There are a number of individuals and organisations who have been instrumental in the realisation of these exhibitions. First and foremost, we would like to thank Luke Fowler for accepting the invitation to present his work in Zurich and in London, and for his thoughtful and focused engagement with both the exhibitions and the catalogue, the latter being the focus of the collaboration between the Kunsthalle Zürich and the Serpentine Gallery. Both organisations are very grateful to him for creating a limited edition work, allowing them to benefit from these sales. We are also indebted to his collaborator, Toshiya Tsunoda, for devoting his time and great expertise to the film and sound installation at the Serpentine Gallery.

We would like to offer our warmest thanks for the generous contributions made by supporters of the Kunsthalle Zürich and the Serpentine Gallery. The LUMA Foundation generously supported the artist's exhibition at the Kunsthalle Zürich, as a part of its overall funding of the programme for emerging artists. We must also thank the Council of the Serpentine Gallery, an extraordinary group of individuals whose ongoing commitment is invaluable.

We are delighted to include a text by Will Bradley and a conversation with the artist by Stuart Comer in this publication, and we thank them both for their thoughtful contributions. It has been a fruitful collaboration between the Kunsthalle Zürich and the Serpentine Gallery, and we are grateful to Rahel Blättler for the editorial coordination.

Our thanks also go to Toby Webster and Kitty Anderson at The Modern Institute, the artist's representative in Glasgow, for their support and assistance in realising the exhibitions.

Finally, the teams at the Kunsthalle Zürich (including Rahel Blättler and Katharina Pilz, Curatorial Assistants and Guided Tours; Susanne Stortz, Press, Members and Sponsors; Alfonso Negri, Website, IT and Graphics; and Sylvie Ledermann, Personal Assistant), and at the Serpentine Gallery (including Sophie O'Brien, Exhibition Curator; Mike Gaughan, Gallery Manager; together with Sally Tallant, Head of Programmes, and Leila Hasham, Exhibitions Assistant) worked hard to deliver the exhibitions. We would like to extend our thanks to these teams, whose commitment and enthusiasm are essential to realising projects such as this.

Julia Peyton-Jones
Director, Serpentine Gallery, and
Co-Director, Exhibitions & Programmes

Hans Ulrich Obrist
Co-Director, Serpentine Gallery, Exhibitions & Programmes, and Director, International Projects

Beatrix Ruf
Director and Curator, Kunsthalle Zürich

'Implicit in this attitude is a belief in freedom'[1]?

Will Bradley

If the conclusions of critical theory had more direct power over the shape of the world, the genre of documentary filmmaking might have been dead by the 1970s. Once it became clear that, from the point of view of cinema, truth was an argument to be constructed rather than a simple collection of facts to be transmitted, it would seem that the fundamental claim of the documentary mode was discredited. In fact, the 1970s saw an accelerated expansion of documentary making, driven by handheld cameras, direct sound, new portable video technologies and a post-'68 enthusiasm for bringing unheard voices and under-represented viewpoints into the mass media forum. Truth in film was no longer an ideal to strive for, but a battleground to be won, a polemical space in which even the radical strategies of self-reflection or self-exposure quickly became simply useful rhetorical tools.

Luke Fowler's filmmaking begins where this line of questioning ends, which is to say that it accepts the evident conclusions, but proposes a critical response. The psychiatrist Ronald D. Laing believed that the most important relationship in human society is that between our individual selves and the way in which we are understood and represented by other individuals, but that this relationship is necessarily, and problematically, mediated by our own perception. Laing's thought is both the subject and basis of much of Fowler's work, and the way in which film represents the individual is, perhaps, the central question it addresses.

Laing's theories were temporarily embodied in a short-lived therapeutic community established at Kingsley Hall in London, where people diagnosed as schizophrenics lived in a communal household with the radical therapists who sought a context that could encompass all comers without the coercive use of drugs or other restraints. Fowler's films *What You See Is Where You're At* (2001) and *Bogman Palmjaguar* (2007), as well as the installation *The Nine Monads of David Bell* (2006–2007), are direct engagements with the history of the Kingsley Hall experiment, while *The Way Out* (2003) and *Pilgrimage from Scattered Points* (2006) both bear the imprint of Laing's thinking.

What Fowler takes from Laing, however, is not the pop-psychiatric theory – unlike, for example, David Lamelas, who turned sections from Laing's bestseller *Knots* (1967) into his *Reading Film from Knots* (1970) – but the social radicalism of Kingsley Hall. Mainstream psychiatry rejected Laing's methods, and their efficacy as treatments is both disputed and hard to assess from within a social order that was itself identified by Laing as harmful. The underlying principle, however, is a moral one, with clear political consequences. Simply put, it is to assert that people suffering from what society currently defines as psychoses are still people, to be accorded the same rights as everybody else. Which is not to say that the crazy people don't need help, but almost the opposite: that if they need aid, they are morally entitled to receive it in a way that does not place them outside society. Laing's work not only raises this political question, but also another about the way in which society functions, which is to ask on what grounds society defines somebody as fit to take part.

Fowler's use of film also faces up to the central criticisms of the documentary mode of filmmaking. Instead of a claim to truth in his constructions, Fowler offers a critique of the idea that a single truth could possibly emerge from the filmmaking process. His films are about the political struggle over the idea of truth, about how the subject might resist being categorised, resist being turned into a simple image that can be understood, situated and manipulated by dominant social forces, but also about how the filmmaking process short-circuits the two-way relationship between our perception of others and their understanding of our perception.

Beyond Laing, Fowler's acknowledged influences connect an interest in the social-democratic radicalism of post-war Britain with the ideas of Structuralist film, the Situationists and free improvisation, and it is possible to propose the unlikely quartet of Hollis Frampton, Lindsay Anderson, Alexander Trocchi and Cornelius Cardew as representing, at least symbolically, Fowler's most salient precursors.

1   Lindsay Anderson, 'The Free Cinema Manifesto, 5th February 1956', Paul Ryan (ed.), *Never Apologise: The Collected Writings*, Plexus Publishing Ltd., London 2004.

2 *The Room*, Tate Modern, London, 28 November, 2008.

3 Luke Fowler, 'Expanded Cinema: Time/Space/Structure', *Map magazine*, Dundee, no. 9, Spring 2007, p. 4–6.

4 Ibid., p. 6.

5 Anderson, 'The Free Cinema Manifesto'.

6 Alexander Trocchi, 'A Revolutionary Proposal: Invisible Insurrection of a Million Minds', published as 'Technique du coupe du monde', *Internationale Situationniste*, no. 8, January 1963.

7 Ibid.

Fowler has made clear his affinity with Structuralist filmmaking, not only in his recent collaborations with Peter Todd and Keith Rowe,[2] but also in his essay 'Expanded Cinema: Time/Space/Structure'.[3] Fowler frames his text as an 'outsider's view', which is inevitable given the time that has elapsed between the 1970s heyday of Structuralist film and the 2007 viewpoint of his article. But he proposes that the Expanded Cinema movement prefigured contemporary video art, and goes on to suggest that its practitioners aimed for 'complete control over the means of production, presentation and distribution'.[4] In other words, he concurs with a school of thought that would situate expanded cinema as a politicised approach to filmmaking that took part in a struggle over the means of representation as well as the means of production.

These questions about the political conditions of filmmaking were also at the heart of the Free Cinema movement in late-1950s Britain, which the director Lindsay Anderson was most responsible for shaping. Free Cinema marked the beginning of a politically engaged approach to film in Britain that paralleled the beginnings of the French New Wave, and was in part powered by the same technological developments – quiet, hand-held cameras and new, fast film stock that enabled direct sound shooting in available light and opened up the possibility of 'fly on the wall' documentarism. Its maxims – 'No film can be too personal. The image speaks. Sound amplifies and comments. Size is irrelevant. Perfection is not an aim. An attitude means a style. A style means an attitude'[5] – became the centre of a movement that was in clear synchronisation with the changes in British society produced by the post-war social democratic settlement. A new generation of working-class playwrights, poets, novelists, screenwriters, television producers, journalists and artists not only affirmed the efficacy of free higher education in promoting social mobility, but saw themselves as part of a revolution in prevailing social values. The unspoken assumption was, perhaps, that this shift in the institutional terms of representation might be more than just a symptom of Keynesian economic compromise and could become a self-amplifying system that would ultimately overpower the dominant myths of British capitalism, at least in the media sphere.

Fowler adopted the title of Alexander Trocchi's essay, 'The Invisible Insurrection of a Million Minds'[6] (1963) for a compilation of electronic music, made mostly in Glasgow, that he released on his SHADAZZ label in 2001. It would be wrong to make too much of Trocchi's influence on Fowler's work, but there are meaningful, if tangential, connections to be made between 'The Invisible Insurrection of a Million Minds' and the milieu of British Free Cinema. At one point in his essay, Trocchi quotes the Welsh Marxist literary critic Raymond Williams, who wrote that 'the question is not who will patronise the arts, but what forms are possible in which artists will have control of their own means of expression, in such ways that they will have relation to a community rather than to a market or a patron'.[7]

The other salient influence on Fowler's films is the most obvious, that of the idea of free improvisation, which Fowler acknowledges and interrogates in his film on Cornelius Cardew and The Scratch Orchestra, *Pilgrimage from Scattered Points*. Of all Fowler's films to date, *Pilgrimage from Scattered Points* is both the one that comes closest to the conventions of the documentary genre, and the one that strays furthest from Laingian territory. It is a retelling of the story of The Scratch Orchestra, founded by Cornelius Cardew, Michael Parsons and Howard Skempton in 1969 (the title is borrowed from a The Scratch Orchestra's recording titled *Pilgrimage from Scattered Points on the Surface of the Body to the Brain, the Inner Ear, the Heart and the Stomach* [1970]), and in part a reworking of Hanne Boenisch's film about the orchestra, *Journey to the North Pole* (1971). *Pilgrimage from Scattered Points* interrupts archive footage with contradictory contemporary interviews and develops a narrative around The Scratch Orchestra's eventual split, bringing questions of ideology into focus within the realm of individual interactions.

The Scratch Orchestra was founded – with a draft constitution published in *The Musical Times* (June 1969) – as an explicitly utopian association, bringing together both musicians and non-musicians to make music in the light of the avant-garde dissolution of aesthetics in politics. It was defined as 'a large number of enthusiasts pooling their resources (not primarily material resources) and assembling for action (music-making, performance, edification)'.[8] But these already wide terms were immediately expanded by the note that 'the word music and its derivatives here are not understood to refer exclusively to sound […] what they do refer to is flexible and depends entirely on the members of The Scratch Orchestra. The Scratch Orchestra intends to function in the public sphere […]'[9]

At the beginning, then, it was a question rather than an answer, but it was a specific question. The aim was not to realise a particular outcome, but to explore a particular relationship between the individual and the collective. The outcome of this exploration would be 'music-making, performance, edification',[10] but it would also be The Scratch Orchestra itself.

Where *Journey to the North Pole* records this outcome, Fowler's film focuses on the question. The Scratch Orchestra is seen not only as a performance ensemble, but a society in microcosm whose members are enmeshed in political power formations and hidden hierarchies. Though many participants find the experience of being part of the orchestra a liberating one, the freedom they discover there is ultimately revealed as insufficient. What constitutes authentic individual expression becomes a point of issue, and in any case individual freedom of expression is realised only in the circumscribed realm of performance; the wider questions of the structure, direction and meaning of the project remain resolutely, and unavoidably, political.

This situation became more complicated in 1971, when Cardew, along with several other members of the orchestra, began to adopt an explicitly Maoist view of the relationship between culture and the class struggle. Turning against what they saw as bourgeois individualism, the Maoist faction in The Scratch Orchestra tried to reconfigure the group as an activist propaganda unit whose performances should use vernacular forms to educate the public. An unsupportable tension developed between the newly minted Maoists and the now-created bourgeois individualists who still held to Cardew's initial ideal. The attempted transformation of the group from an isolated utopian model into an activist cadre led ultimately to an unproductive stasis, and in 1973 Cardew joined in founding a new collective endeavour, People's Liberation Music.

In Fowler's hands, Cardew's experiment echoes Kingsley Hall in the way that it tried to overcome, or rather explore, the erasure of a social boundary. Just as the Philadelphia Association (the mental-health charity started by Laing and others,[11] which founded Kingsley Hall) began with the radical assumption that the voices of those diagnosed as schizophrenic should nonetheless be listened to, Cardew assumed that music made by people 'diagnosed' by society as non-musicians also had value. And just as Kingsley Hall established a community where the (previously segregated) psychotic and sane hoped for a productive exchange, The Scratch Orchestra sat classically trained virtuosos together with tone-deaf first-timers and made the political assertion that the results were music. It is worth adding that, in both cases, it took the intervention of a socially sanctioned expert (Laing a qualified psychoanalyst and Cardew a Fellow of the Royal Academy of Music) to give permission.

Fowler's preceding film *The Way Out* (a collaboration with Kosten Koper) revolved around a subject who had explicitly refused to give the filmmakers an honest or straightforward testimony. Mostly assembled from home movies, archive footage and interviews, but augmented with fragmentary footage from scenes improvised specifically for the film, *The Way Out* was a non-portrait of a missing individual. Somewhere, perhaps, there exists a flesh and blood person, who, from the late 1970s up to the present, recorded the musical parts – basslines, vocals, keyboards, guitar – variously attributed to Jim Welton, L Voag, Amos, Xentos Bentos, Xentos Jones and others, on records and tapes that were independently distributed to a tiny audience by various more or less underground bands. But the film

8   Cornelius Cardew, 'A Scratch Orchestra: Draft Constitution', Michael Parsons (ed.), *Twenty Five Years from Scratch*, London Musician's Collective, London 1994, p. 20.
9   Ibid.
10   Ibid.
11   Clancy Sigal, Aaron Esterson, Joan Cunnold, David Cooper and Sid Briskin.

deliberately fails to construct a coherent image of Xentos from its montage of audio recordings, DIY Super-8 movies, performative recollections and invocations. Instead, it collaborates in Xentos's own project, and underlines the broken, transitory, yet also two-way nature of the connections between the processes of an individual life and their social perception. What, in the terms of conventional documentary investigation, should have been the search for the source, the unifying truth behind these multiple personas, becomes a film about why that search must fail. *The Way Out* does not suggest that the real Xentos has somehow escaped from the net of documentarism, but that this 'real' person was not and could never be the subject. That it left one reviewer questioning whether Xentos even 'really existed', or had in fact been invented by the filmmakers, was surely not down to that one journalist's lack of critical insight but to *The Way Out*'s refusal to comply with the accepted terms of validation.

Fowler himself is, of course, caught up in this system that validates authors on the basis of their successful works, and works on the basis of their successful authors, that produces cultural capital out of cultural attention and follows chains of association, cultural links, only to temporarily come to rest at points where these conjunctions correspond to a marketable myth. Fowler's attention to The Scratch Orchestra put Cardew's work back in the art world eye, and the resulting feedback surely raised the filmmaker's reputation by association, even among those who had never seen *Pilgrimage from Scattered Points*.

It is significant then, that for his next full-length film, *Bogman Palmjaguar*, Fowler stepped back from this process. Bogman Palmjaguar is no ready-made counter-cultural hero – he is apparently a troubled, middle-aged man living reclusively in northern Scotland, and engaged in an intractable bureaucratic struggle with minor state functionaries – and what is at stake is unfilmable: Palmjaguar's legal status, his administrative freedom. Fowler's film is not so much intended to contest the state's diagnosis of Palmjaguar as schizophrenic – that is the role of Dr Leon Redler, a former colleague of Laing, who is supporting Palmjaguar's legal battles and who appears in the film – not to 'tell his story' in the hope of gaining the activist sympathy of the audience, but rather to produce a restrained and poetic polemic in favour of the idea that individual behaviour is deeply dependent on situation and environment.

Fowler's previous films relied largely on archive material. *Bogman Palmjaguar* is the first to be based primarily on Fowler's own footage, augmented with Lee Patterson's sound recordings. The perversity of making a film about an individual who shuns interpersonal contact, and who refuses to show his face on camera, fits with Fowler's previous paradoxical use of the medium of film to expose the unreliable and contingent nature of any attempt to represent a personality as an image rather than as a social process.

Still, the film walks a difficult line, between uncritically presenting and affirming its subject, and reproducing a stereotypical portrait of the schizophrenic other. Fowler approaches this problem – which is an unavoidable problem of representation already produced by the prevailing social categories – by splitting the cinematic presentation of Palmjaguar into three different modes. In the first, we see the landscape and hear its field-recorded soundtrack, interspersed with Palmjaguar's own reflections on the landscape and his relation to it. In the second, we see Palmjaguar fleeing from the camera, his face hidden by a mask. In the third, we hear him interviewed and speaking, off camera, about the legal battle he is involved in to be recognised as sane, which means to be allowed to live in an unconfrontational relationship to mainstream society and be accorded all associated human rights. This threefold approach corresponds to an analysis of Bogman Palmjaguar himself as a political subject, or perhaps rather of the processes that construct him as a political subject. But this analysis, this breaking down of the object of enquiry, is not conducted aggressively. Instead, it is undertaken as an analysis in opposition to the simple categorisation of Palmjaguar proposed by the administrative institutions to which he is legally subjected.

When Palmjaguar talks about the Flow Country, the particular undeveloped part of the Scottish landscape in which he has found his place, his words become an incantation, a weaving together of legitimising bureaucratic measurements, tourist board slogans, facts drawn from authoritative sources, with personal observations, meditations and confirmations of therapeutic changes, bringing together the overlooked biospheric significance of the landscape and his own happiness at finding his place in it. In these monologues there is an apparent over-identification, but also the clear and joyous recognition of a functioning context for a particular subjectivity. In fact, Palmjaguar's meditations seem very close to Henry David Thoreau's celebrated descriptions of his experiences of living in solitude at Walden Pond, where 'the most sweet and tender, the most innocent and encouraging society may be found in any natural object, even for the poor misanthrope and most melancholy man'.[12]

Likewise, Palmjaguar is able, indeed keen, to represent himself, and he finds a way to work with the filmmakers despite his reluctance to show his face. It is in the film's third mode that real questions begin to be asked, but Fowler productively establishes these questions in relation to the first two approaches to Palmjaguar's life. If the majority of what seem to be Palmjaguar's symptoms can plausibly be redescribed as socially-sanctioned – if undeniably eccentric – positions in relation to the individual's place in the social/natural order, what remains is only Palmjaguar's confrontational relationship to the normalising institutions of society. In other words, Fowler suggests that what keeps Palmjaguar in conflict with society is not any specific anti-social transgression, but simply that his way of living and thinking, which otherwise has quietly found its place, cannot be explicitly recognised.

Palmjaguar is guilty of no crime, but is effectively criminalised because he has become paranoid. For deep-seated reasons, social and personal, he feels persecuted, so he lashes out with the limited means available to him, and the institutional response is an attempt to suppress him. This gives him a legitimate basis for his paranoia, and enmeshes him in an impossible game with the psychiatric authorities.

Fowler's film does not suggest itself as an answer to Palmjaguar's situation. It does, however, offer Palmjaguar's situation as a question, a question that is not framed in strictly polemical terms but that is built from the verified facts of filmic observation and live recording. It is a question about a real situation rather than about an imagined individual, and one that refuses to go away once the film has ended.

Luke Fowler's work upsets the conventions of the documentary mode, but in an unexpected and productive way. It reverses the now-banal questions of the veracity of the image, the trustworthiness of the edit. Fowler often uses pre-digital technologies to promise the truth of the recording, in order to question the perception of the social interactions that created it. He uses the techniques of montage neither to construct an apparently seamless representation, nor to alienate or problematise it, but to construct an argument. His work is unashamedly polemical, but the polemic is in favour of the proposition that the same discontinuities, paradoxes and breakdowns in communication that are at issue in cinema are also at work in our unmediated lives. Fowler's work seems to suggest that the disjointed, biased, incomplete construction that cinema offers is a better reflection of the real processes in operation. This is not to claim that, as a result, Fowler's films somehow capture a more authentic representation than others, but rather to suggest that they are made in the real spirit of authenticity, which in its negotiations with a public can only be explicitly provisional, partial and personal.

12   Henry David Thoreau, *Walden, or Life in the Woods*, Hayes Barton Press, Raleigh NC 1975, p. 88.

Luke Fowler in Conversation
with Stuart Comer

sc – Your work emerged out of a collective activity, tapping into various transgressive art and music subcultures and presenting a bricolage of documents, screenings and performances. Although an interest in collaboration and subverting hierarchies still resonates in recent projects such as your work with Toshiya Tsunoda in Yokohama and with Keith Rowe and Peter Todd in London, you've turned increasingly to consolidating this multipartite approach into individual 16mm film 'portraits'. What possibilities do you think an obsolete medium like 16mm film offers you in contrast to platforms like musical performance or the internet?

LF – My attraction to 16mm came out of using Super-8 film as a texture within my films and looking for a medium that I had more control over and that could eventually be self-sufficient (i.e. to project from film rather than to transfer to video). 16mm is a far more versatile medium than Super-8, though I still like the roughness of the latter. But because both are – as you say – largely obsolete, the price difference in stock and transfer is negligible.

I think it's interesting that you draw a contrast between my gravitation towards independent and artists' 16mm films and my movement away from the earlier multifaceted projects. There are several reasons why I made the shift. Essentially, I see it as a continuation of earlier concerns, yet with more concentration on the aesthetic and temporal structure of how a viewer receives the ideas and research. Filmmaking for me is still very much a social process, incorporating cross-discipline collaboration with musicians, academics, other artists, etc. I'm just much more interested in the processes and possibilities of doing that in film than in installations or curated projects.

sc – Since your work can clearly be seen to have come out of various 'intermedia' histories, could you flesh out your thoughts about using a 'romantic' medium like 16mm? How do you balance a 'post-medium' position with an interest in materialist filmmaking?

LF – I think artists have always been interested in obsolete mediums, haven't they? I mean, why are artists still using Victorian presses for printmaking? Or physically cutting up photocopies to make a collage when they could be scanning and doing it all in Photoshop? Why do certain musicians prefer to record to analogue tape or play an analogue synth when they could use modern digital alternatives? Surely it's because they prefer the distinct quality of their medium and its peculiar idiosyncrasies and feel dissatisfied with whatever modern tools have superseded them.

We're at an unprecedented moment in history where 16mm film-stock technology is still being developed by Fujifilm and Kodak and can be used in conjunction with digital editing either to output as print or transfer to digital. I've tried both and would prefer, in most cases, to project a film than to use video – but of course, it's expensive and in some cases impractical.

16mm has a specific set of signifiers when used within the gallery context; often artists employ films with loopers as sculptural objects, or as a throwback to early conceptual work. If I had the choice, I'd much prefer to show my films in cinemas, where the comparison to those kinds of tactics can't be drawn and people are more involved in the content than the mode of presentation.

sc – What prompted your interest in histories of experimental and Structuralist filmmaking, and in investigating specific radical cultural figures such as Cornelius Cardew and Ronald D. Laing?

LF – A serious interest in researching and tracking down some of the canonic experimental/Structural films came quite late on for me – probably only in the last few years. At Art School in Dundee it was very hard to see any of the classic avant-garde films (British or otherwise) due to the fact that the time-based art department, which was established by one of Britain's early pioneers of video art, Stephen Partridge, promoted and fostered artists working with new media (Bill Viola was their God). At that time, the end of the 1990s, video art was really booming. There was a tendency towards the spectacle of monumental video projections that dwarfed the viewer and limited engagement.

Fortunately, a tutor of ours, Alan Woods, somehow managed to get hold of a preview copy of Johan Grimonprez's *Dial H-I-S-T-O-R-Y*

(1997), which was showing at that year's *Documenta X*. A bit later, at college, I saw Dan Graham's *Rock My Religion* (1982–1984) and Patrick Keiller's *London* (1994). These works and other classic documentary films had a profound effect on me, and probably led to my own 'essay film' *What You See Is Where You're At* (2001) about Ronald D. Laing's Kingsley Hall experiment. The language and sophistication of my first film was nowhere near as accomplished as those that I was influenced by, but it was both an affirmation – towards a research-based form – and a rejection of the current dominant strands in video art: performance-to-camera works and those looping grand spectacles.

My interest in tracking down and researching the history of British and American experimental/Structural works came out of a desire to understand the history and legacy of a field that I was beginning to be more involved in. In a way, making a 'pilgrimage' was born out of the same motivation, only in this case the field was British experimental and improvised music and in particular the development of a politically conscious movement of composers/musicians.

The interest in Ronald D. Laing came much earlier, when I was at college. If you grew up in the intellectual hub of Glasgow's West End as I did, Laing was a figure of pride and great repute. When I was at art school and my sister Meg was working on her PhD, I remember her discussing *The Divided Self* (1960) with my folks. I listened intently and must have made a mental note to look into it myself.

Then, in my final year, I was working on a series of projects that were informed by social and psychological experiments. The show for Transmission Gallery, *The Social Engineer* (1999), involved setting up an incredibly ambitious network of blind-date interviews that I 'engineered' between political or social opposites (the governor of Barlinnie Prison talking to a body artist, etc). It was around this time that Meg suggested I read up on Laing's Kingsley Hall experiment because I'd been researching people like Stanley Milgram and Philip Zimbardo's experiments. I found a fascinating account of Kingsley Hall in Adrian Laing's biography of his father, which laid the germs of an idea for a film project.

sc – The notion of mental illness, in particular Laing's 'divided self', is a recurrent theme in your films, as is the work of radical or eccentric figures in music, such as Cardew and Xentos Jones. There seems to be a resonance between Laing's interest in group therapy, rethinking notions of 'family', and Cardew's People's Liberation Music and his notion that the act of improvisation is one of shared ownership and responsibility. How does their work come to bear on your own interest in community, collaboration and synchronicities between sound and image?

lf – With Laing, it was partly due to his inclusion in this Glasgow intellectual legacy, and my previous research into social experiments. The other significant factor was to attempt to see a rationale for the multiple breakdowns that I experienced within my own family during that time. Reading Laing and seeking out Leon Redler provided great solace for me.

The motivation to work on Cardew and The Scratch Orchestra stemmed from my burgeoning involvement in the free improvisation scene in Glasgow and its historical roots in the UK. If you look at the membership lists of The Scratch Orchestra at its height, it was almost like a 'who's who' list of British composition and free improvisation: Gavin Bryars, Brian Eno, AMM, Michael Nyman, Howard Skempton, David Jackman, Michael Parsons, Christopher Hobbs – the list was 100-plus individuals.

Also some of the political questions that Cardew and his cadre raised chimed with basic political questions that most artists ponder: Who does your art serve? What is the function of art? Can art have a political or revolutionary role? Is this social and political function always at the cost of artistic innovation?

My interest in how to tackle these two great individuals was always going to hinge on how their work fostered a community that challenged and offered a real alternative to prevailing norms. With Laing, this challenge was to ask how our society treats the mentally ill; with Cardew, it was more about countering an elitism in avant-garde music, which eventually turned into a question of whether the avant-garde itself was of any relevance within a political dimension, or if there were more effective methods of engagement. It was always my intention to look at how these 'charismatic leaders' built and defined their own communities and how that played out on a human level.

On a formal level, I was interested in building up layers of sound and image tracks that quite often pull against and away from each other. The voice and music didn't necessarily have to sync up and reinforce the image track. This is probably one of the areas in which it strays most from the Griersonian documentary, where the emphasis is often on fixing interpretation and thus meaning. Of course, there is a small but rich tradition of the essay film or anti-documentary (e.g. Dziga Vertov, Guy Debord, Chris Marker, Jean-Marie Straub & Danièle Huillet, Harun Farocki, Peter Watson, Berwick Street Film Collective, Black Audio Film Collective) where this disruption of illusionism and fixed meaning is par for the course. Their recent recuperation in the museum context marks their increasing relevance in the search for precursors to the current generation. In my view, this marks a general breakdown of the old division between independent filmmakers showing in cinemas and visual artists occupying the galleries. In a way, it ups the ante for artists in terms of combining critical engagement with a high level of formal sophistication.

SC – That raises the issue of a phenomenon that Peter Wollen termed 'the two avant-gardes' during the mid-1970s. The first group Wollen described was identified loosely with the Co-op movement and included many of the Structuralist filmmakers whom your recent work has invoked, such as Peter Gidal, Malcolm Le Grice and Gregory Markopoulos. The second included the filmmakers you mention, such as Marker, Jean-Luc Godard, Straub & Huillet, Farocki and others making discursive essay films.

Okwui Enwezor's *Documenta 11* in 2002 helped to cement a growing trend towards presenting documentary-oriented film and video practices in the gallery space. Much of this work is generally more indebted to legacies stemming from Vertov and Sergei Eisenstein than to the formal optics of the Co-op. Subsequently, while there has certainly been a renewed interest in interrogating modes of documentary practice, there's also been a notable popularity for 16mm film

in the art world, as you've suggested, with artists such as Tacita Dean, Mark Leckey and Daria Martin all eschewing large-scale, multiple-screen video installations and instead presenting more discrete 16mm film projections.

Your work is what Wollen would call a 'multiple system'; it seems to occupy a space between these various positions. It's indebted equally to documentaries, essay films and formalist or personal filmmaking. Wollen claimed: 'Though a simple convergence is very unlikely, it is crucial that the two avant-gardes should be confronted and juxtaposed.'[1] Do you feel a need to further resolve these different systems and histories, or to create a space for dialectics and argument? How would such an approach allow you to address vanguard figures from the past and open up the possibilities for representing the full radicality of their contribution?

LF – In many ways, I think Wollen's postulation about the confrontation of two avant-gardes – although a sharp analysis for the time – has been well and truly absorbed into post-medium practice. It doesn't seem like there are two warring camps anymore – or that narrative and didactic interests are inimical to the position of the independent artist filmmaker. So no, I don't feel a need to resolve these histories; I'm engaged in seeking out, looking at and respecting these broad histories for what they are. Now that the gatekeepers of the avant-garde are slowly retiring from the field, we can perhaps begin to see film, cinema, TV documentary, etc for their own individual merits, rather than simply as pawns in an ideological battlefield.

One of the reasons why the avant-garde has broken down has perhaps to do with the loss of community that occured due to stratified production and distribution networks (this split began when London Video Arts was established in the late 1970s). Whether you think this is a good thing or not, there's no longer a central committee like the London Filmmakers, Co-op that came together to produce, share and disseminate theory and practice. This means the central, critical kernal of what would be an avant-garde has fallen away, producing instead an atomised collection of filmmakers and artists whose work is distributed through

1   Peter Wollen, 'The Two Avant-gardes', *Studio International*, London, no. 190, November–December 1975, p. 171–175.

public and private institutions, in both cinemas and the art world.

SC – Could you discuss in more detail your interest in specific filmmakers like the Free Cinema movement, Markopoulos, etc. Your work seems to have developed gradually into a more historically referential practice. How do you think the past resonates in your work, and how does your interest in the live event complicate this?

LF – I find the work of Robert Beavers and Hollis Frampton extraordinary. Frampton argues that film has fallen into a trap of genres, that film should be made over again to include everything from the complexities of the natural world to human consciousness. In Beavers' work I also find this move away from verbal language to uncharted territory in film; he builds fascinating relationships between place, sound, image and the self, offering complex matrixes of images and sounds, in both a cerebral and sensual manner.

I've enjoyed seeing certain Structural works but it feels very connected to a set of concerns and polemics that were being explored at a specific time. I'm not sure how much they resonate outside of that moment. Nathaniel Dorsky, the great American filmmaker, said a nice thing about how making a film was like a heartfelt conversation with a friend – one should always try and be a good communicator, responding equally from the heart and the intellect. In his opinion, all too often artists are very bad communicators; they're patronising, didactic, repetitive and boring. Their aim, it often seems, is only to torture the audience.

In terms of resonating with the past, I don't know – it would depend what past you're talking about. Of course, the films resonate personally with my own past and clearly many of them engage with historical turning points – Kingsley Hall, The Scratch Orchestra, punk. I hope that this engagement is one that's questioning and re-activating, rather than merely representing tired old clichés.

SC – In terms of your own past, your early work, such as the SHADAZZ project, was very much rooted in the Glasgow music scene. Music and sound investigations still play a primary role in your work, such as your recent collaboration with Toshiya. How would you relate this to your earlier projects?

LF – Actually, I see them as quite separate entities. SHADAZZ is a vehicle for releasing my music and that of my friends – it has no remit other than putting out things I'd like to hear and champion. It's a very small, sporadic labour of love.

The first music project I was involved in was at the age of fourteen or fifteen with a friend called Luke Arnold who played bass. I had a four-track and he'd been given this copycat (an early tape echo) machine by a musician friend of his parents. We always used to run out of blank tapes to record onto, so we'd record over my Mum's interview tapes; quite often the voice would seep through like a ghost in the mix, or else it would come through between tracks. Later on, during art college, when I made *The Social Engineer* project, I created these contrived interviews, as I said, and used them as source material for compositions. This marked my predilection for combining the voice, sometimes purely as a texture, against more dissonant sounds and music. These were the sorts of different media that I was trying to fuse when I came to using film. I find the trajectory in the new works comes from striving to create something that excites me, that affords the possibility to collaborate and investigate ideas, arguments, people and places in new configurations. Past works often inform this process, in that I'm trying to push further or even against my own established methodologies.

The collaboration with Toshiya came out of the invitation to participate in the Yokohama Triennale and from an intense interest in his sound works. I'd met him the year before, when he was invited by Arika to make some sound installations for a project in Argyll called *Half Life*. I was working on a film with Lee Patterson at the time, and so I doubled up as both a driver on their field-recording expeditions and a documentarist. Toshiya and I had some interesting discussions during that time. His interest, he said, was not in field-recording per se. He doesn't just go out with his equipment and collect or hunt for sounds; it stems from a more philosophical base. In trying to record the shifting conditions of objects or features of familiar places, he's attempting to create the sonic equivalent of the draughtsman's 'perfect circle', to document unusual sound phenomena (e.g. air-borne or solid vibrations) that are omnipresent but imperceptible to the ear. In many ways, it's a very structural approach to sound. The work has no pretensions towards being music on the one hand or pseudo-scientific research on the other. They're recordings made by a consummate observer. The value lies in the inherent qualities of the sounds themselves and the subtle differences he reveals as he presents several instances of these phenomena while collecting them, in different conditions. I thought it would be a fascinating experience to work with him on a film. And so I invited him to collaborate on a joint work for Yokohama.

Toshiya sent me this beautiful statement where he draws up an intention to create simple artworks that are devoid of signification or wider meaningful strategies. He wanted to see what artworks would be like if they were freed as much as possible from artistic intentions. Perhaps in a way he's describing a situation analogous to the phenomena he seeks to record. The vibrations have no narrative or conceptual meaning; they're simply by-products of material relations between an object and its environment.

Immediately, Toshiya's interest was drawn towards, for him, a new set of conditions – the film projection. By adding these quite theatrical props (fan, lights, wire) into the film installation we were aiming to challenge the illusory nature of the image and disrupting the viewer's immersion in it. The images in our film derive from both an empathy for each other's approach and disparity in our histories and different modes of production, while firmly avoiding a compromising resolution.

sc – You've also recently collaborated with Keith Rowe, a founding member of AMM and a key figure in improvisational sound practice. What was it like to work with him after having made a film about Cardew?

LF – I met Keith once when he played with John Tilbury in Glasgow. Because Tilbury was doing the biography of Cornelius it seemed more appropriate to talk to him about the project than Keith. When I was doing the interviews, I did write to Keith, who lives in France, but I didn't receive anything back, so I just went ahead without his contribution, which I always thought was a shame because it would have been important to have included his opinion on things. Isn't there an old proverb that says the absent person is always in the wrong? It seems, based on a remark he makes in the archive footage and an interview with John, that Keith was somehow responsible for the Maoist agitation that led to factions within the orchestra. It was good to eventually get his side of the story. Keith was very close to Cardew and his politics; he quite selflessly dedicated himself to left-wing campaigns (against imperialism, racism, 'the troubles'), playing very traditional guitar in what was the essentially agit-prop, marching-band context of People's Liberation Music. Eventually he returned to the more abstract concerns of AMM.

Working with Keith and the filmmaker Peter Todd was really great because there seemed to be a complete trust and respect for each other's capacities. I think there's a lot of confusion about Keith's methodology as an improviser; several people have been disparaging of the fact that Keith doesn't seem to respond to what his fellow collaborators are doing. Well, if he is doing that, in my mind that doesn't make him a bad improviser, it raises questions of why improvisers seem to tacitly rely on agreed modes of behaviour and interaction. Why isn't it valid to improvise with the conditions of a room or the aleatory events that randomly tuning a radio raises? I think it's a quite a generous contribution to create a blanket, underlying colour for others to cut into and shape. In this way, I think Keith is a very enthusiastic, innovative and non-judgmental improviser.

sc – I'm interested in how your interest in collaboration across artistic generations extends to, or might connect with, your 'portrait' films. How do you think your approach to documentary liberates the subjects of your films from mere biography? Do the subjects of your films become meta-figures for a broader interest that you seem to have in radical politics?

 Firstly, whatever my sympathies, it would be disingenuous to call myself an activist, or to suggest that I had any profound engagement with radical political groups. I'm attempting to make personal films that find new forms and ask questions.

Bogman Palmjaguar (2007) is a film that raises questions about the coherence and narrative construction of documentary and biography. Narratives on mental illness often disguise the underlying social conditions and conflicts that can create, in the individual, an angry or mistrustful relationship towards others. In my film, I first outline several experiences of Bogman's life as a conservationist; these slowly unravel into painful narratives of abuse and betrayal. Mediated through the film's namesake, one builds up an idea of how Bogman has been shaped by a complex series of social processes. It's only through our own personal experiences that we can form a reaction to these processes, which will allow us to either empathise or evoke suspicion towards his position.

The normative modes of communicating a story of mental illness tend to look at the individual in isolation – as a case study – rather than try to understand these complex social processes that have created the 'troublesome' behaviour. Cinéma vérité or more recent forms of 'Reality TV' attempt to break with the notion of the person as persona. They deceptively attempt to reveal 'the man behind the mask'. This fails to accept that the individual is often playing a conscious role in their own self-presentation.

I think documentary often falls into the trap of being restricted by the notion of 'reality' and impartiality, since it clearly can't be hinged on objective realities. Conversely, I'm striving to create a set of experiences, views or fragments that resist becoming a neatly packaged and mediated experience, but instead struggle to question the complex and contradictory accounts that together make up 'collective representations', that attempt to realise the potential for film to embrace the complexities and contradictions of lived experience and shared histories.

As an artist, I've decided to ask these questions using an aesthetic language, not simply as a historian or biographer would. Ultimately, the worth of my works can only be judged through the laws of images and how durable these images are.

The conversation was held on 28–29 February 2009.

Filmography

All Production, Direction, Camera, Editing
and Sound Design by Luke Fowler unless
otherwise stated.

What You See
Is Where You're At

DVD, colour and b/w, sound
24 min.
Production: Dundee Contemporary Arts,
Dundee
Editing Assistance: Torsten Lauschmann
Sound design: Rob Kennedy
Music: Hassle Hound
Interview narration: Dr Leon Redler
and Luke Fowler
Archive: Dr Leon Redler, Richard Adams,
Estate of Ronald D. Laing, Oddvar Foss

Selected exhibitions
2008
Kunsthalle Zürich, Zurich
2007
Widening Horizon, Pleasure Dome,
Toronto
2005
Beck's Futures, ICA – Institute of
Contemporary Arts, London; CCA – The
Centre for Contemporary Arts, Glasgow
2004
Anti-Psychiatry Film Festival, Nova
Cinema, Brussels
2003
What You See Is Where You're At,
Spacex, Exeter
Art/34/Basel, Basel
Electric Earth (British Council touring
exhibition), State Russian Museum,
St Petersburg; Radio Laboratory
Museum, Nizhni Novgorod; Yaroslavl
Museum of Fine Art, Yaroslav; Na
Solyanke Gallery, Moscow etc.
2001
Beyond, Dundee Contemporary Arts,
Dundee

Luke Fowler's film *What You See Is Where You're At* was inspired by the pioneering work of the psychiatrist, psychoanalyst and writer, Ronald D. Laing, who set up an experimental residential community at Kingsley Hall. The experiment constituted a daring and innovative approach and response to 'madness'. A breakdown – perhaps of a way of being that was no longer tenable, perhaps a breakdown of way of not being oneself – was seen to be a possible beginning of a breakthrough in the healing of the fragmentations and disturbances of mind, body, soul and spirit.

Conventional psychiatric diagnosis (rarely the 'seeing through' implied by its etymology), in reducing complex experiences within particular social contexts to categories of illness, could not do justice to the complexity and depth of the experiences of many people in mental distress. Conventional treatment, while often achieving dramatic 'results' with people who were disturbed and/or disturbing to others, too often suppressed, obfuscated or deferred the facing up to urgent, painful and perplexing emotional, existential, spiritual and ethical issues. At Kingsley Hall, people were allowed to find their own way, in their own way and in their own time, whether on their own or in whosoever company they chose to keep.

Was the Kingsley Hall experience a success? It was and it wasn't, depending on who you were and on your definition of what constituted 'success'. It was a success in raising questions that need to be asked in every generation: What do we mean by 'sanity' and 'madness'? On what basis, and involving what and whose interests is that distinction made? What is at stake in how such questions are asked and answered by each of us and by those empowered to pronounce and act on these matters? It was a success in so far as it gave space and respect to the human spirit of inquiry into who we really are and what might be better ways of being-in-the-world with one another, especially when in real distress or on difficult 'journeys'. Such spirit resists the constraints of convention and transcends temptations to deaden our pain and anguish without thoughtful consideration of the cost of such deadening with regard to a passion to live with greater integrity, vitality and responsibility.

Fowler was attracted by the courage, drama, pathos, poetry and sometimes near surrealism unfolding between the diverse characters at Kingsley Hall. 'First and foremost I was drawn to the Kingsley Hall experiment because of personal circumstance, i.e., my own experiences of contemporary psychiatry […] disillusion with the way in which my father was treated by the system, and an overall healthy, cynical attitude towards institutions.' (Luke Fowler in conversation with Dr Leon Redler, 2000)

Fowler has added his dissenting voice to others critical of what looks very much like a psychopharmacological industry, the legal drug cartels with vast and effective influence over psychiatric training, practice and research. The unholy alliance of psychiatry with the pharmaceutical industry, encouraged by governments run increasingly as corporate states, effectively marginalises those who question prevailing materialist values and seek sources of mental suffering in the way in which we live together and treat each other.

—Dr Leon Redler

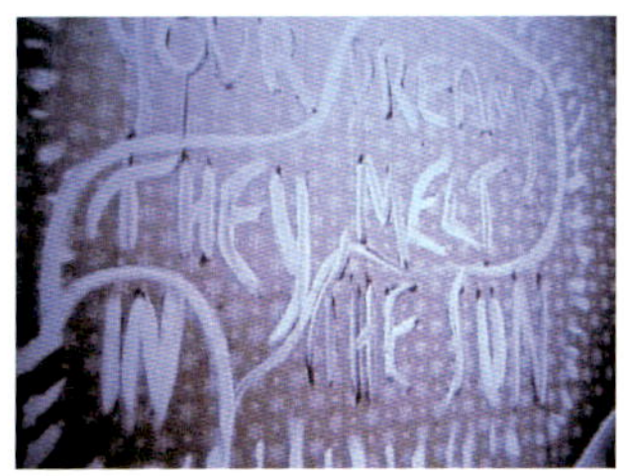
THEY MELT
IN
THE SUN
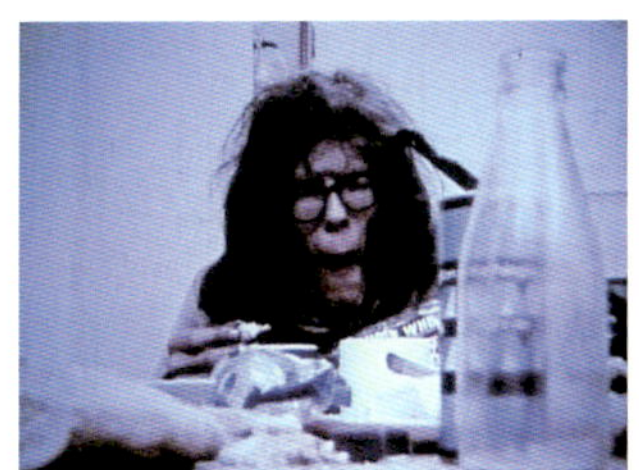
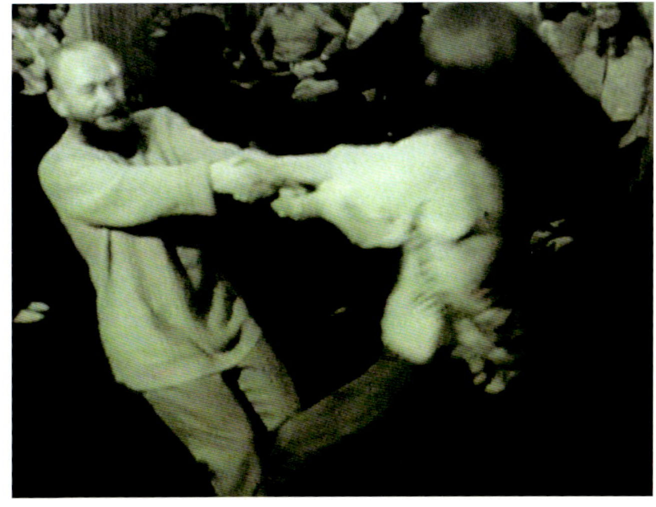
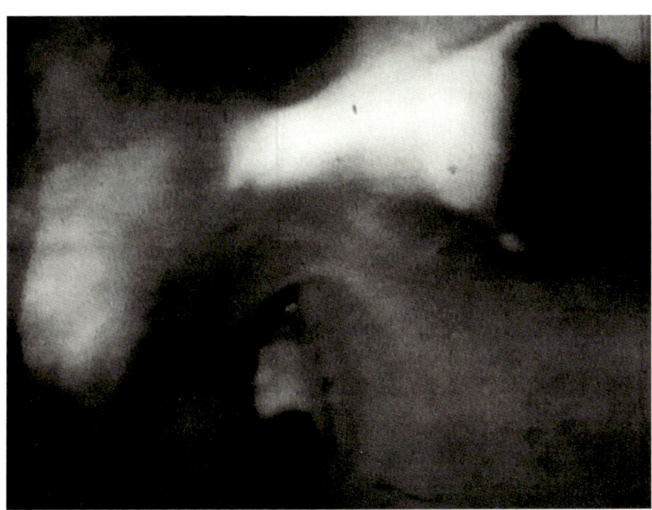
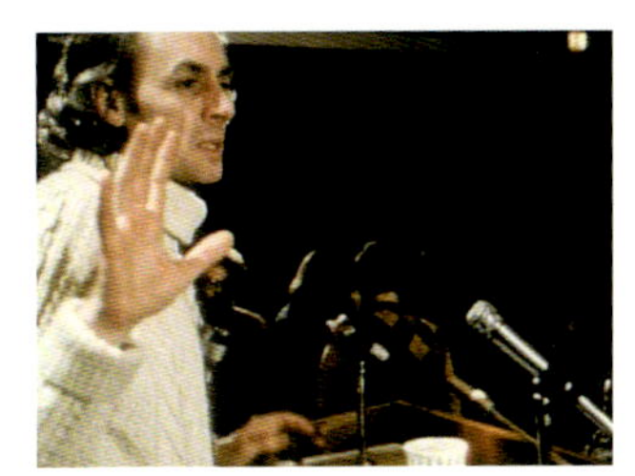
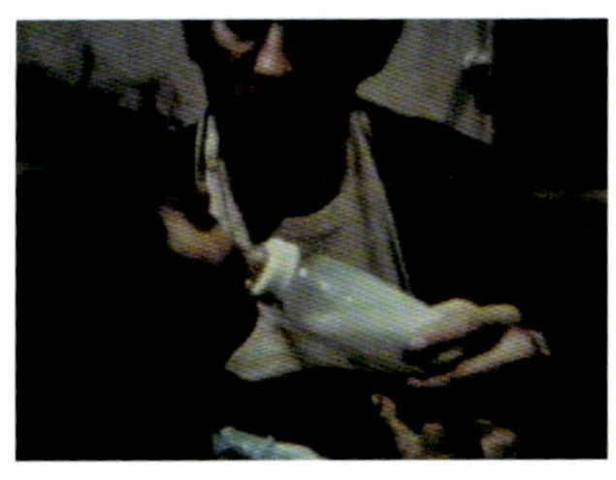
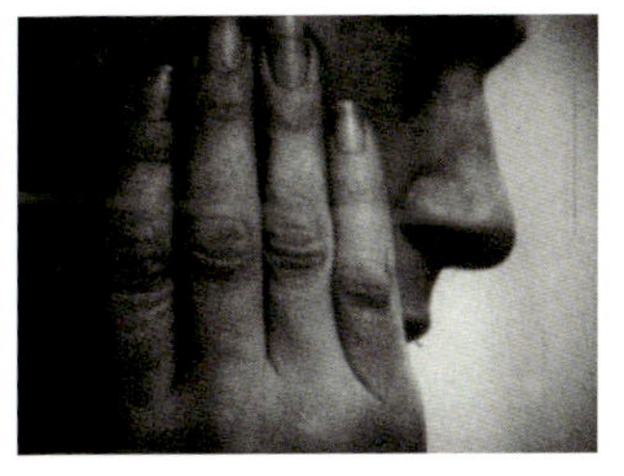
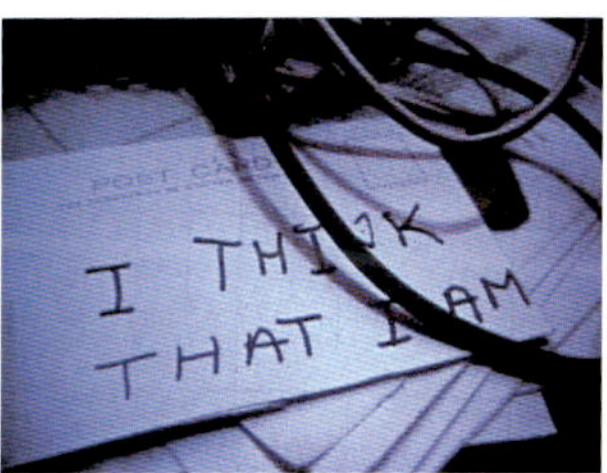
POST CARD
I THINK
THAT I AM
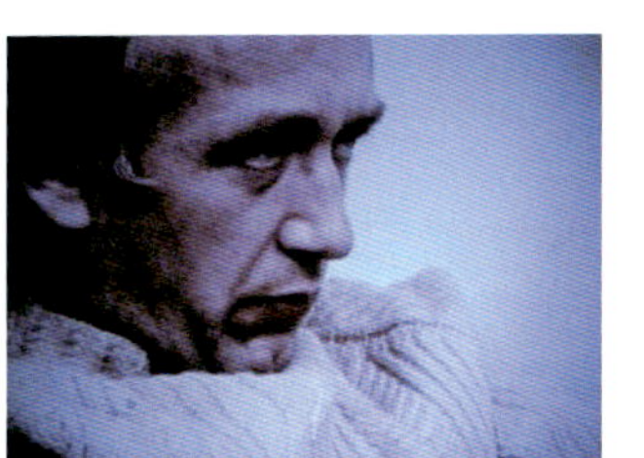
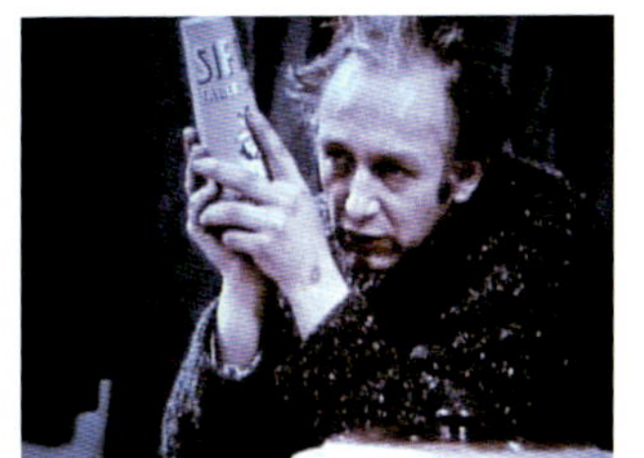
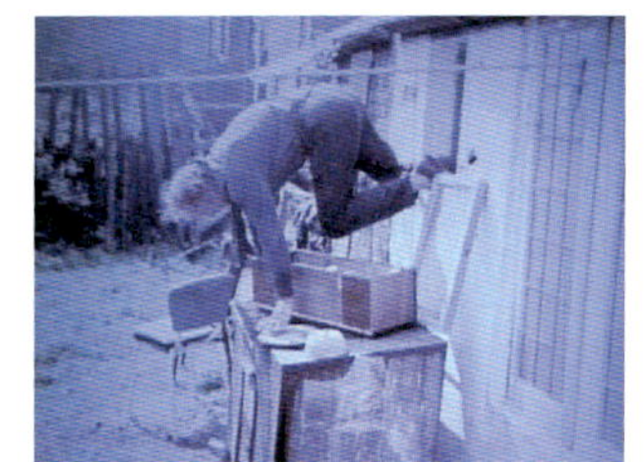

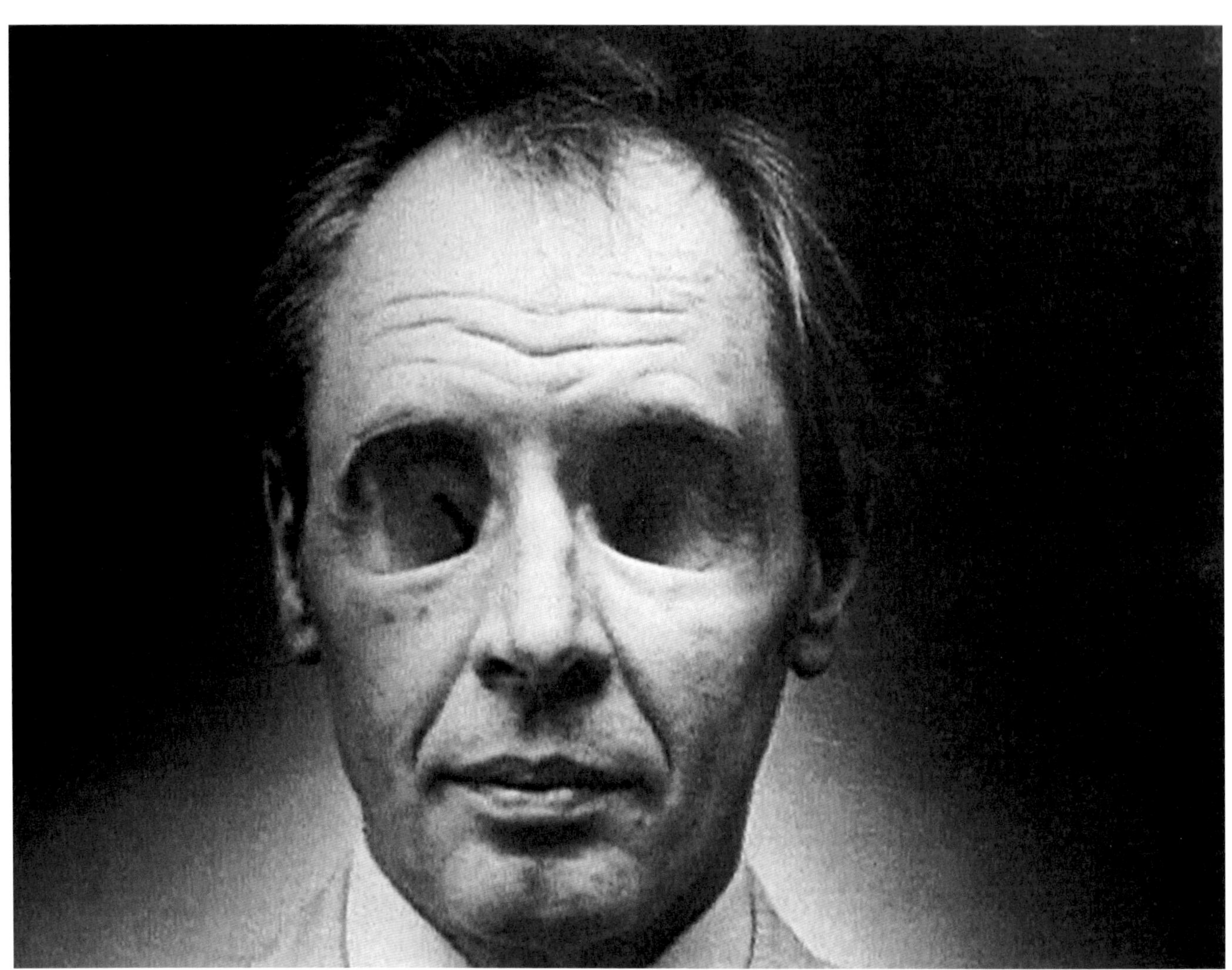

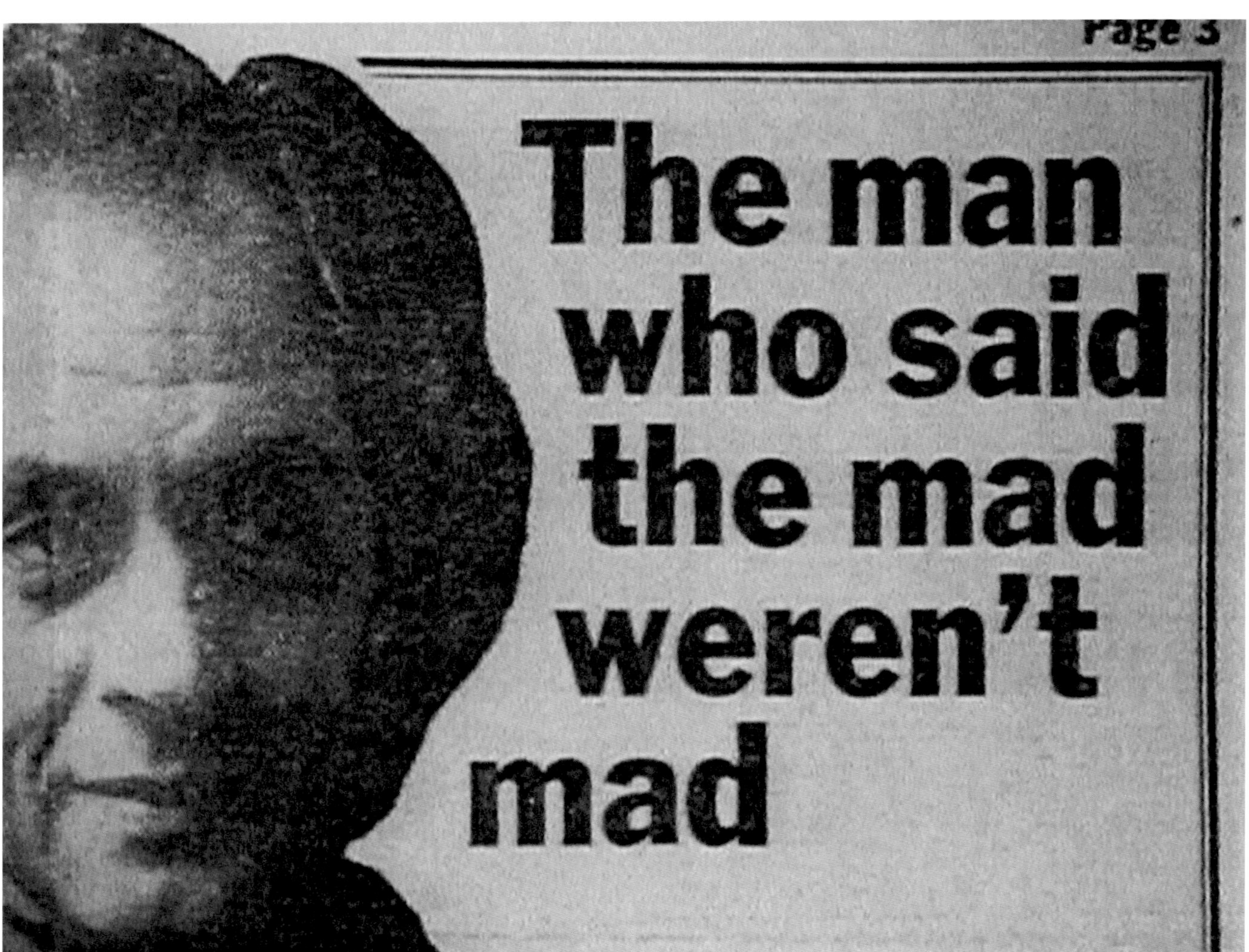
The man
who said
the mad
weren't
mad

The Way Out
(with Kosten Koper)

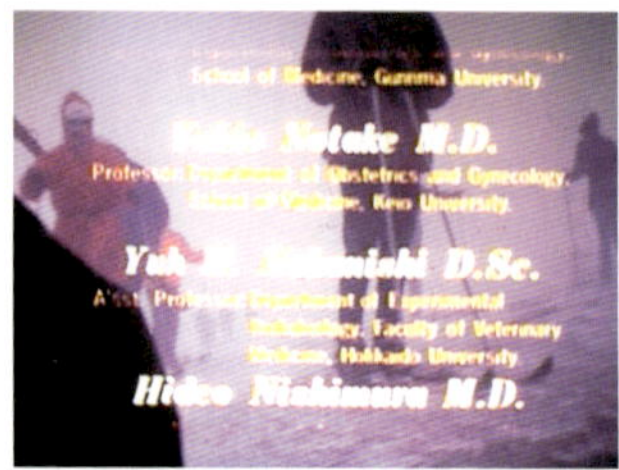

DVD, colour and b/w, sound
33 min.
Production: Cubitt Gallery (Emily
Pethick), London; Zenomap; The Modern
Institute/Toby Webster Ltd, Glasgow
Camera: Luke Fowler, Kosten Koper,
Will Hunt
Editing Assistance: Duncan Campbell
Music: Die Trip Computer Die,
The Homosexuals, Harmon E. Phraisyer,
Xentos Jones, Milk From Cheltenham,
L Voag, Leonard and Rodger,
Comrad O'leau
Narration: Danny Saunders
Cast: Bing Selfish, Ed Baxter, Lepke B,
Charlotte Prodger, Kosten Koper, Franz
Ferdinand, Optimo
Archives: Xentos 'Fray Bentos', Lepke B

Selected exhibitions
2009
Serpentine Gallery, London
2008
Kunsthalle Zürich, Zurich
2007
Widening Horizon, Pleasure Dome,
Toronto
Whenever It Starts It Is The Right Time,
Frankfurter Kunstverein, Frankfurt
am Main
2006
Adventures in Modern Music, The Gene
Siskel Film Center, Chicago
2005
Beck's Futures, ICA – Institute of
Contemporary Arts, London; CCA – The
Centre for Contemporary Arts, Glasgow
2003
*Jakob Kolding, Luke Fowler/Kosten
Koper*, Cubitt Gallery, London
*ZENOMAP – New Works from Scotland
for the Venice Biennale*, 50. Biennale
di Venezia, Venice
Art/34/Basel, Basel

The Way Out, profiles Xentos 'Fray Bentos'
Jones, one of the founding members of
The Homosexuals, a band that lapsed into
obscurity after self-releasing a number of
groundbreaking records in the post-punk
period. Although The Homosexuals dis-
banded without ever releasing an author-
ised album, L Voag (aka Xentos) released his
own solo project, *The Way Out*, in 1979. *The
Way* Out was a cut-up DIY concept album
that imagined a musical context situated
in an inverted parallel universe where pop
music is made by modernist, serialist com-
posers and the avant-garde is left to those
on the fringes of acceptance. Amos (aka
Xentos) continued to produce and distribute
a mass of diverse tape projects throughout
the 1980s on his own label, It's War Boys,
spanning most known and unknown musical
genres, under a myriad of multiple identities.
The Way Out interweaves new interviews,
scripted scenes, found and filmed footage
with unearthed Super-8 films by Xentos
himself.

—Luke Fowler

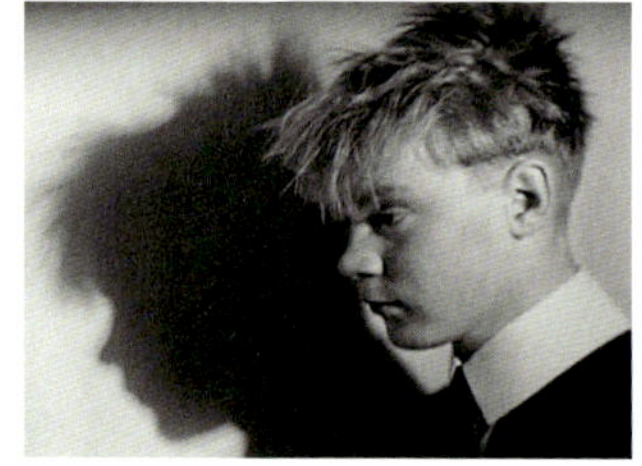

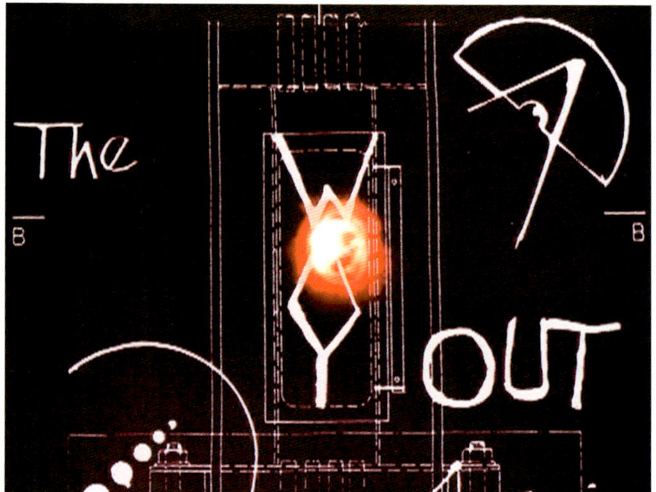

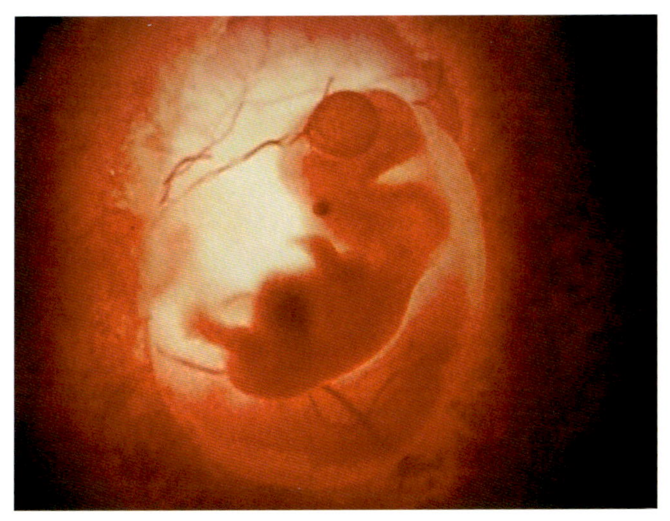
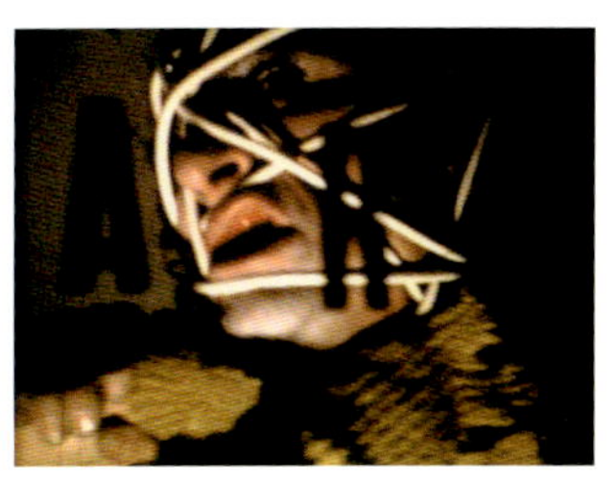
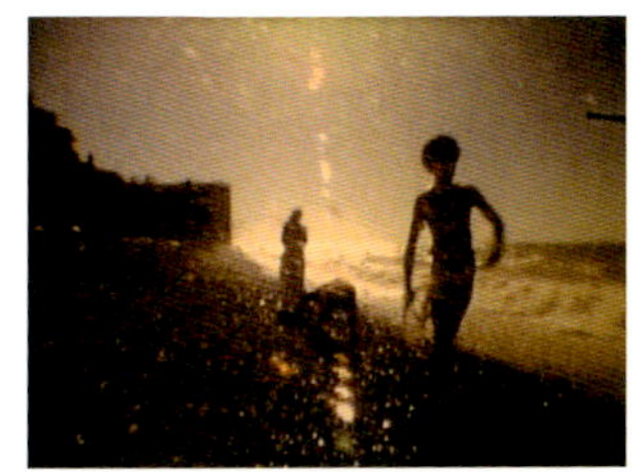
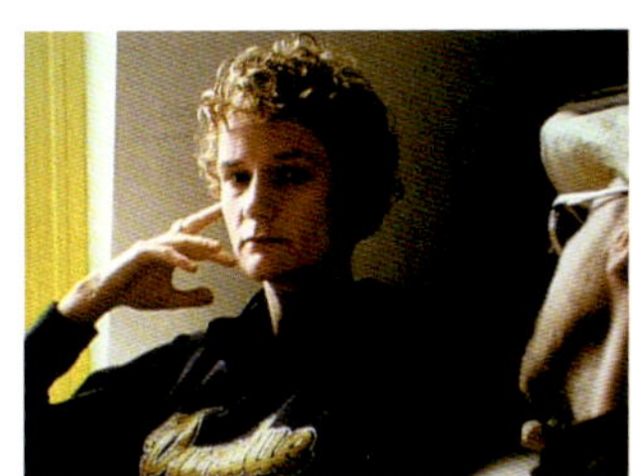
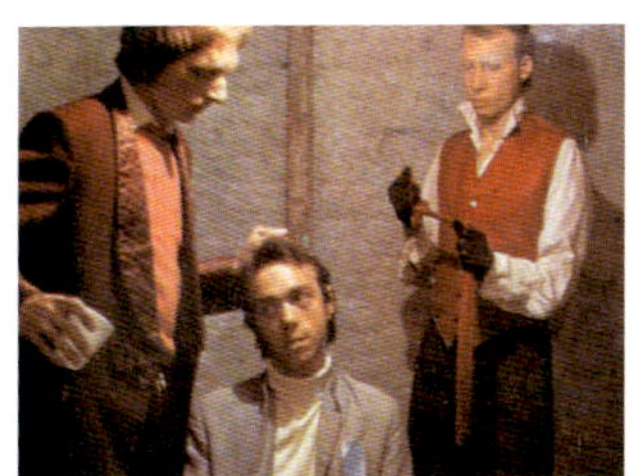
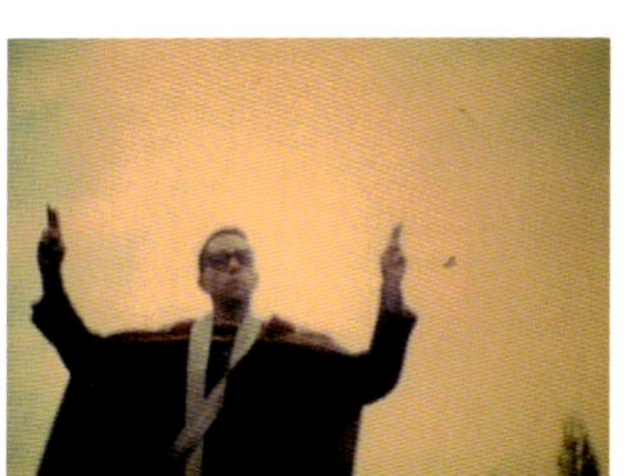
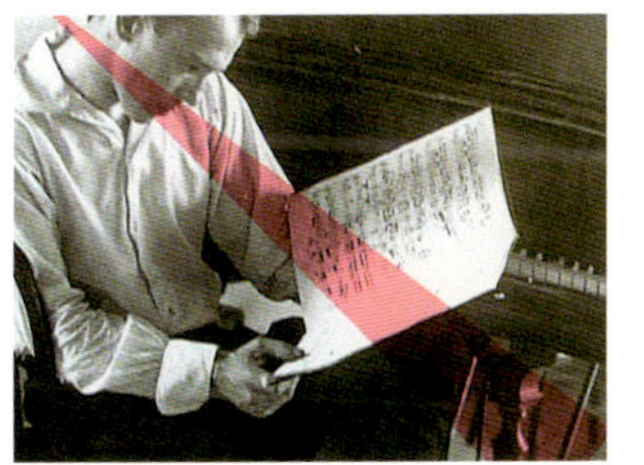
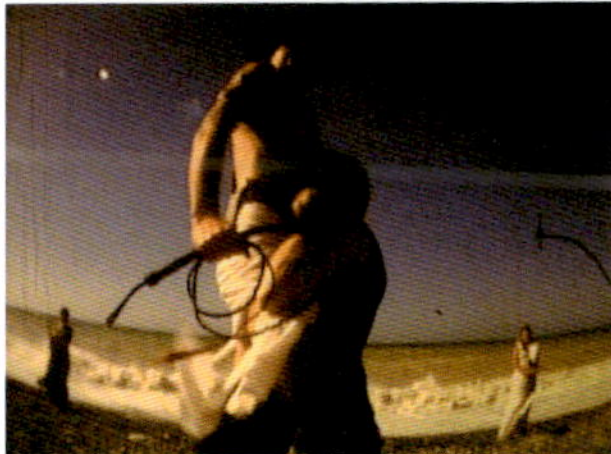
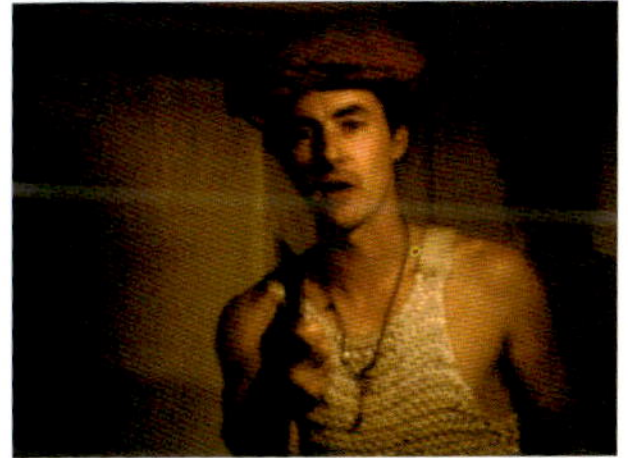
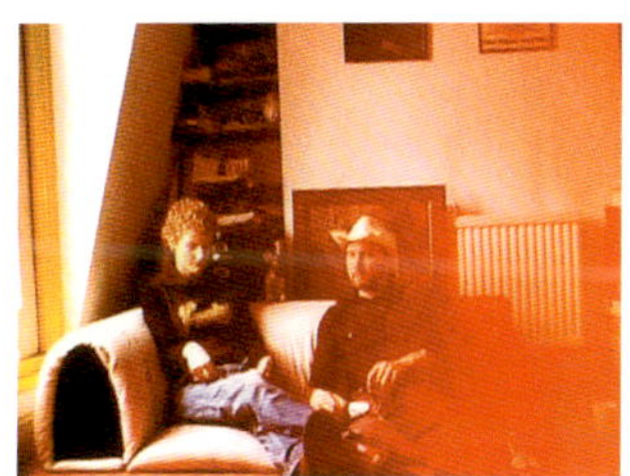

Pilgrimage from Scattered Points

DVD, colour and b/w, sound
45 min.
Production: Dewar Arts Award,
Kirkcudbright; The Modern Institute/
Toby Webster Ltd, Glasgow
Camera: Luke Fowler, Guy Corbishley,
Lucile Desamoray, Alasdair Willis
Music: Cornelius Cardew and The
Scratch Orchestra, Michael Chant and
Hugh Shrapnell, Thurston Moore, John
Tilbury, Richard Ascough, Chris May,
Christian Wolff, David Jackman
Cast: Cornelius Cardew (from archive),
John Tilbury, Michael Chant, David
Sladen, Bryn Harris, Christopher Hobbs,
Edwin Prevost, Richard Ascough,
Laurie Baker, Stella Cardew, Psi Ellison,
Hugh Shrapnell, Carole Finer, Michael
Parsons, Dave Smith
Archive: Cardew Estate, Hanne
Boenisch, Arts Council England, BBC,
Werner Bethsold, Michael Chant,
Richard Ascough, Psi Ellison, Carole
Finer, Alec Hill, Bryn Harris, David
Jackman, Hugh Shrapnell, Dave Smith,
Victor Schoenfield, John Tilbury

Selected Exhibitions
2009
The NOW now festival, Sydney
Serpentine Gallery, London
The Associates, DCA – Dundee
Contemporary Arts, Dundee
2008
Milton Keynes Gallery, Milton Keynes
Sónar 2008, Barcelona
*CPH:DOX International Documentary Film
Festival*, Copenhagen
Hot Docs, Austin
Courtisane Film Festival, Arts Centre
Vooruit & Sphinx Cinema, Ghent
*KVIFF – Karlovy Vary International
Film Festival*, Prague International Film
Festival, Prague
OFF: Other Film Festival, Brisbane
Artists's Films, Camden Arts Centre,
London
The New Museum, New York
2007
Widening Horizon, Pleasure Dome,
Toronto
You Have Not Been Honest, Museo
d'Arte Contemporanea Donnaregina,
Naples
*Never Still. MAP Magazine presents
new artists' film*, CCA – The Centre for
Contemporary Arts, Glasgow
Twighlight Adventures in Music,
Whitechapel Art Gallery, London
Kraak Festival, Hasselt
2006
White Columns, New York
The Modern Institute/Toby Webster Ltd,
Glasgow
Tate Triennial. New British Art, Tate
Britain, London
*State of Innocence. International Film
Festival Rotterdam*, Rotterdam
Adventures in Modern Music, The Gene
Siskel Film Center, Chicago
Normalisering, Rooseum Centre for
Contemporary Art, Malmö
Avanto Festival, Muu Galleria, Helsinki

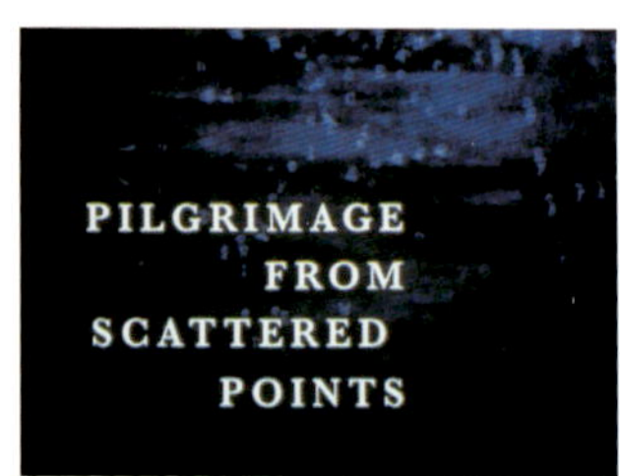

Pilgrimage from Scattered Points is a film
about the English composer Cornelius
Cardew (1936–1981) and The Scratch
Orchestra (1968–1973). Cardew formed The
Scratch Orchestra with Michael Parsons and
Howard Skempton in 1968, and published
its draft constitution in *The Musical Times*
in June 1969. The constitution set out the
framework that would dominate the orchestra's musical work for the first half of its
existence. It proposed a fluid community
where students, office workers, amateur
musicians and some professional compos-
ers would gather together for performance,
music-making and edification.

The only full-length recording of The Scratch
Orchestra available is a performance of
Cardew's *The Great Learning* (1968–1970), a
six-hour choral work written for the orchestra based on the Confucian scriptures. The
work calls for a large number of trained and
untrained musicians to sing, speak, drum,
perform actions and gestures, improvise and
use conventional and unconventional sound
sources.

The Scratch Orchestra's concerts often
consisted of the following: 'Scratch Music',
which relied on graphic or verbal instruc-
tion instead of traditional musical nota-
tion; 'Popular Classics', where established
works, mainly from the classical canon, were
subverted; 'Improvisation Rites', a communal starting point for semi-structured, free

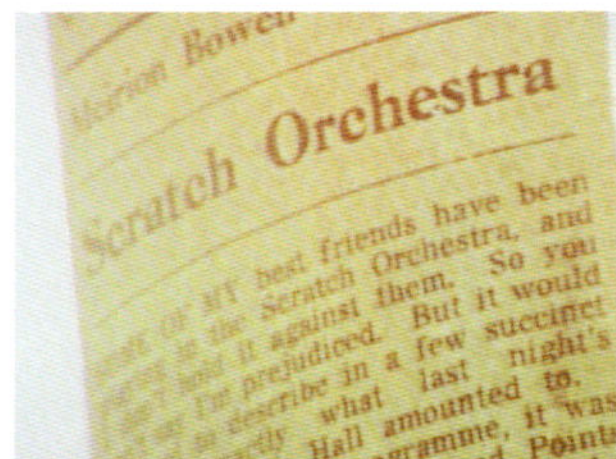
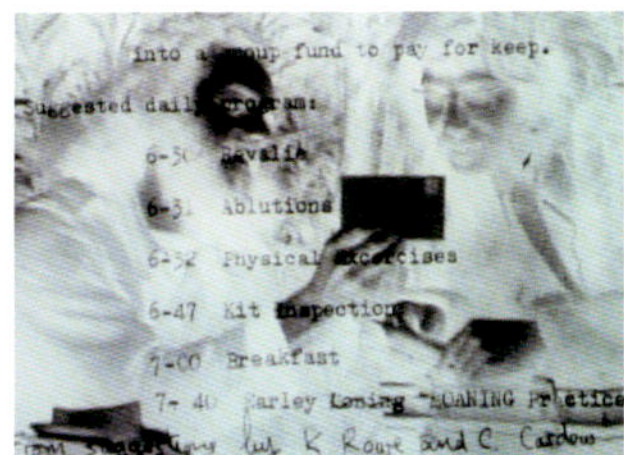
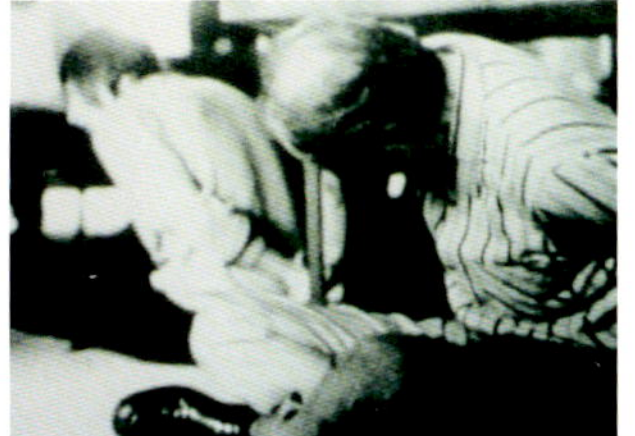
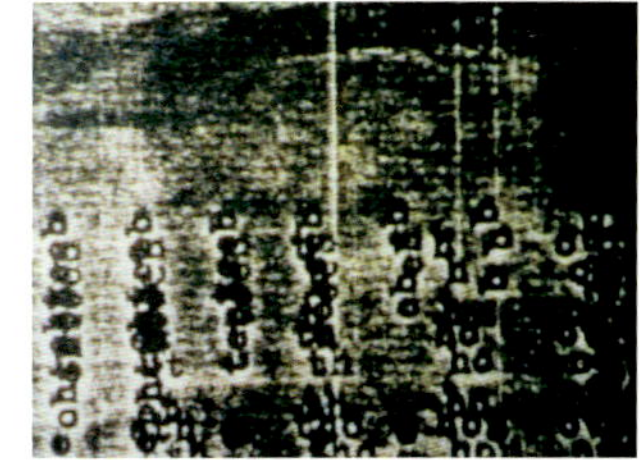
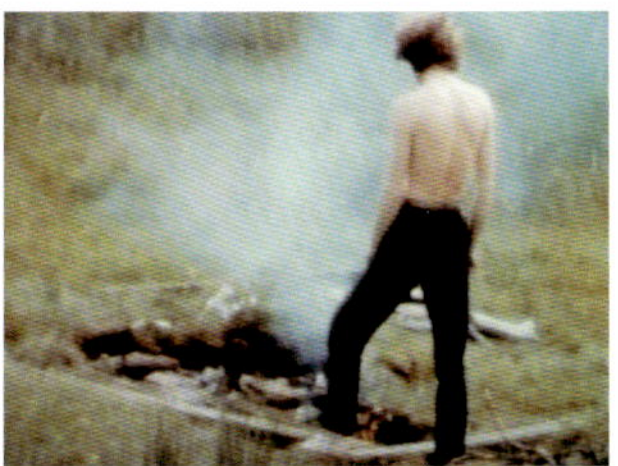
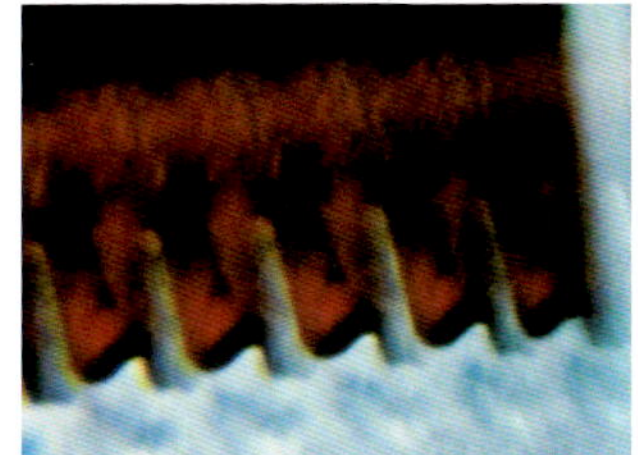
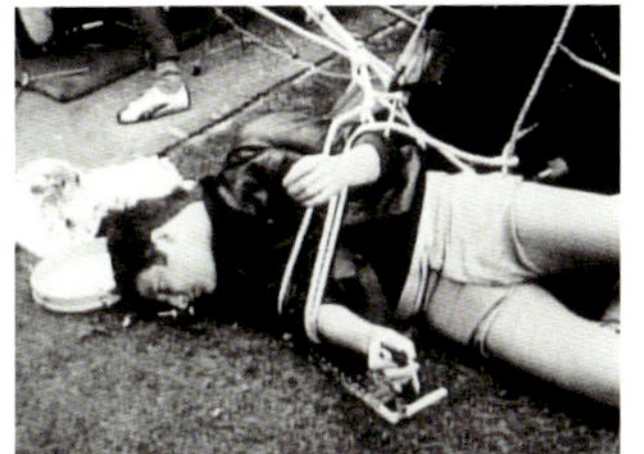
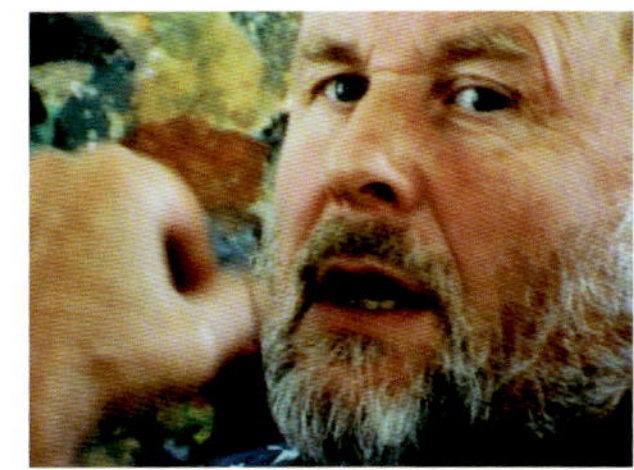
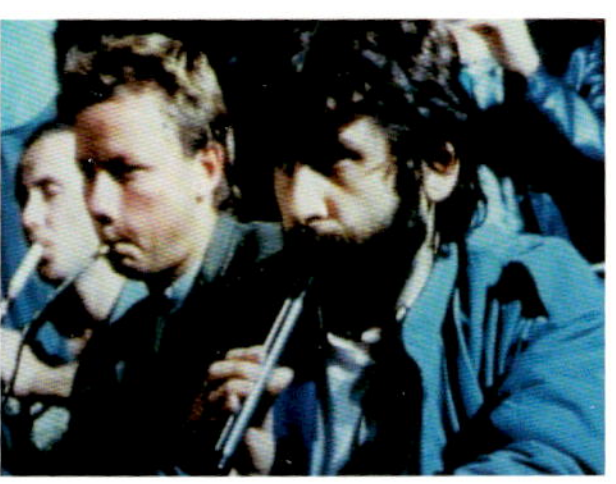
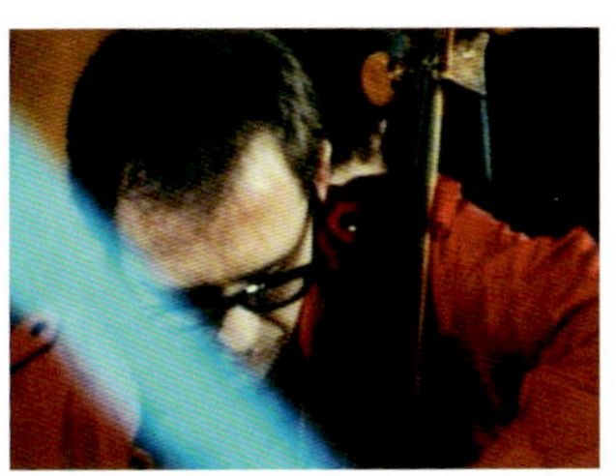
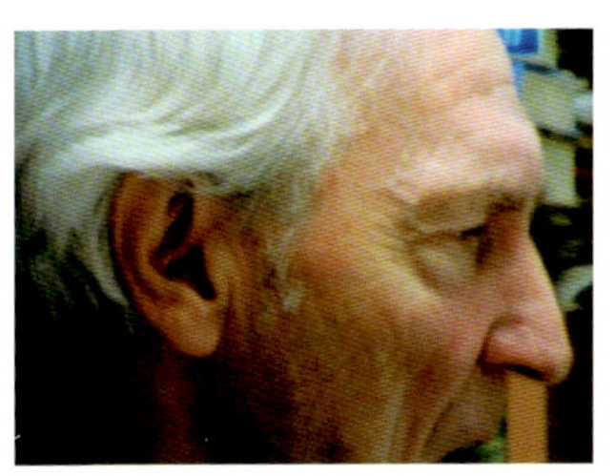
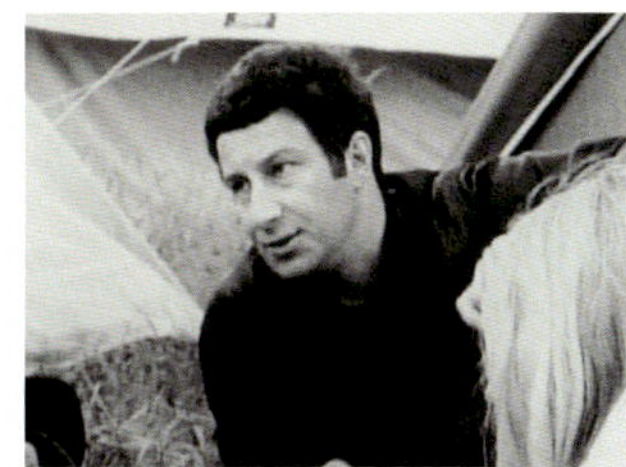

improvisation; 'Research Projects', journeys that were undertaken in many dimensions — temporal, spatial, intellectual, spiritual and emotional. Rejecting the musical establishment, the orchestra sought out new locations and audiences for its music. Concerts could take place in town halls, train stations, shopping centres and boating lakes, at weddings or remote village halls.

After two years, this musical and social experiment became rigorously self-critical, with debates about the function of its art and whom it served. To manifest this criticism, meetings were held and a 'discontent file' drawn up. This triggered a split in the orchestra into two opposing camps. The first camp, 'the ID group', believed in the Maoist dictum that music should serve the struggle of the broad masses. The second, the 'bourgeois idealists', struggled for an autonomous art that primarily served formal, musical experiments and self-expression.

In Pilgrimage from Scattered Points the internal contradictions and struggles of The Scratch Orchestra are related through interviews, recent and archival footage and predominantly unreleased music.

—Luke Fowler

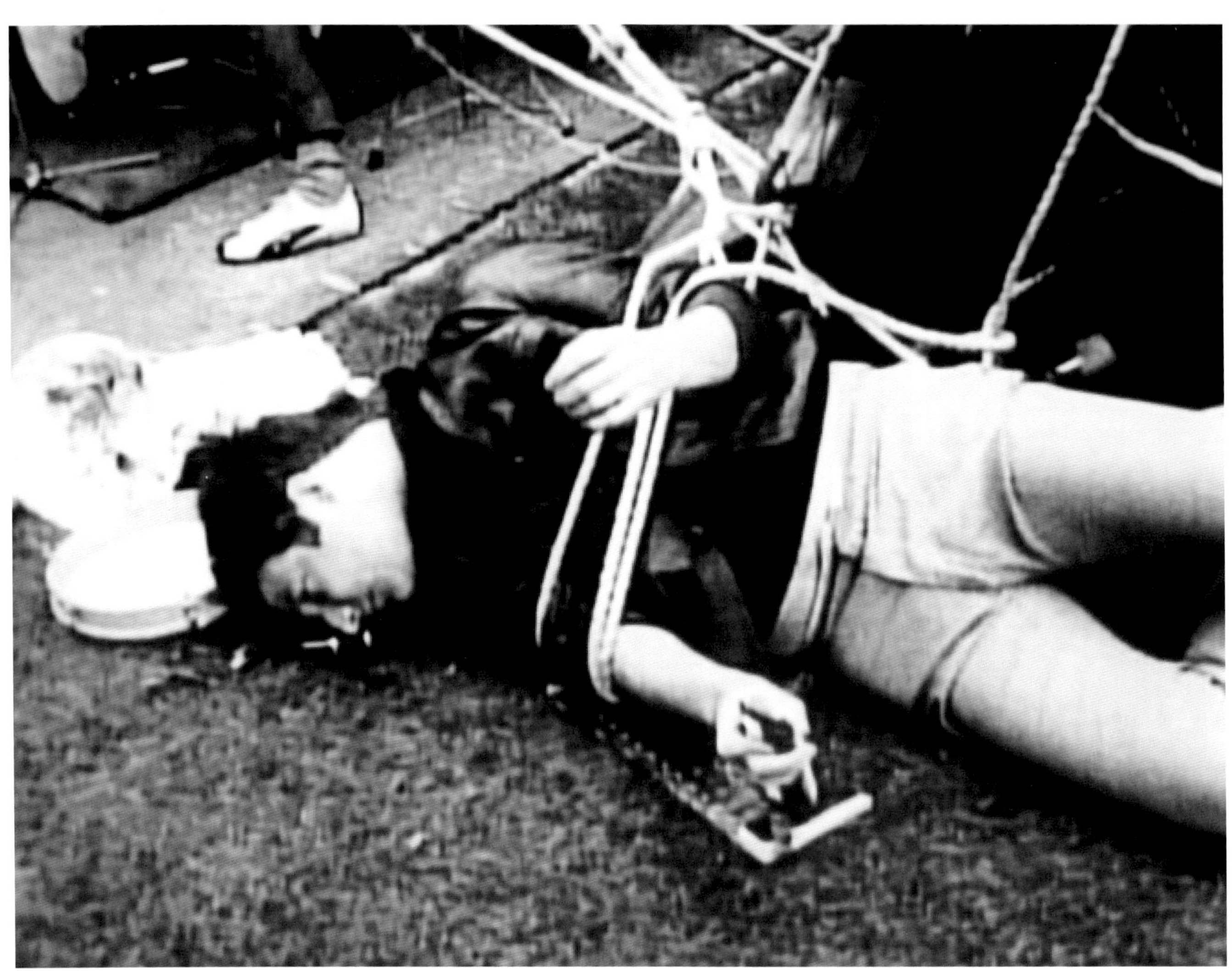

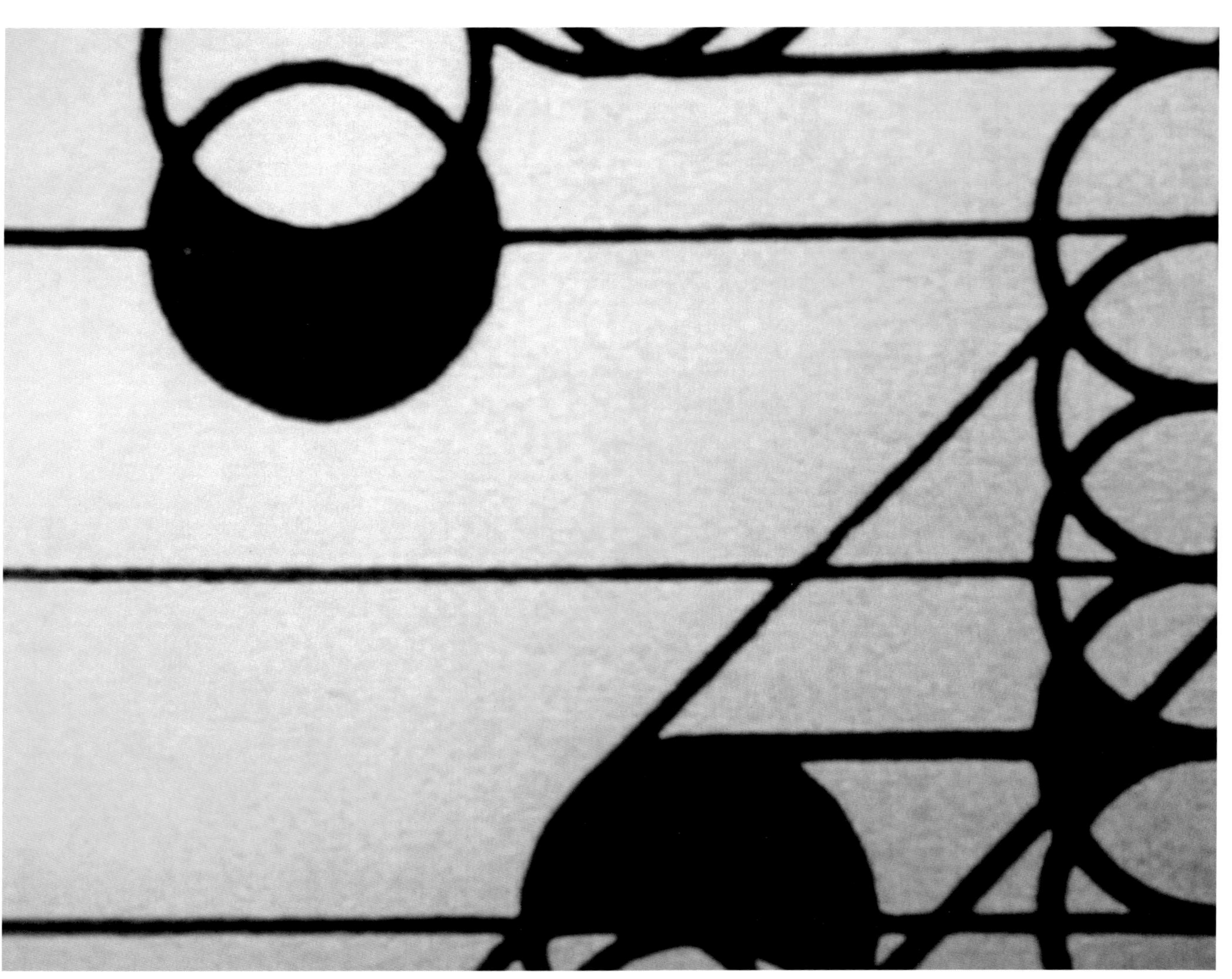

The Nine Monads
of David Bell

Installation of sound, b/w, Super-8 film and archive materials
50 min.
Production: The Modern Institute/Toby Webster Ltd, Glasgow; Dr Leon Redler
Music: Stuart MacRae
Cast: Stephan Bach, Ursel and Felix Gumbsch, Ulrich Bohnefeld, Bambam (film), David Bell, Leon Redler (sound)

Selected exhibitions
2009
Serpentine Gallery, London
2007
Extra City – centrum voor hedendaagse kunst, Antwerp
2006
Villa Concordia, Bamberg

The installation *The Nine Monads of David Bell* consists of a new body of work that departs from Luke Fowler's earlier film *What You See Is Where You're At* (2001), a portrait of the Kingsley Hall community (1965–1969) set up by maverick psychiatrist Ronald D. Laing and the Philadelphia Association to offer a place of refuge for those who were disturbed, distressed or mentally ill. *The Nine Monads of David Bell* is an investigation into the world of David Bell, one of Kingsley Hall's most poetic and verbose residents. Bell was a mathematician who moved to London in the 1950s to work as a computer programmer. After being rejected by his girlfriend, Bell's eccentric behaviour became a cause for alarm and he was sectioned. This led to his move to Kingsley Hall and his befriending by Dr Leon Redler, a young American psychiatrist who came to London to work with Laing. Despite the local mental hospital's characterisation of Bell's language as pure 'schizophrenese', at Kingsley Hall his words were valued and documented. Further documents pertaining to Bell, who died in the 1990s, where preserved by Redler, material on which the present installation is based.

The central component of this installation is a sound element lasting fifty minutes. This material has been edited from tapes recorded between 1965 and 1976 at Kingsley Hall and later at Redler's private practice. Fowler structured the material in order to highlight a linear representation Bell's changing states. While the first part documents Bell in various social situations around Kingsley Hall, the second half focuses on internal struggles between his three distinct personages, 'he', 'she' and 'boy'. The last section offers a stark contrast to this; here we find him under strong medication and in therapy with Redler, offering a lucid, yet lacklustre self-reflection on his behaviour over the years.

The transferred Super-8 film displayed on a monitor shows a recent film that Fowler made with amateur actors enacting Bell's dreams. Memories of these dreams were also recorded on tape. Fowler has depicted four dream sequences.

The photographic documentation is comprised of three series. The first shows a series of newspapers that Bell used as writing paper, juxtaposing articles, advertisements and Bell's own notes. The second series shows extracts from Bell's loose-leaf notebook. The final series comprises photographs taken at Archways Community, the Philadelphia Association's successor to Kingsley Hall. The photographs depict Bell and his fellow residents in various social situations. These photographs have been attributed to Mike Yokum, resident and caretaker at Archways Community. The exhibition also features two miscellaneous handwritten cards and a passport that Bell has defaced.

—Anselm Franke and Dr Leon Redler

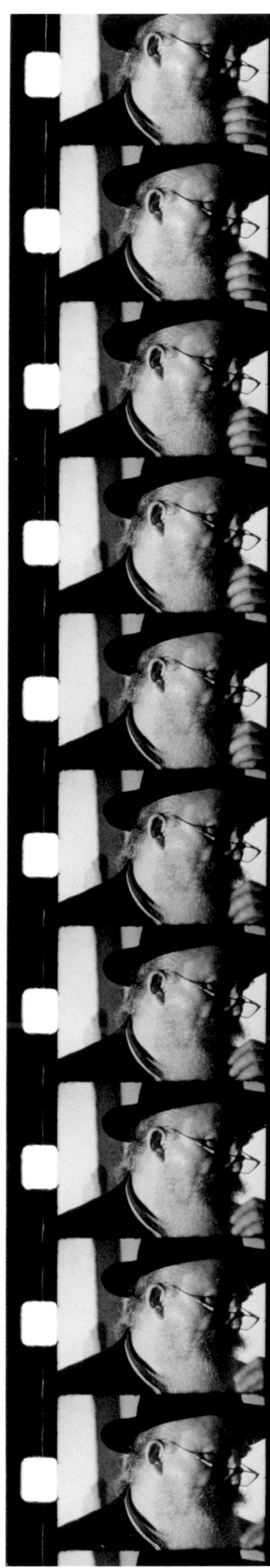 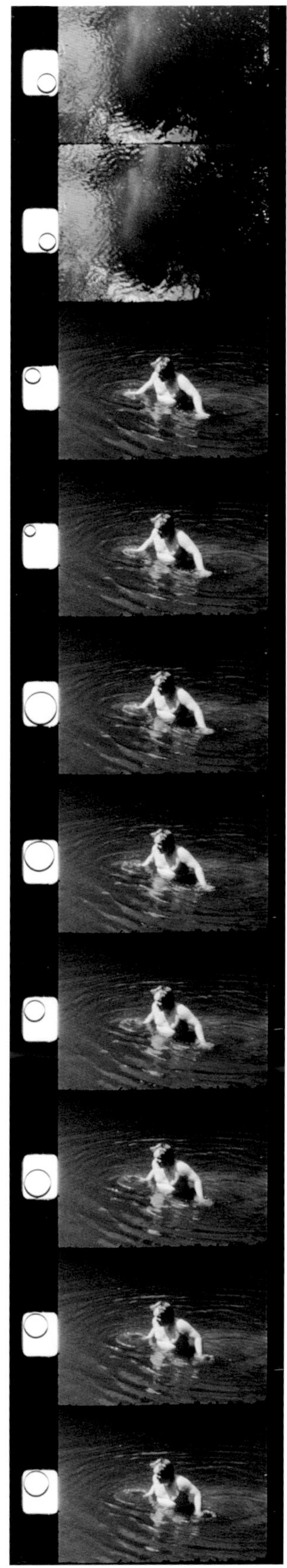 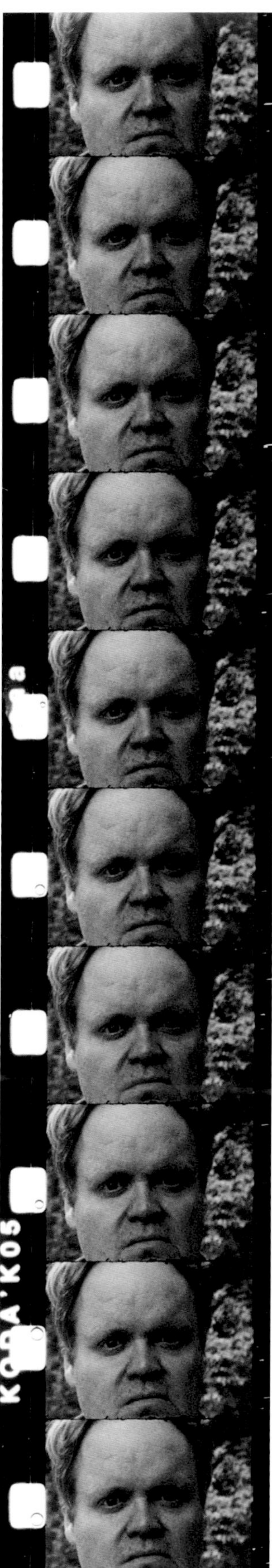

Bogman Palmjaguar

**16mm film and Super-8 film trans-
ferred to video, colour, sound
30 min.**
Production: Arts Council England; EAST-
International, Norwich
Sound: Lee Patterson
Cast: Bogman Bluequartz Palmjaguar,
Dr Leon Redler, Lee Patterson

Selected exhibitions
2008
Kunsthalle Zürich, Zurich
International Film Festival Rotterdam,
Rotterdam
Transmission Gallery, Glasgow
Scottish Shorts Showcase, Edinburgh
Film Festival, Edinburgh
2007
EASTInternational 2007, Norwich

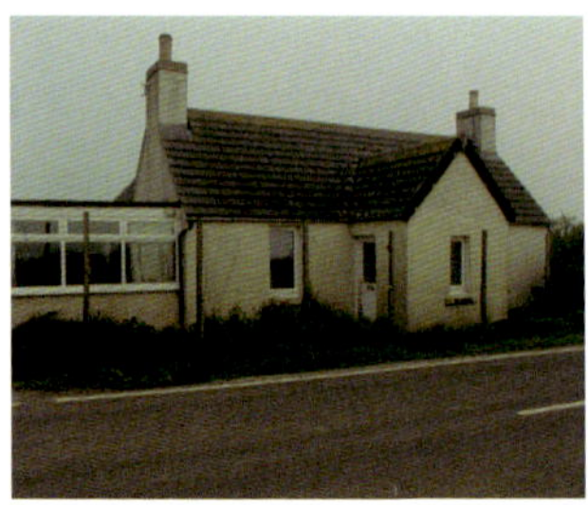

Bogman Palmjaguar is a portrait of a man who, after a series of disturbing events, became distrustful of people and withdrew into nature. Bogman describes himself as 'the hidden cat' and 'wild outlaw of paradise' and is fighting against a diagnosis that brands him as a 'paranoid schizophrenic'. Bogman's early life and the diagnosis, conditioned his relationships with others, both within and beyond the medical establishment. The decision to take legal action to remove this label is of paramount importance to him, both as a search for justice and to understand the course that his life has taken over the past three decades.

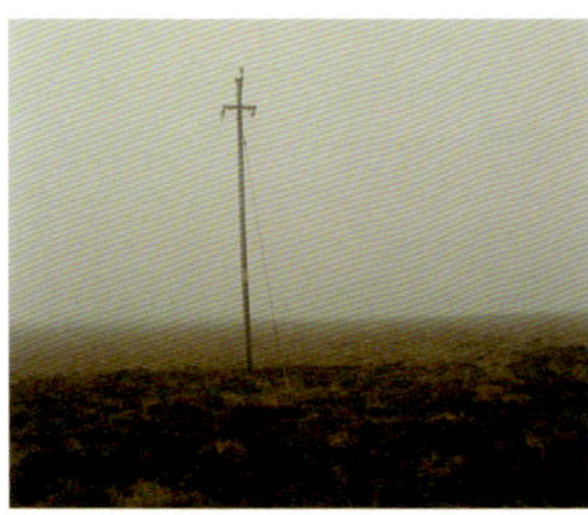

The film was shot across two visits to Bogman's home in a remote village in the north of Scotland. The former was motivated by a request from Bogman's solicitor for an independent report by Dr Leon Redler (author, and colleague of Ronald D. Laing), to assess whether the label 'paranoid schizophrenic' was justified. The latter was in collaboration with sound artist Lee Patterson, documenting the environment that Bogman sought to preserve during his time as a conservationist. Bogman had been passionate about the threatened habitat of Scotland's Flow Country, a wilderness of blanket bogs and peatlands that houses a unique diversity of wildlife. The peatlands, however, also became a hideout, where Bogman fled attempts by authorities to section him. The film is a reconciliation of the young conservationist with his older self, isolated and withdrawn from society.

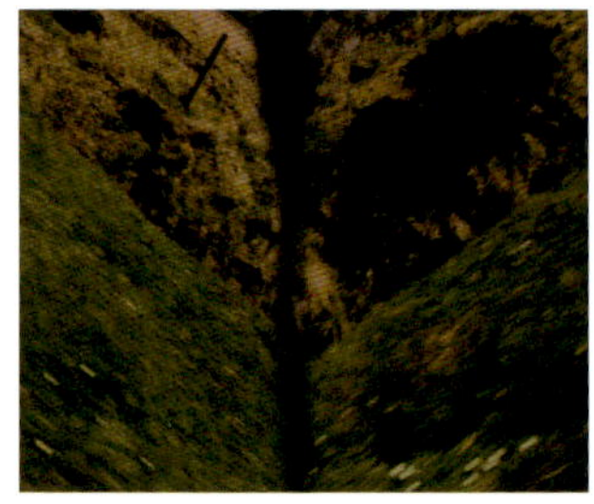

—Luke Fowler

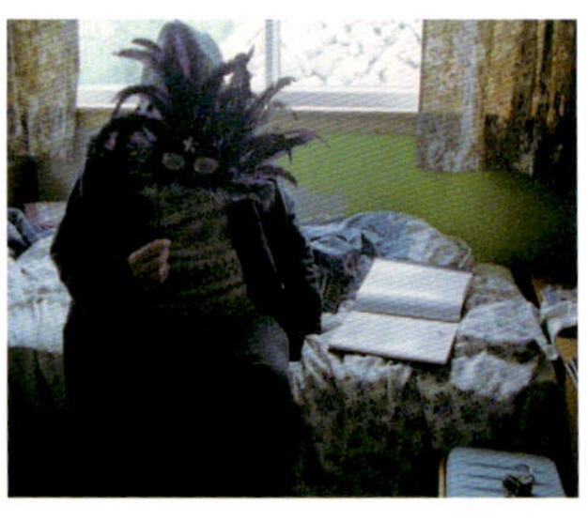

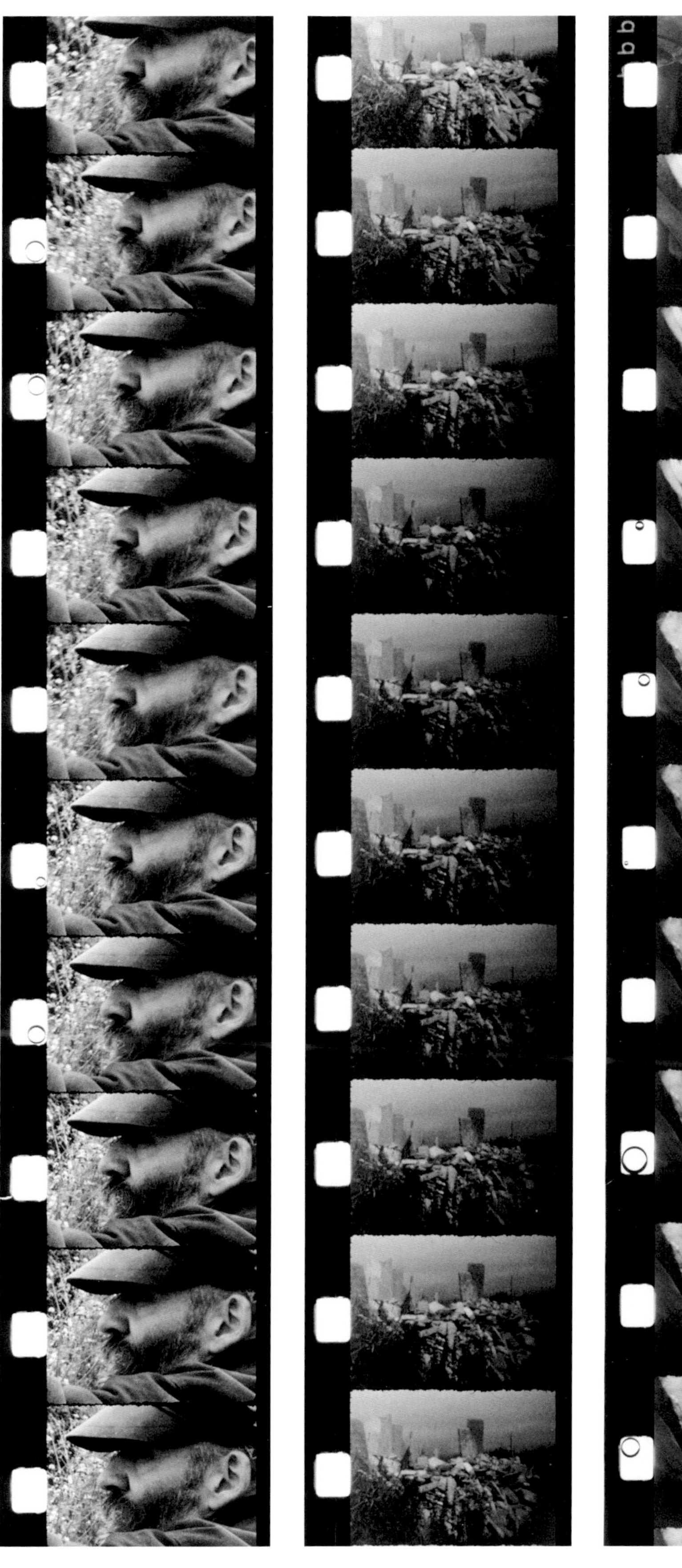

2007

Achterhaven Splinters (with Barry Burns and Mark Vernon)

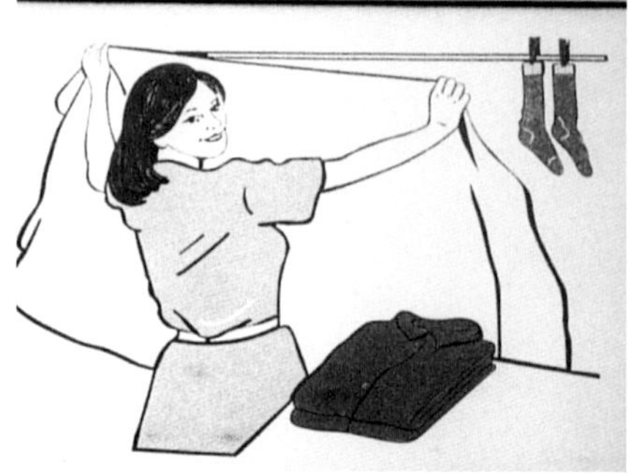

16mm film transferred to DVD, b/w, sound
6 min.
Production: Worm Filmwerkplaats, Rotterdam

Achterhaven Splinters is a fragmented portrait of Achterhaven, a working-class suburb of Rotterdam. Shot over the course of twenty-four hours, a series of fleeting moments of everyday life is scrutinised and exploded in the process of hand printing. The documentary sequences begin to take on new meanings when subject to the physical manipulation of light, chemistry and material. The soundtrack was recorded while on location and then composed to the images. Its dynamic texture mirrors the images in its fluctuation between reality and abstraction.

—Luke Fowler

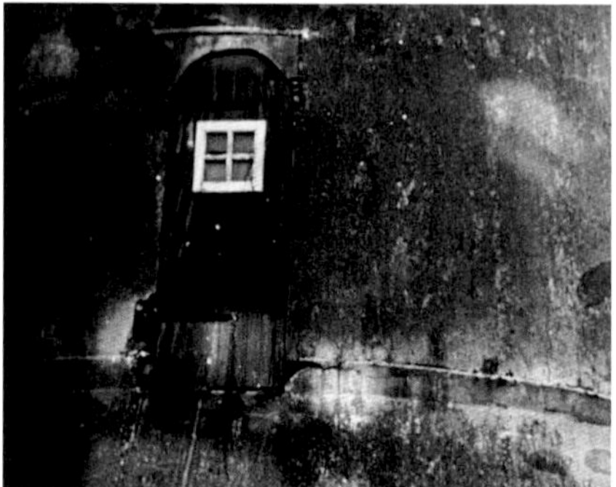

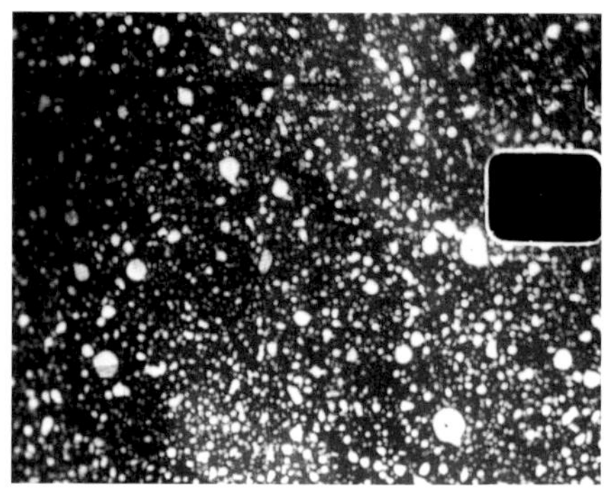

The Harbour Doubts

16mm film transferred to DVD, colour, sound
6 min.
Production: Worm Filmwerkplaats, Rotterdam

Selected exhibitions
2008
The Harbour Doubts, Bad Bad Boys Club, Dundee
2007
Esther Schipper REC Projektraum, Berlin

The Harbour Doubts is Fowler's first 16mm film. It is an autobiographical work that documents the other side of his practice – soundworlds. For over ten years he has been involved in bands and electronic music and since 1999 he has been running the label SHADAZZ. In the groups Rude Pravo and Lied Music he has worked mainly with tape technology and self-invented instruments, partly inspired by the work of pioneering British improvisers of the 1960s, Hugh Davies and Keith Rowe (formerly of AMM).

In the last few years he has been concentrating on compositions constructed largely from field recordings. The starting point for *The Harbour Doubts* was the necessity to combine this aesthetic with his work in film. Through programmer Peter Taylor, Fowler was invited to use the 16mm film facilities at Rotterdam's Worm studio, thus providing the setting and opportunity to make the film.

The film and sounds were recorded, edited and composed by Fowler over the course of a week-long residency in Rotterdam in April 2007, and investigate the transduction of vibrating surfaces, found in everyday locations around the city, into acoustic sound waves. These recordings were made using contact microphones, DIY hydrophones and miniature condensers. The film simply documents the sites where the sounds where recorded. It was edited and composed independently from the sound, in order to create a disynchronous dialogue between the sound and image.

—Robert Meijer

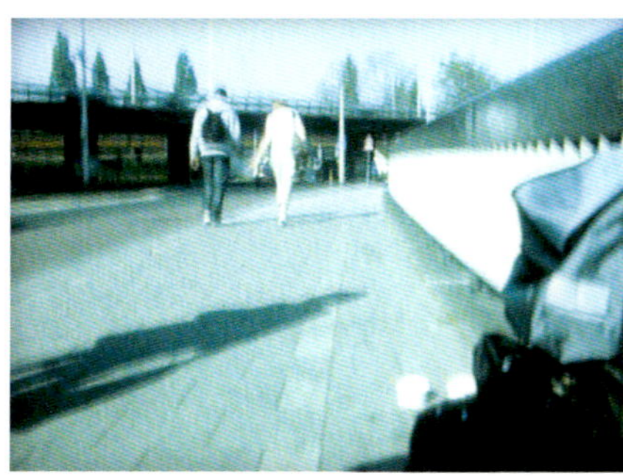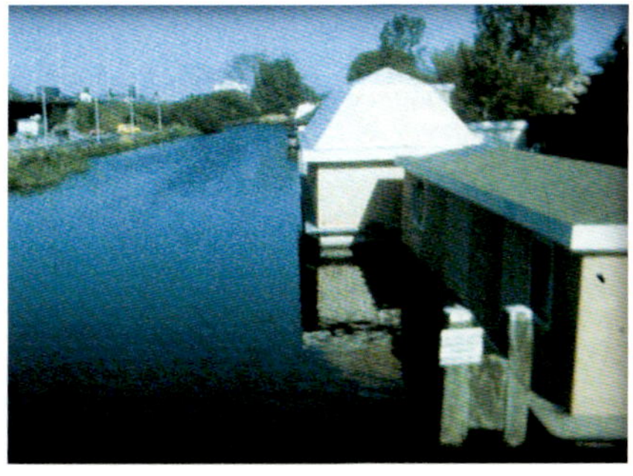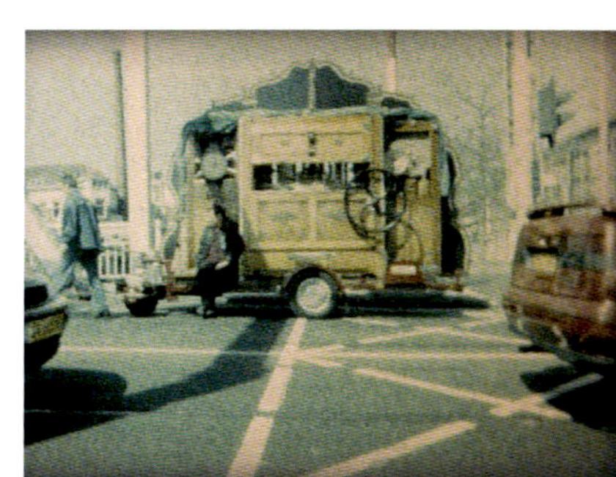

George

16mm film transferred to DVD, colour, sound
4 min.

Selected exhibitions
2008
a passable door for a movable passer,
Buccleuch Street, Glasgow
Aurora Film Festival, Norwich

George was an attempt to reconsider the basic components of my approach to film-making and boil them down to their bare essentials. The act of looking is implicit in my past documentary work but in this study it becomes the focus. The starting point for the film was the area in which I was born and still live – the west end of Glasgow – and its conjunction with the location where the film was first installed – a flat in Garnethill. The walk between these locations, also central to the film, is through the St George's X area. The film deals with the relationship between sounds and images, acoustic phenomena and architectural details.

—Luke Fowler

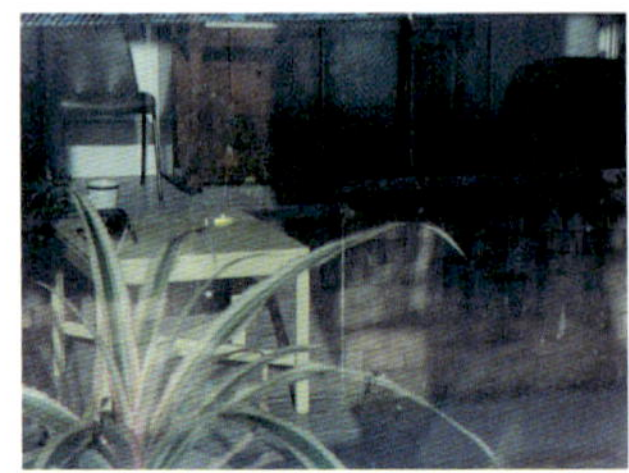

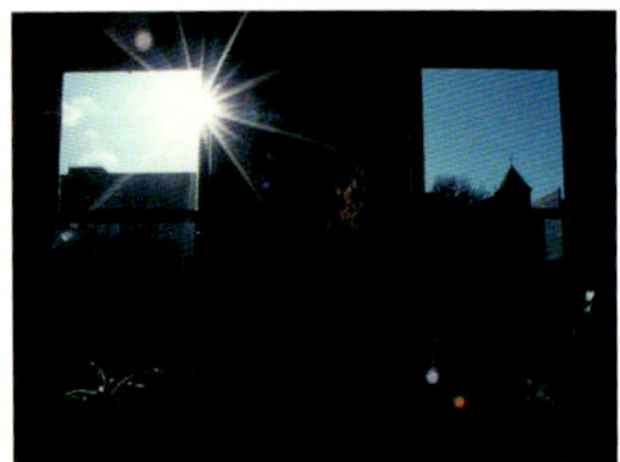

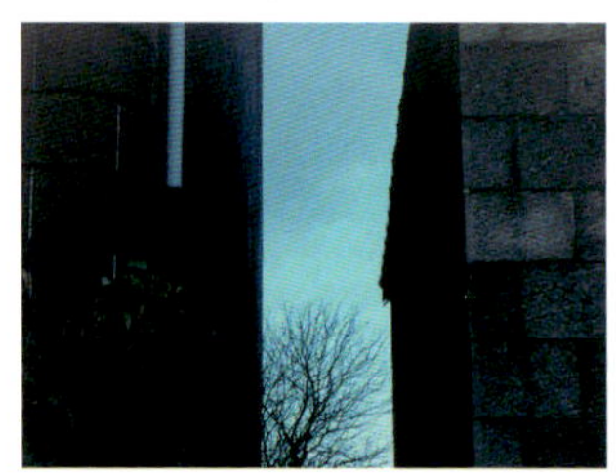

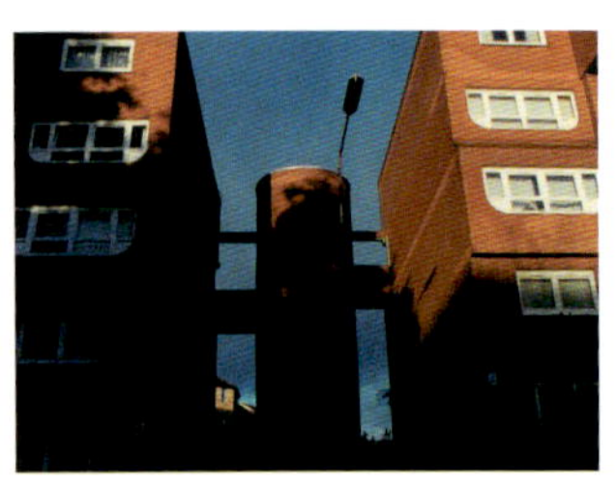

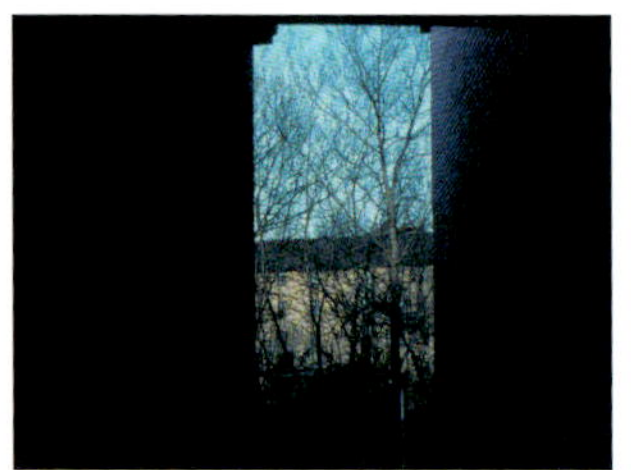

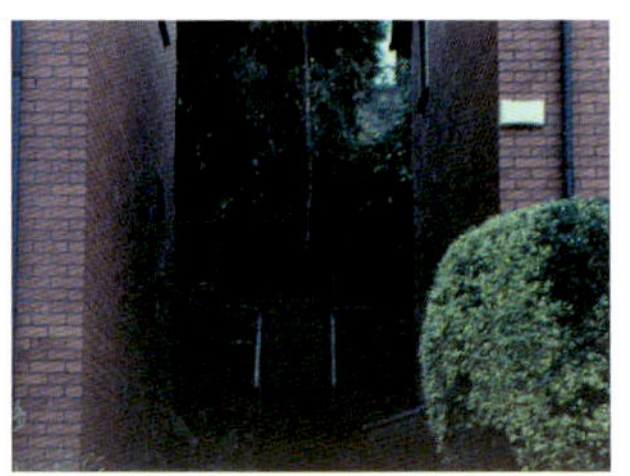

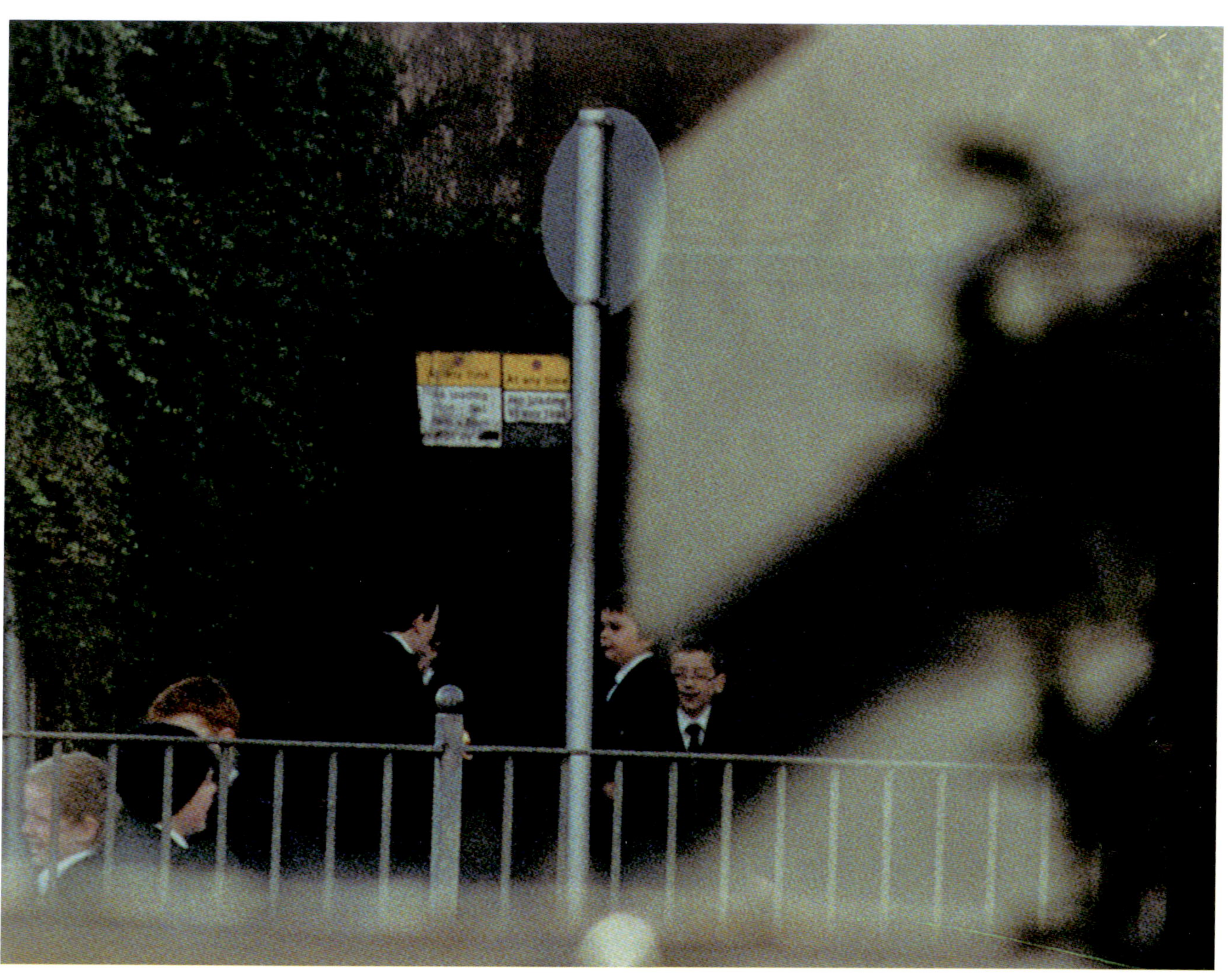

At any time
At any time

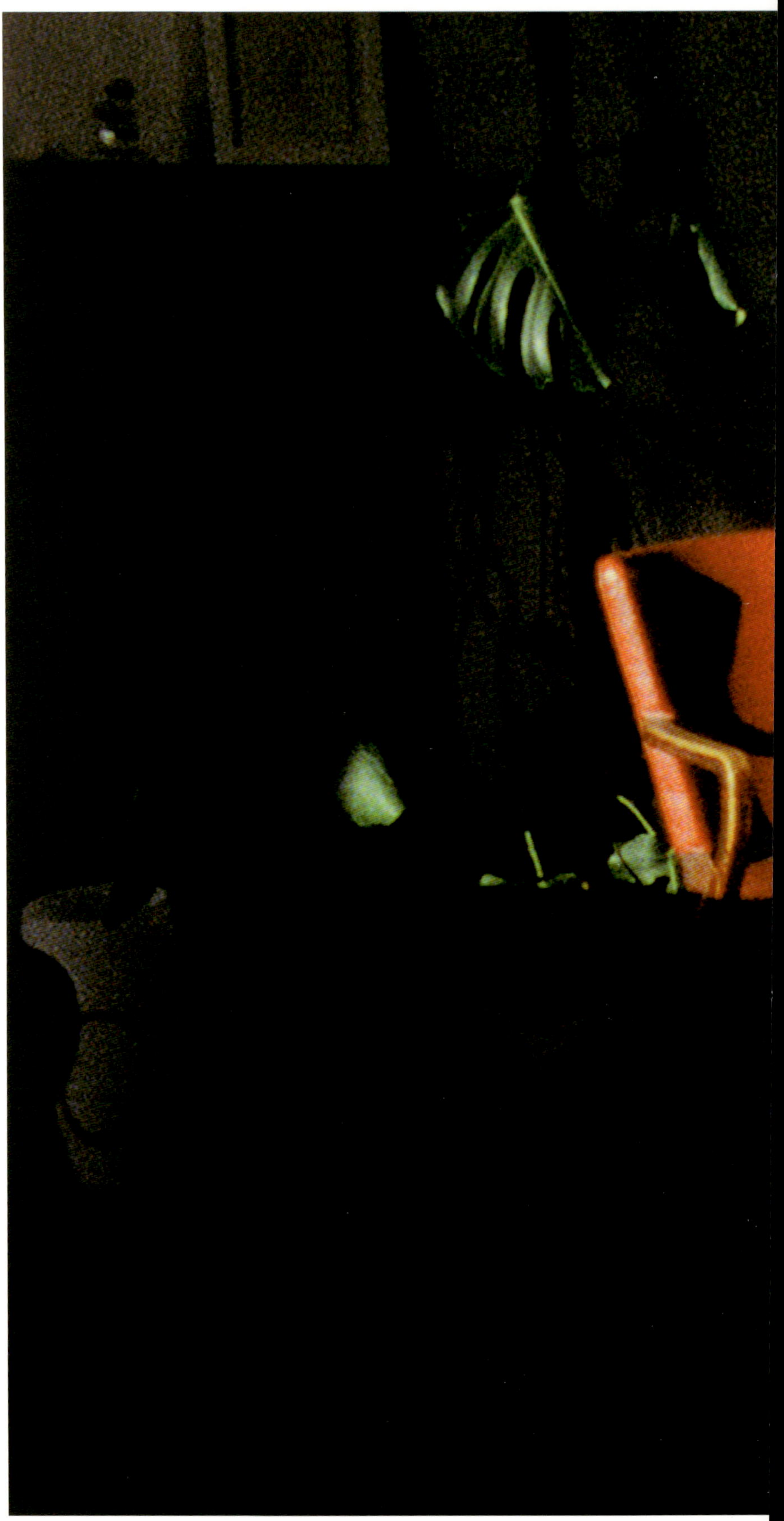

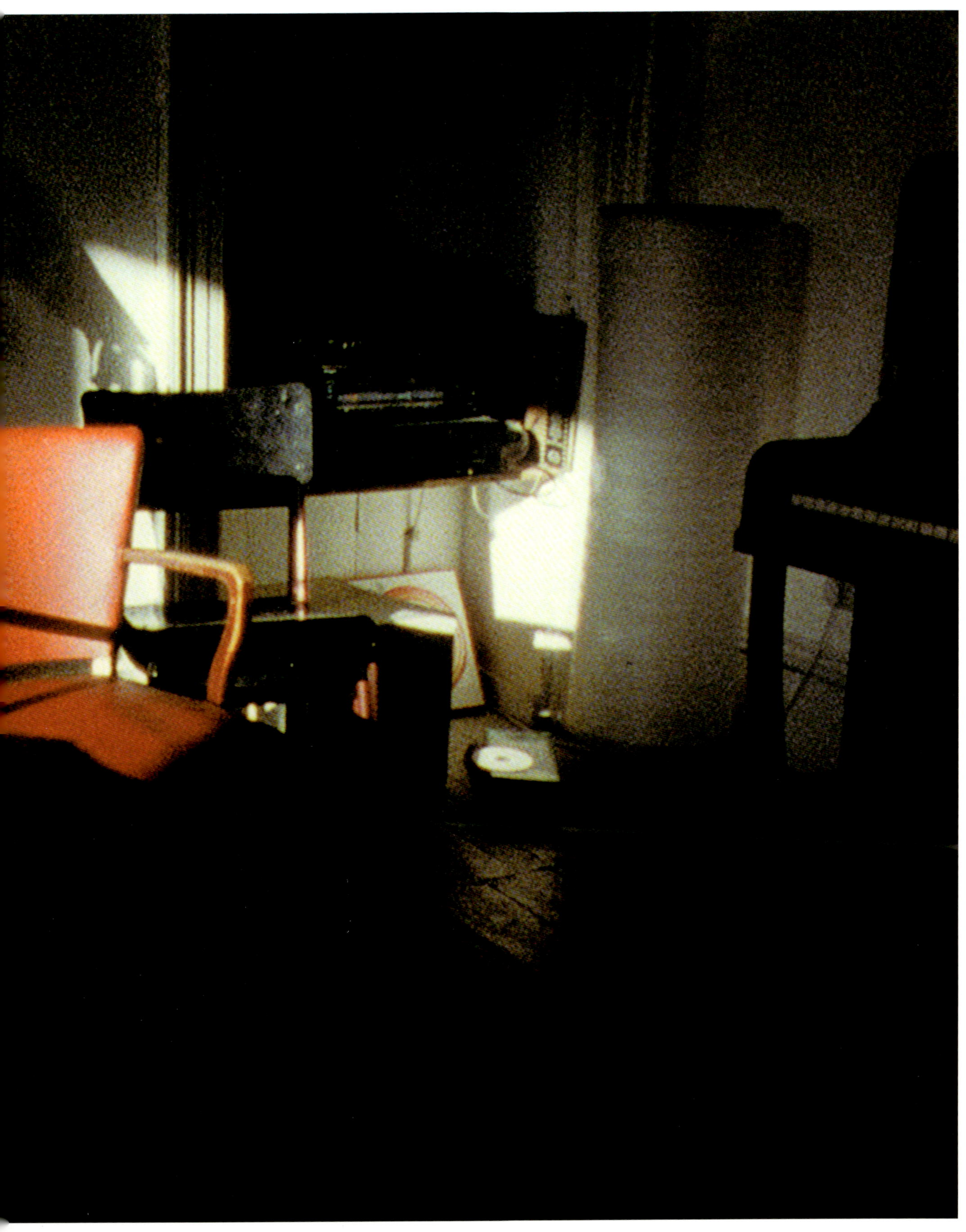

An Abbeyview Film

16mm film, colour, silent
11 min.
Production: Nicola Atkinson Davidson,
Abbeyview Regeneration Office,
Communities Scotland, Fife Council

Selected exhibitions
2008
Permanent vs. Temporary, Abbeyview
Community Centre, Dunfermline
Kunsthalle Zürich, Zurich

An Abbeyview Film was commissioned by
Abbeyview artist-in-residence (2007–2008)
Nicola Atkinson Davidson as part of regeneration funding for a deprived housing
estate in Dumfermline, Scotland. Rather
than choosing a clear stance in relation to
the subject of a deprived area, Fowler offers
a contingent, at times contradictory, poetic
snapshot of a community. The film resists
traditional documentary and cinematic representation of housing estates, striving
instead to build an aesthetic of ambivalence
and hope.

—Barry Burns

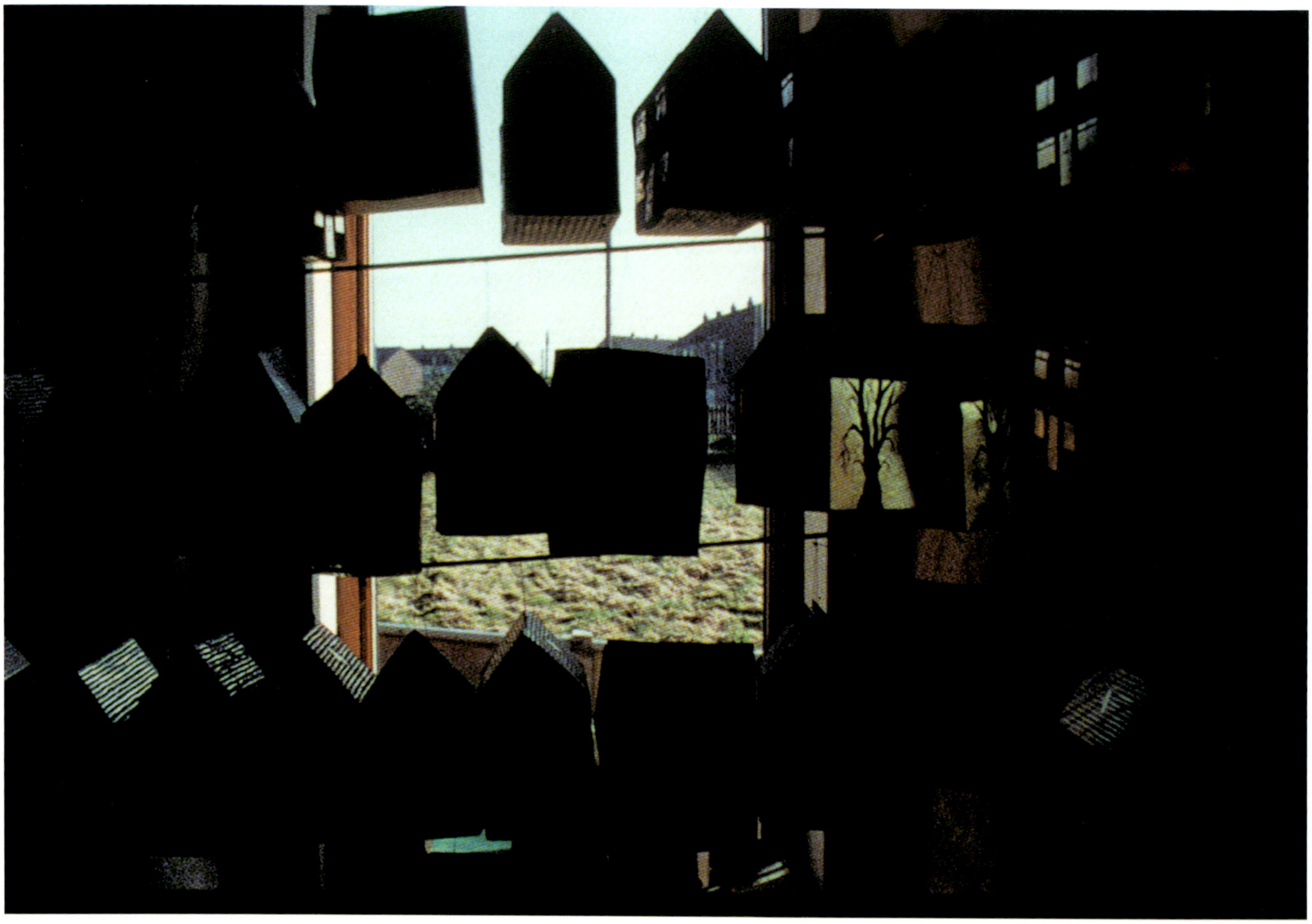

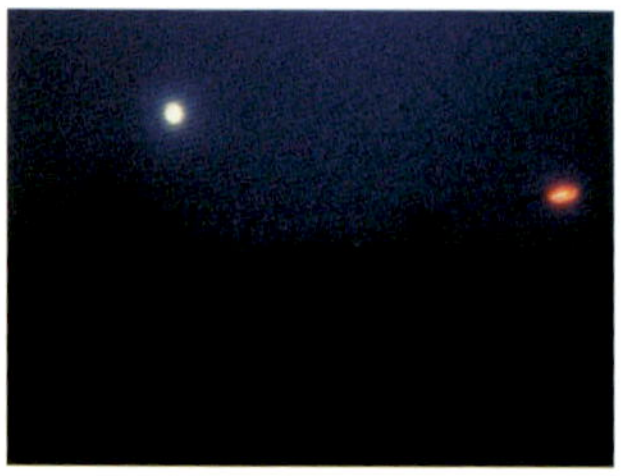

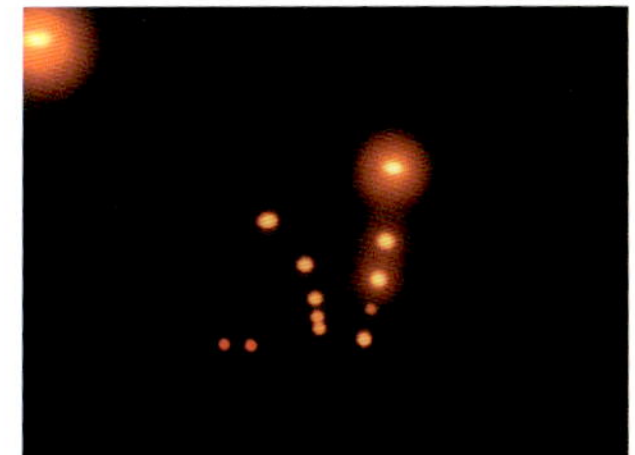

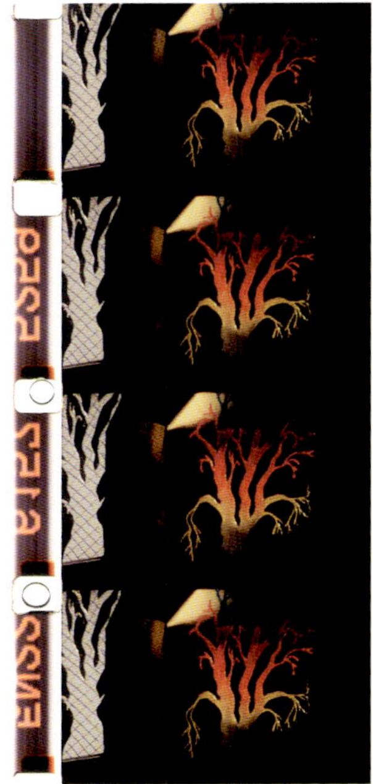

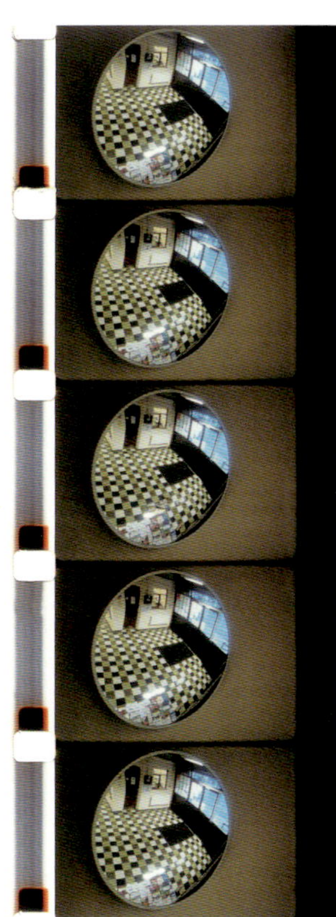

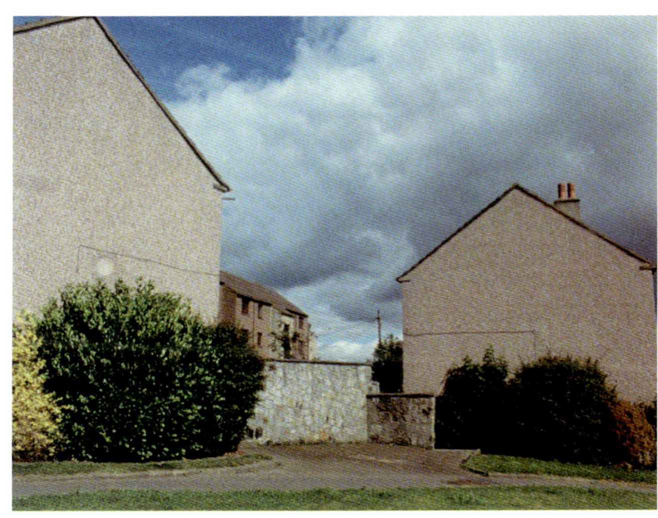

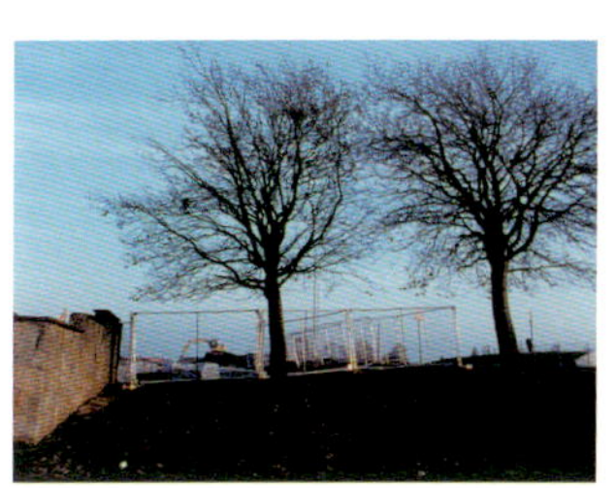

Another Day of Gravity
(with Richard Youngs)

**16mm film transferred to DVD,
colour, sound
4 min.**
Production: Arika, Edinburgh
Music: Richard Youngs

**Selected exhibitions
2008**
Instal 08, The Arches, Glasgowh

Commissioned by Arika for *Instal 08*, the film was structured around acappela verses from English musician Richard Youngs, those recordings are celebrated for progressing the song form by drawing from 'minimalist' and improvised musics. The film was shot over the course of a day in Youngs' flat. For each new line in the song, the camera angle would change; with each new verse, the film would move to the next room. The film was screened at *Instal 08* in The Arches, with a live accompaniment by Youngs and featuring audience participation.

—Luke Fowler

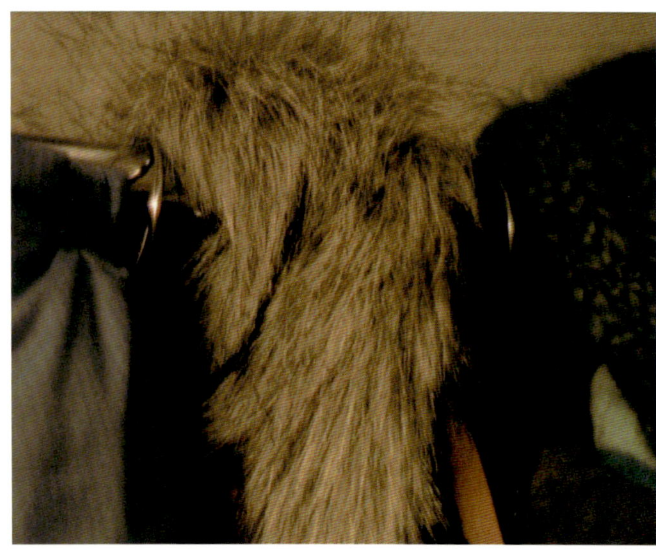

Paddington Collaboration
(with Anna McLauchlan)

16mm transferred to DVD, colour,
sound
2 min. 45 sec.

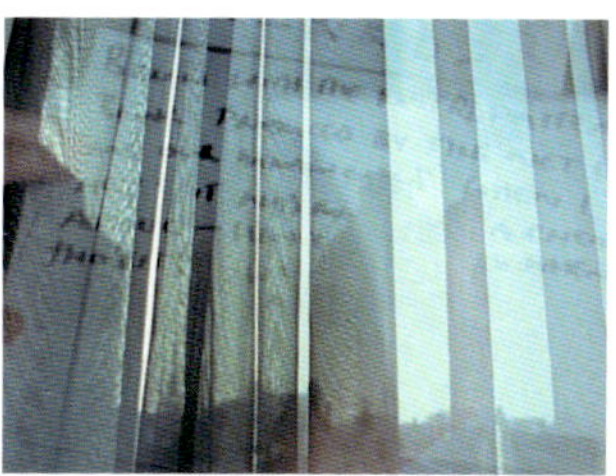

Paddington Collaboration is a collaboration with Glasgow-based artist and writer Anna McLauchlan, filmed in and around her sister's flat in Paddington (London), on the morning of 26 December 2007. The film was invented as an elaborate excuse to escape family duties and also to refamiliarise McLauchlan with the medium, which she had not practised for many years. The film is shot on one roll of film and edited in camera. It is divided into two parts — the first of which is my plan and the second of which is McLauchlan's.

—Luke Fowler

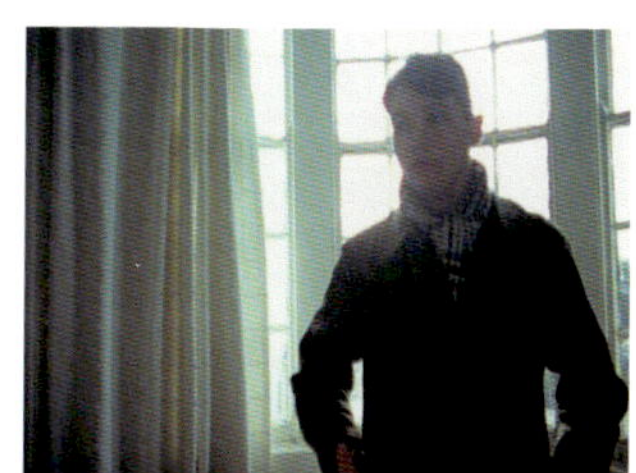

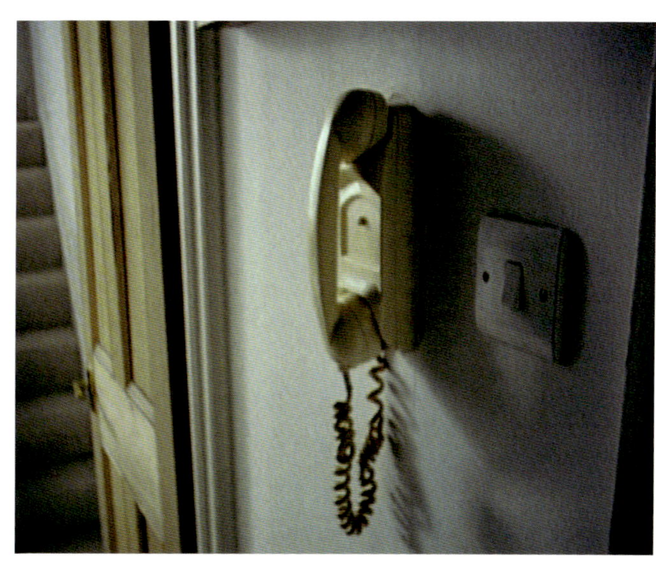

B8016: Draw a Straight Line and Follow It (with Lee Patterson)

16mm film, colour, sound
25 min.
Production: Alice Koegel (for Tate Modern, London)

Exhibitions
2008
Kunsthalle Zürich, Zurich
The Long Weekend, Tate Modern, London

In the film *B8016: Draw a Straight Line and Follow It* we were inspired by La Monte Young's 1960 text score *composition no. 10, draw a straight line and follow it*. Our response to the score was to find a straight road and follow it, documenting the experience in film and sound, while collecting materials – human detritus and natural phenomena – along the way. The hidden potential of these materials as 'sound objects' will become evident as part of the live performance, which brings an improvised element to the otherwise static experience of viewing/projecting film.

We chose the B8016 on the isle of Islay, part of the Scottish Inner Hebrides, to conduct our walk. This road from Port Ellen to Bridgend was chosen not just because it is long and straight, but because it crosses several types of terrain, including areas of the built and natural environment. It was the first time we made this walk. This activity shares concerns that are at the heart of both our practices: the art of observation – looking beneath the surface – and the art of collecting – reclaiming the undesired and overlooked.

—Luke Fowler and Lee Patterson

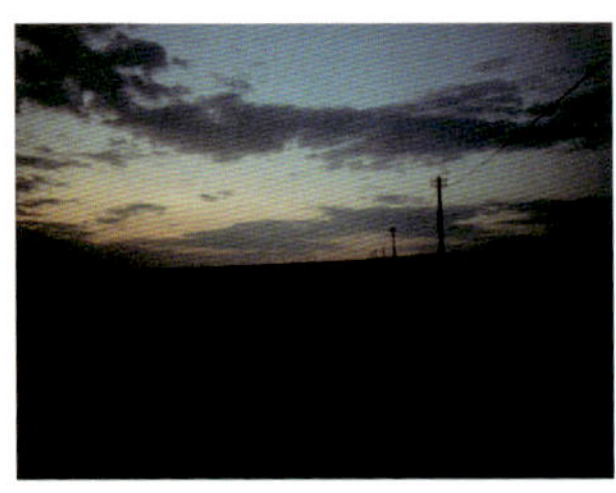
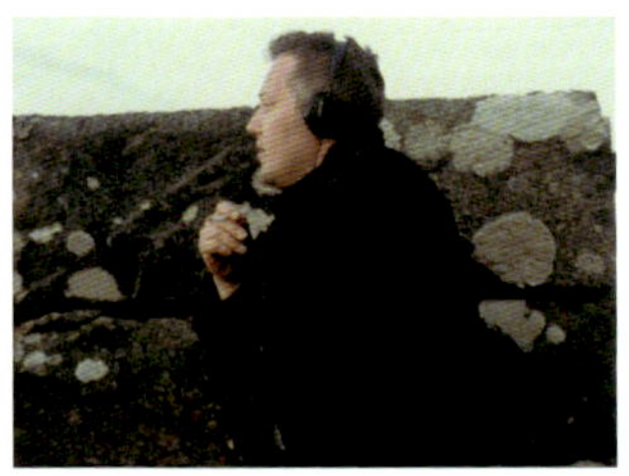

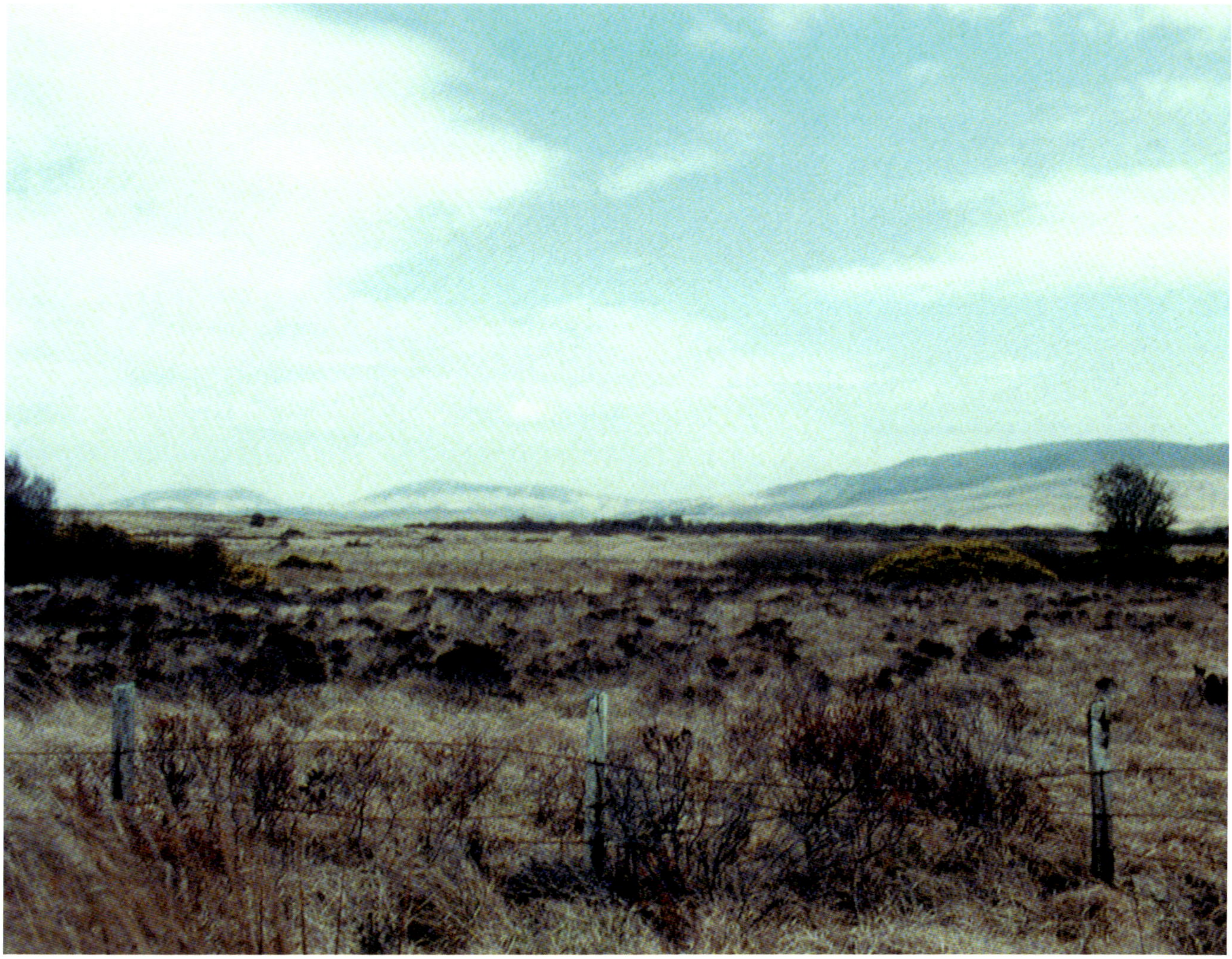

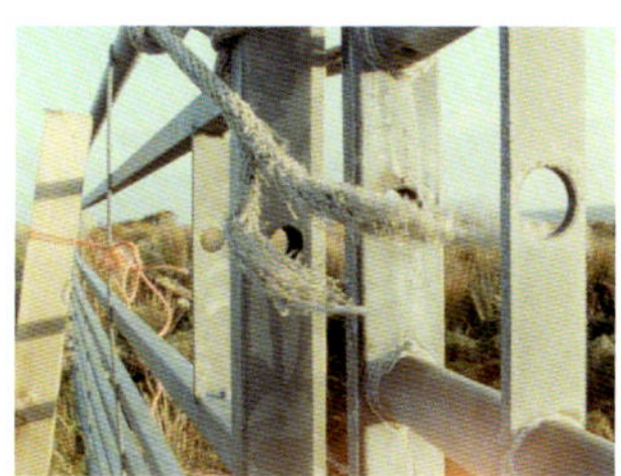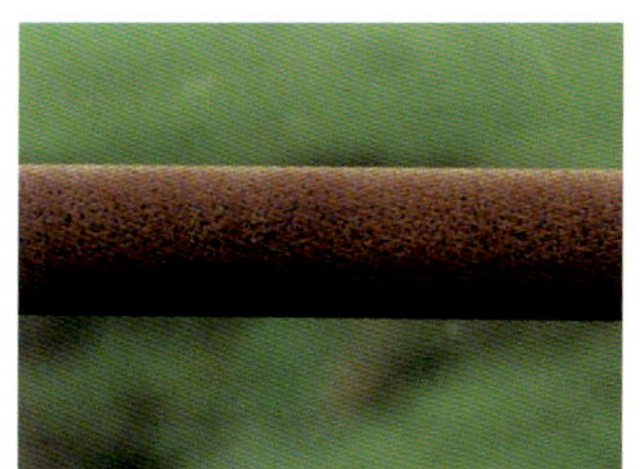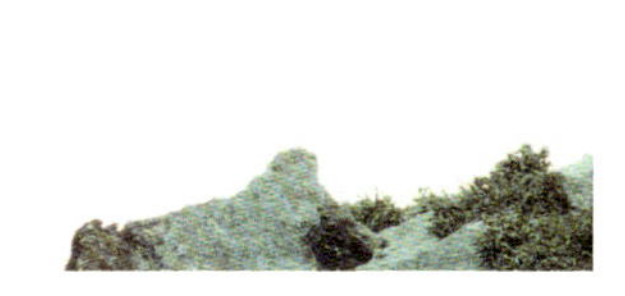

Northwest from Chesterhill:
Draw a Straight Line and
Follow It
(with Lee Patterson)

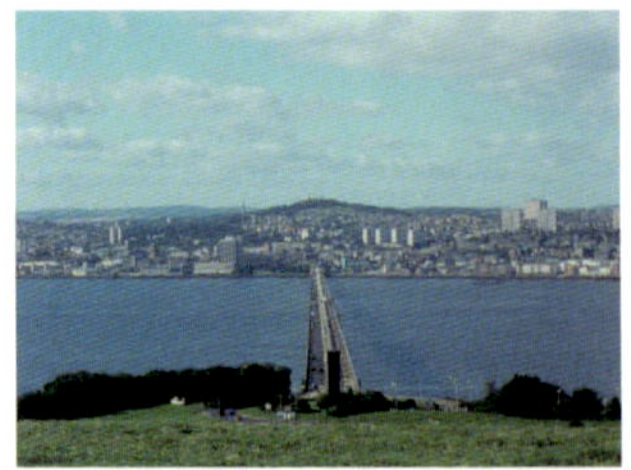

Live performance of 16mm film, colour
sound
Production: Arika, Edinburgh

Exhibitions
2008
KYTN, DCA – Dundee Contemporary
Arts, Dundee

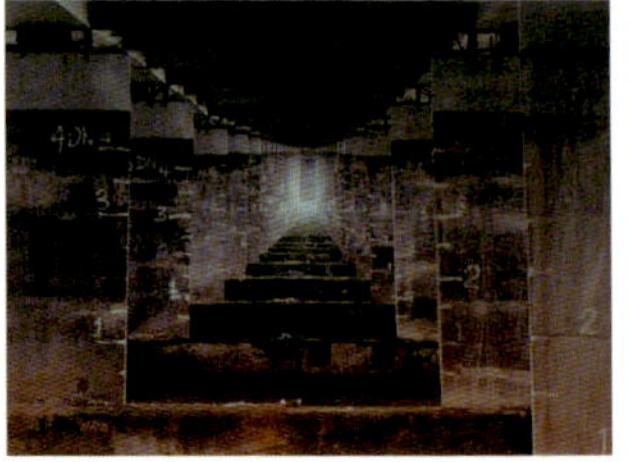

*Northwest from Chesterhill: Draw a Straight
Line and Follow It* is the second performance
of this ongoing project by Lee Patterson and
myself. The starting point for the walk was
in the fields of Chester Hill. We then made
our way across the Tay Bridge into Dundee's
city centre. Departing from a continuous
straight road as we had done in the *B8016:
Draw a Straight Line and Follow It*, we drew a
straight line on a map of Dundee City Centre,
using the Tay Bridge as the central point.
The walk was in two stages and concluded
when we reached Dundee's Law Hill.

—Luke Fowler

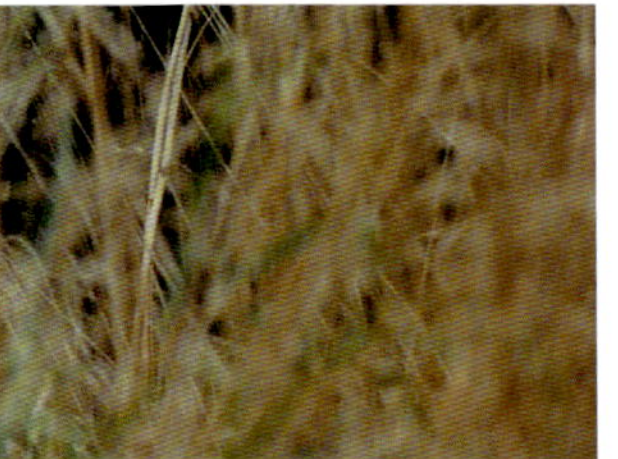

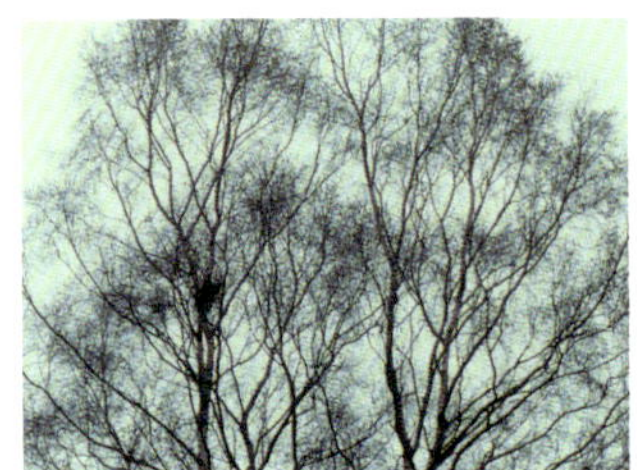

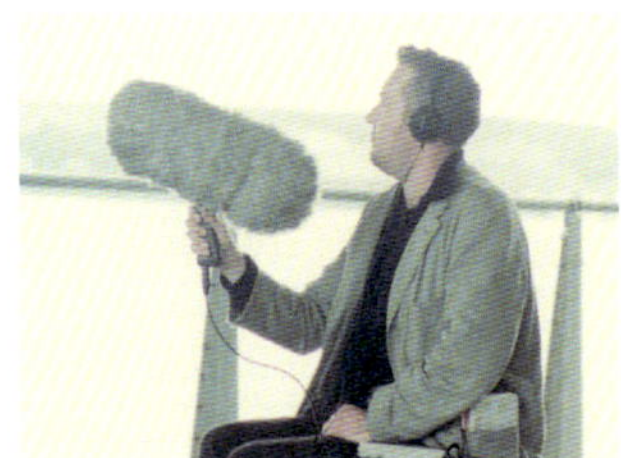

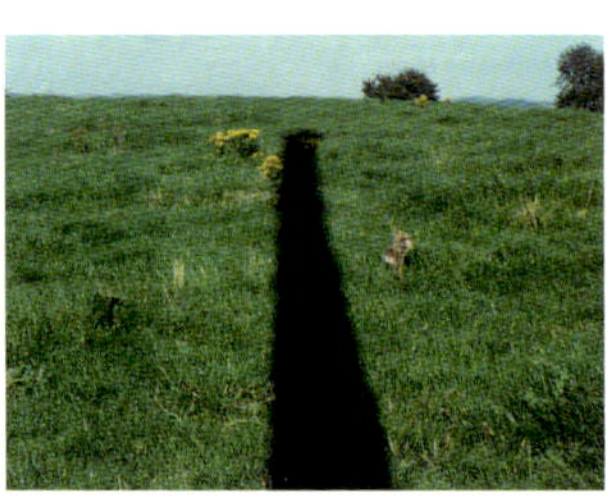

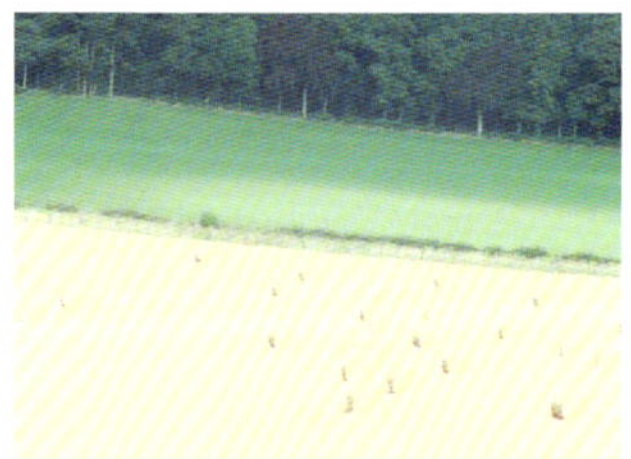

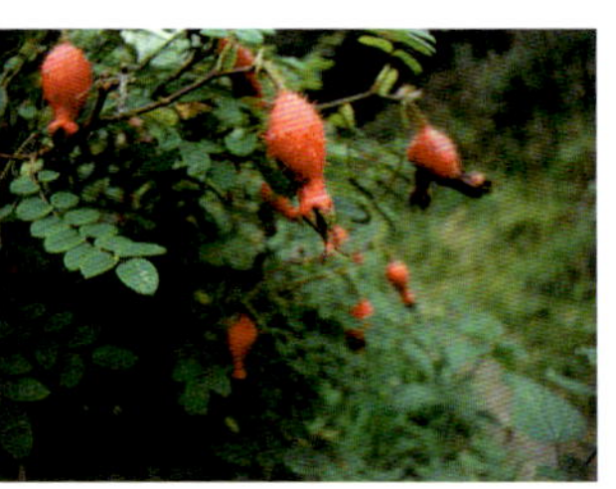

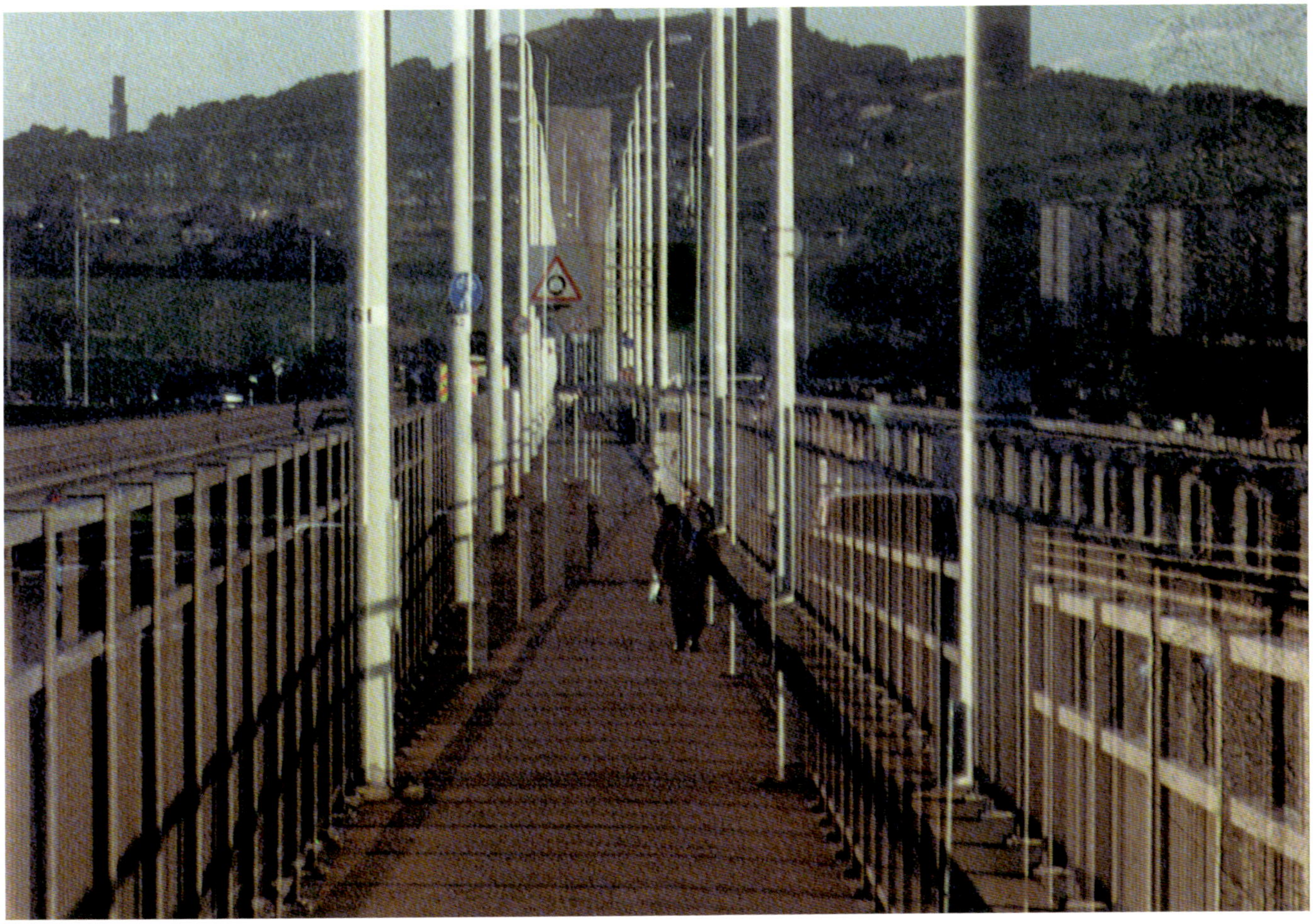

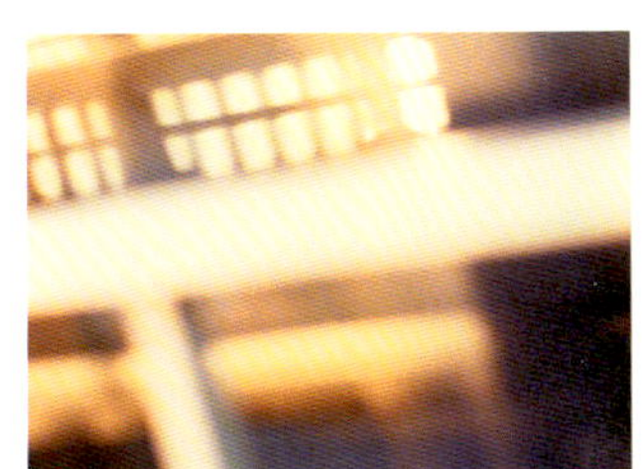
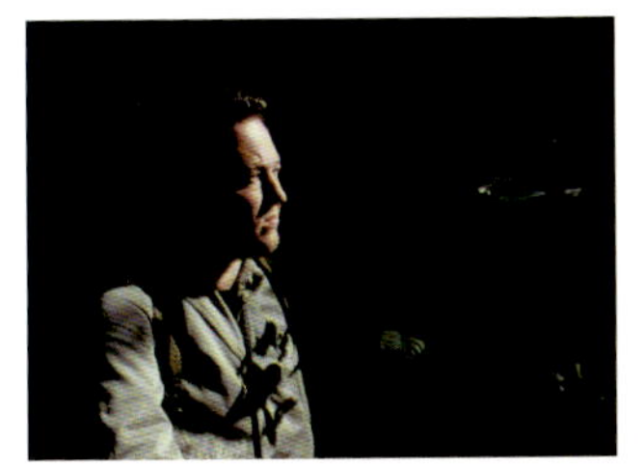
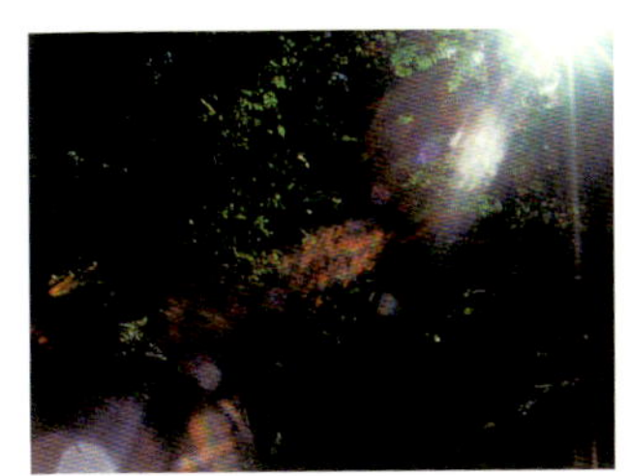

Composition for Flutter Screen
(with Toshiya Tsunoda)

**Installation with 16mm colour film
and projector, homemade screen,
timer, wire, fans, lights**
Production: Yokohama Triennale,
Yokohama

Exhibitions
2009
Serpentine Gallery, London
2008
Yokohama Triennale 2008, Yokohama

The film installation is a result of a collaboration with Toshiya Tsunoda and was shot and conceived in Yokohama for the Triennale there in 2008. The film shows a series of objects (candle, map, wire, etc), which were placed in sites where Tsunoda has spent much of his working life making sound recordings. These objects can be seen as measuring the 'conditions' of the locations in which they are filmed – local conditions (vibrations, light, wind) will be recorded by the movement of flames on two small candles, the surface tension of a glass of water at meniscus point, the light at a harbour as it emphasises different shadow contours on a relief map. The images also employ illusionistic techniques (depth of field, macro, 3-D representation of a mountain range), which throw the viewer into a state of uncertainty as to the authenticity of the images.

Interventions (using a timer, amplified wire, fans, lights and a lightweight screen) are introduced in the film installation, disrupting the possibility of a traditional cinematic experience.

—Luke Fowler

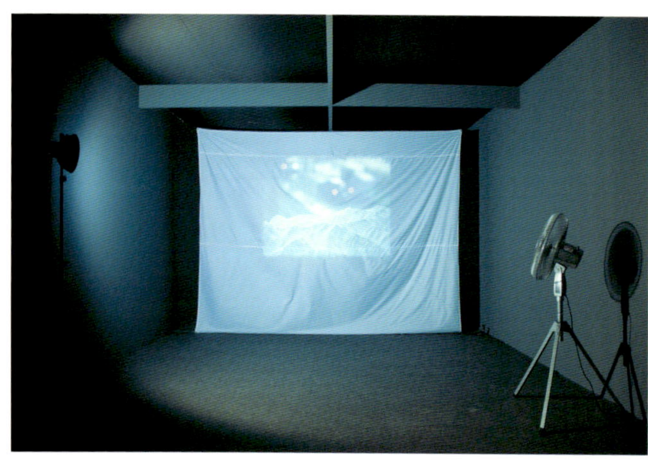

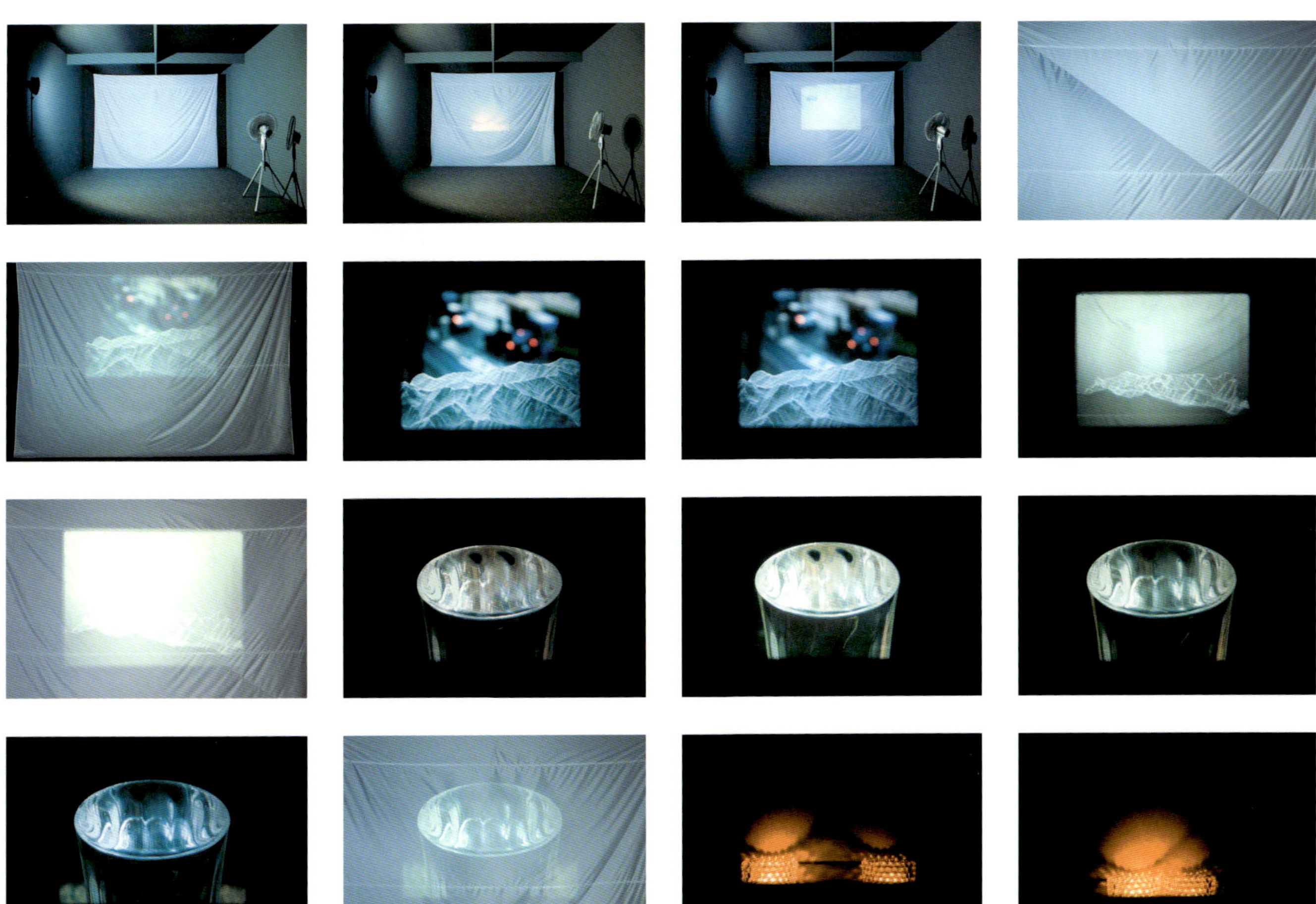

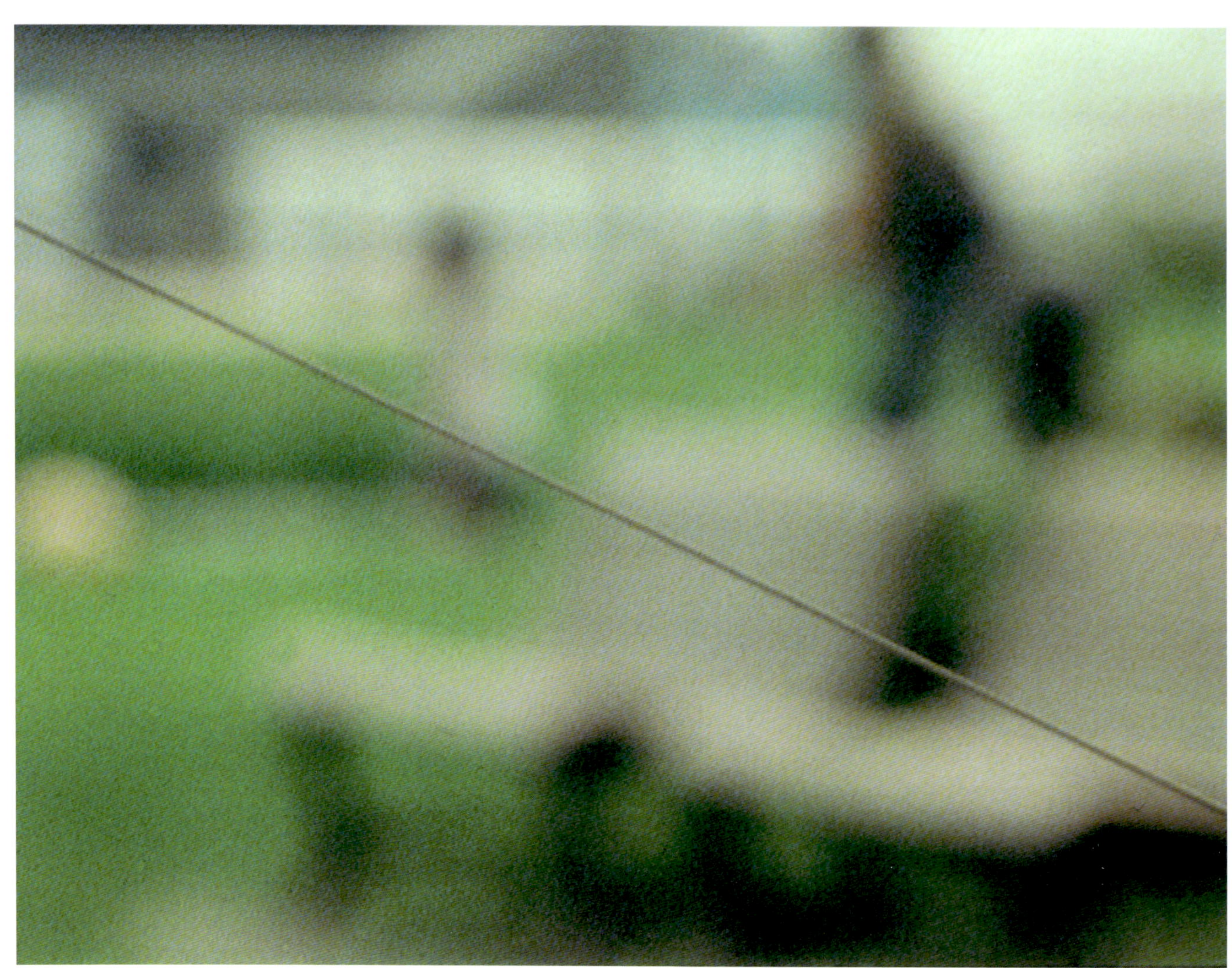

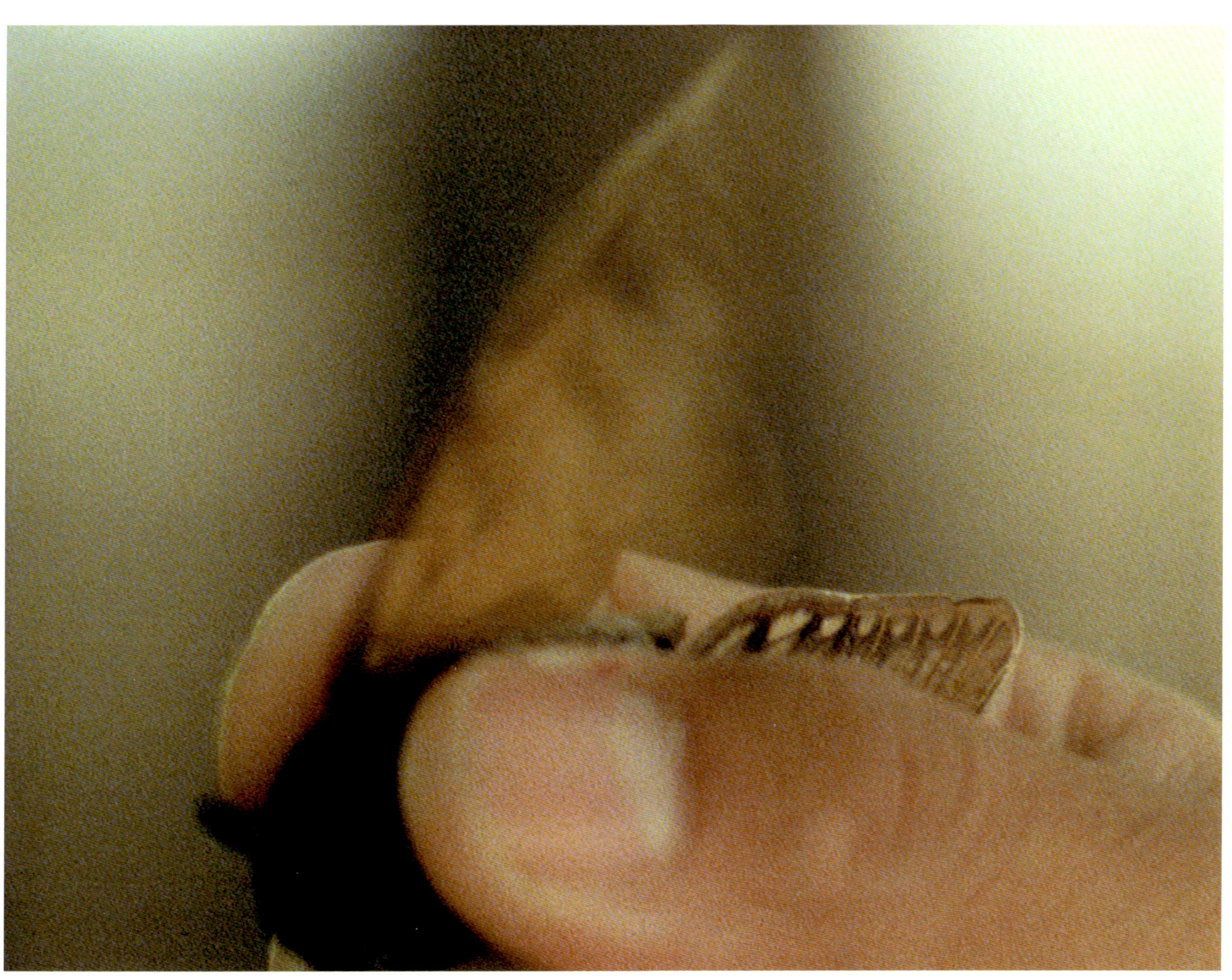

The Room
(with Keith Rowe
and Peter Todd)

Live performance of 16mm colour films and sound
Production (at time of press): Tate Modern, London; CAC Brétigny – Centre d'art contemporain de Brétigny, Brétigny-sur-Orge
Camera: Luke Fowler, Peter Todd
Sound: Keith Rowe

Exhibitions
2008
Expanded Cinema for Rothko, Tate Modern, London

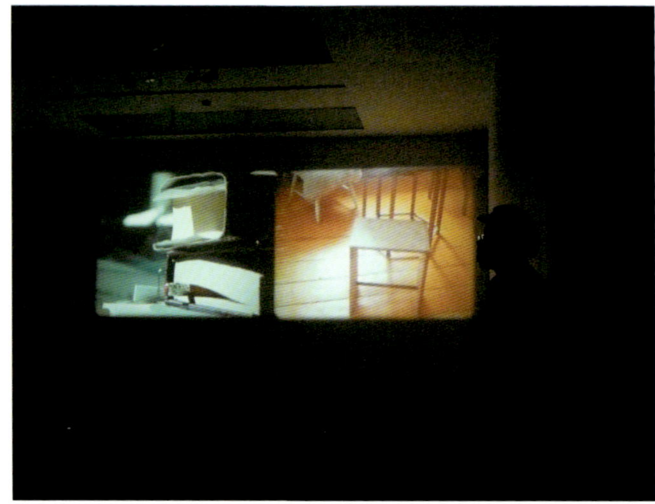

The Room is the first event in an ongoing series of collaborations by three artists. 16mm films are intertwined with live guitar improvisation by Keith Rowe. We work independently, shooting in different rooms, then bring the films together for each unique performance.

Tate Modern presented the first installment of *The Room* on 28 November, 2008. *The Room* is cumulative, building every time it is shown, with another two films added in each subsequent performance. The filmed rooms are unpopulated, yet they harbour residues of human activity, signs of historical and current events, personal effects, the random. The rooms are unique – acoustically and visually. Hidden frequencies are unearthed; radio static and random broadcasts dialled in; fleeting movements of light captured.

—Luke Fowler and Peter Todd

16mm film, colour, silent
18 min.
Production: CCA – The Centre for
Contemporary Arts, Glasgow

Exhibitions
2008
Open Field, CCA – The Centre for
Contemporary Arts, Glasgow

I filmed a diary for the period just before
and during the course of the exhibition *Open
Field*. The film rushes were shown unedited,
and changed fortnightly. During this excep-
tionally bright and cold winter I moved house
twice, visited friends in Berlin, recorded
music, travelled by train etc.

—Luke Fowler

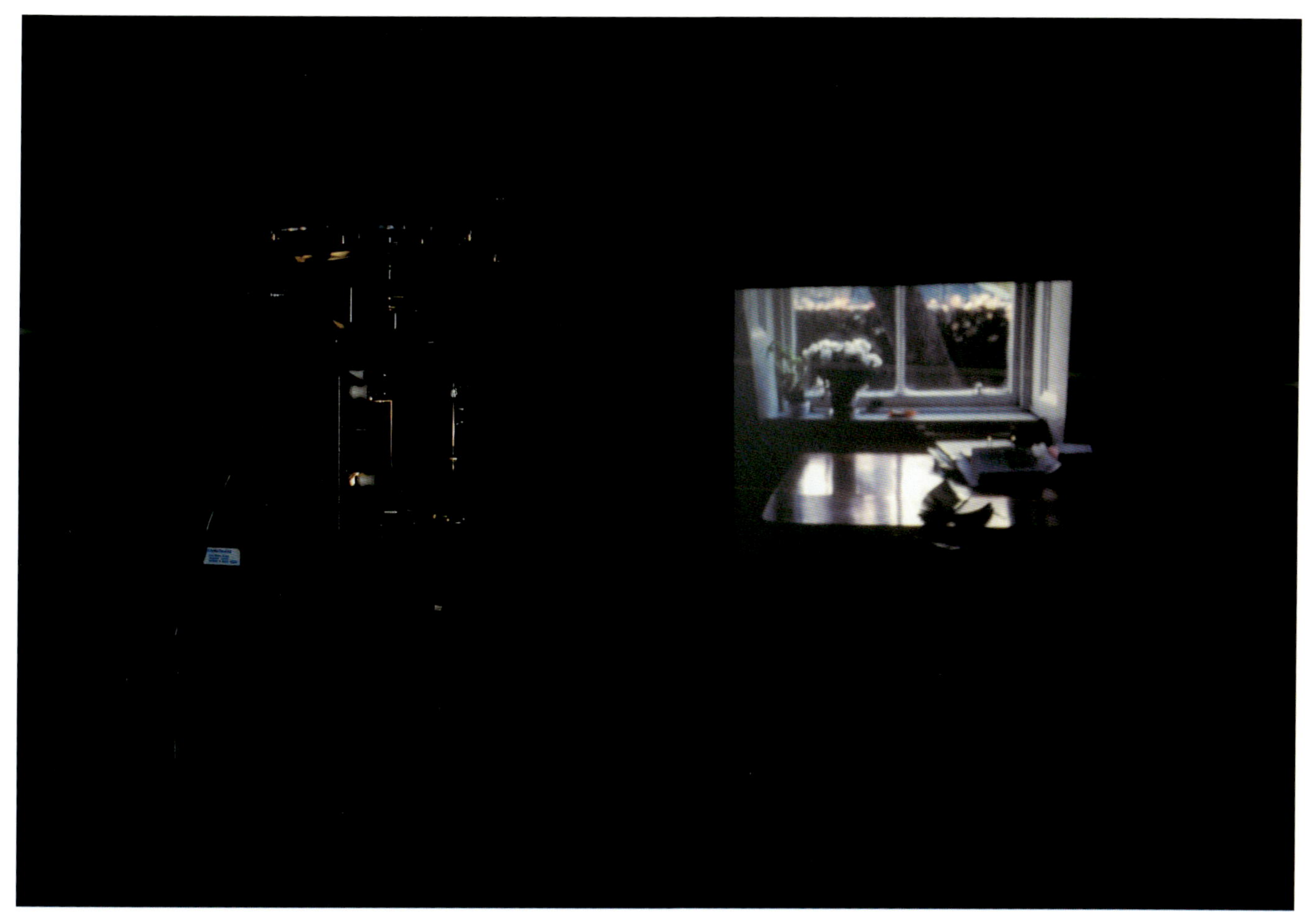

Tenement Films

16mm film, colour, sound
4 × 3 min.
Derek Jarman Award, *3 Minute*
***Wonder* for Channel 4**
First TX date: April 2009
Production: Film London, London;
Channel 4; Derek Jarman Award
Music: Lee Patterson, Toshiya Tsunoda,
Taku Unami, Charles Curtis

Exhibitions
2009
Serpentine Gallery, London

A series of portraits, made for television, of four diverse individuals brought together through shared residence.

These short films were shot in the tenement where I lived for eight years. The first is shot in my bedroom, which doubled up as my former partner's office. The following three were shot in architecturally identical spaces owned by my then neighbours.

Shot and edited on a single 16mm bolex camera using available light throughout, the films invoke reflections on the four individuals, how they occupy these particular spaces and our relationships together. Capturing residual marks traced by the incessantly panning and tracking camera eye, all of these films feel haunted by a series of ungraspable narratives.

The first film, *Anna*, shows my former partner and glimpses of myself, shot in reflection, as I navigate the camera around her and the architectural details of the room. The soundtrack in *Anna* is an original composition by Lee Patterson comprising field recordings, often using contact microphones attached to objects and features of the actual room.

The second film portrays Helen and is set in a distinctively decorated gold room. This film strays even further into a dimension of self-portraiture, using fast cutting between shots in a large mirror, and of bay windows, multiple exposures and disjunctive camera movements. The film weaves a taut web of associations between personal ephemera, a painting, objects, furniture and the outside world. The original soundtrack is composed by Toshiya Tsunoda and features recordings of a previous installation (*Composition for Flutter Screen*), prepared guitar and field recordings.

Moving up the tenement floors, David is the subject of the next film. In contrast to the other films, David's interior is sparse and uncluttered. The timescale of this film is extended to the evening: the viewer is offered scenes filmed from his window of cars and passers-by coming and going, while the daylight changes from twilight to deep night. The soundtrack for this work consists of sine-wave and multiple hand claps, performed in arhythmic fashion and composed by Taku Unami.

The final film, *Lester*, the most mellifluous of the quartet, features a warm, ornate score for solo cello and sine-wave, performed and composed by Charles Curtis. The film suggests a culmination of previous experiments in developing a lexicon of camera techniques, employed in articulating and exploring these personal spaces.

—Luke Fowler

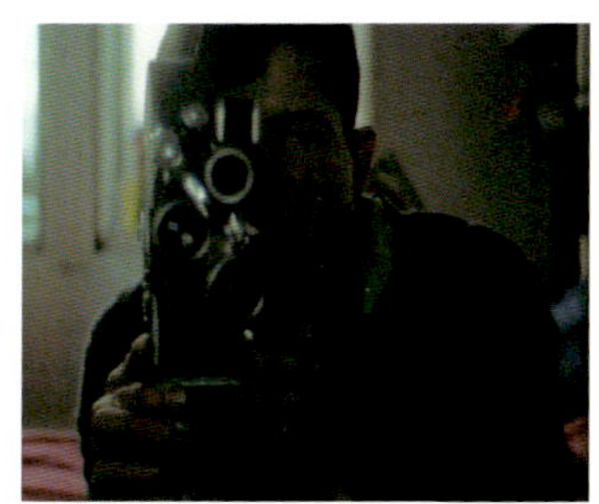
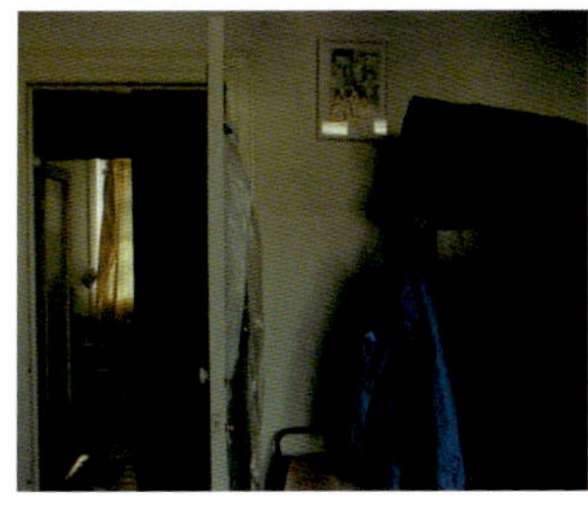
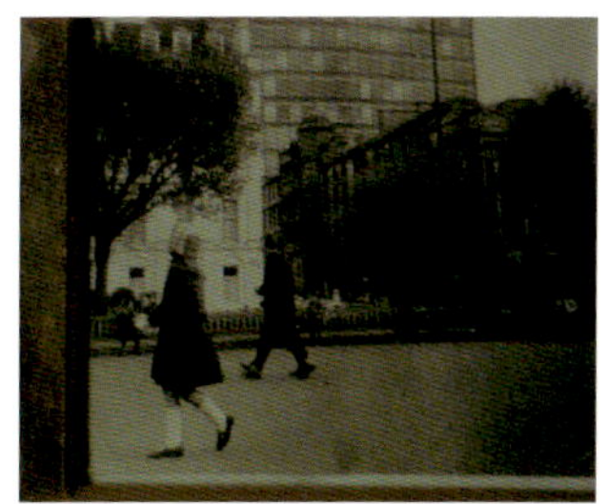
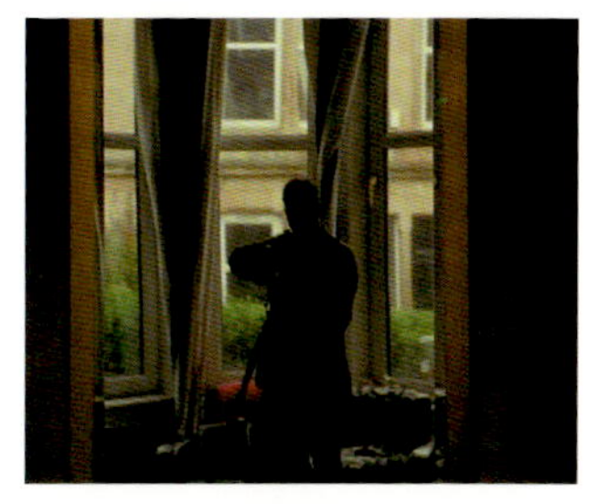
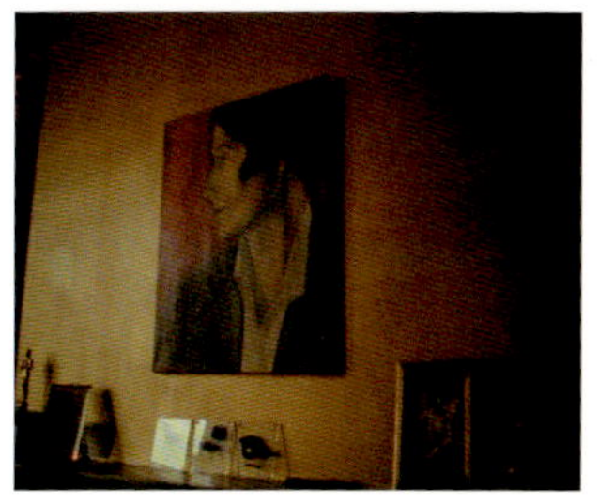
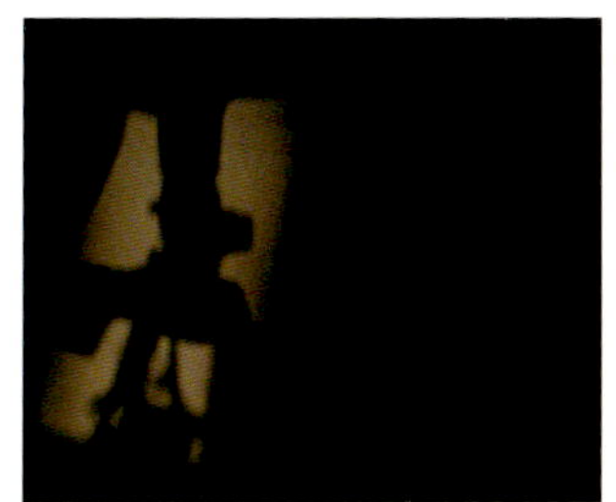
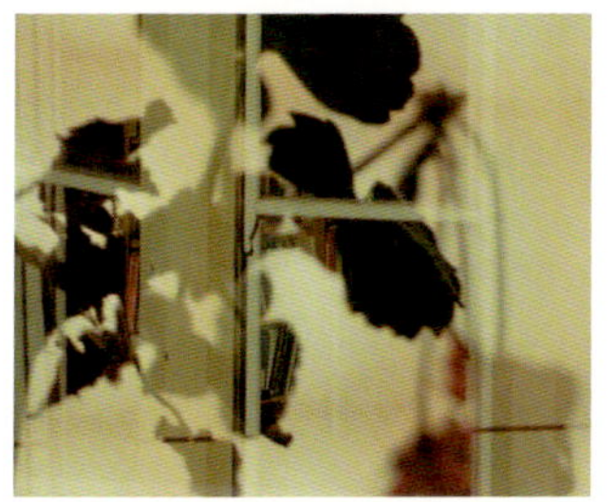
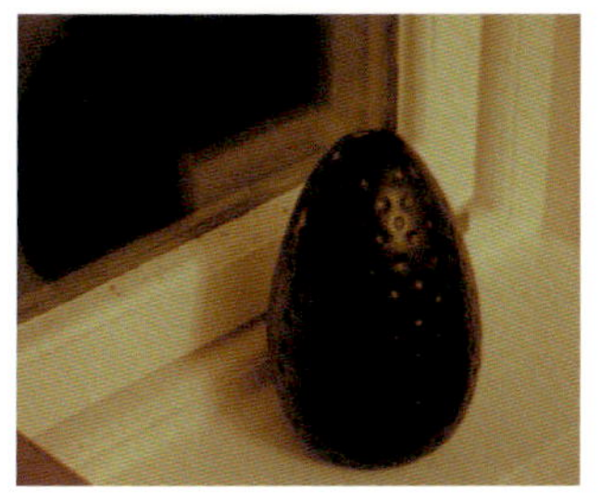
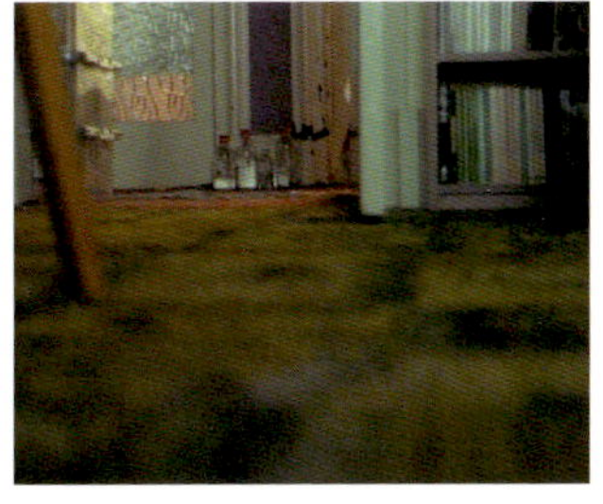
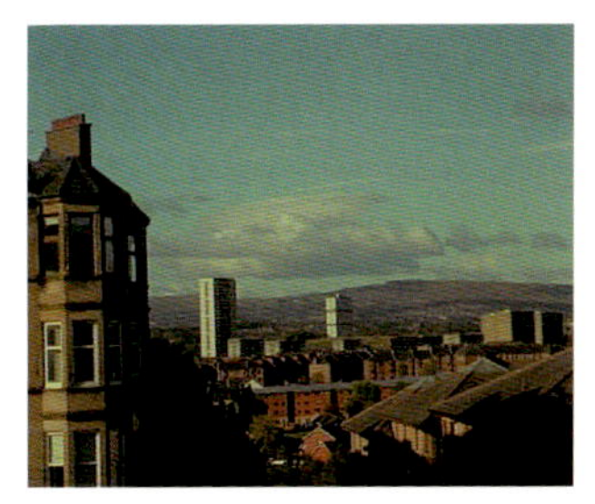
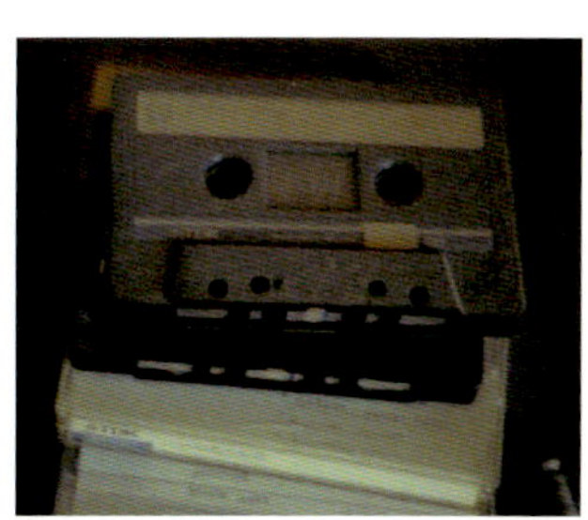

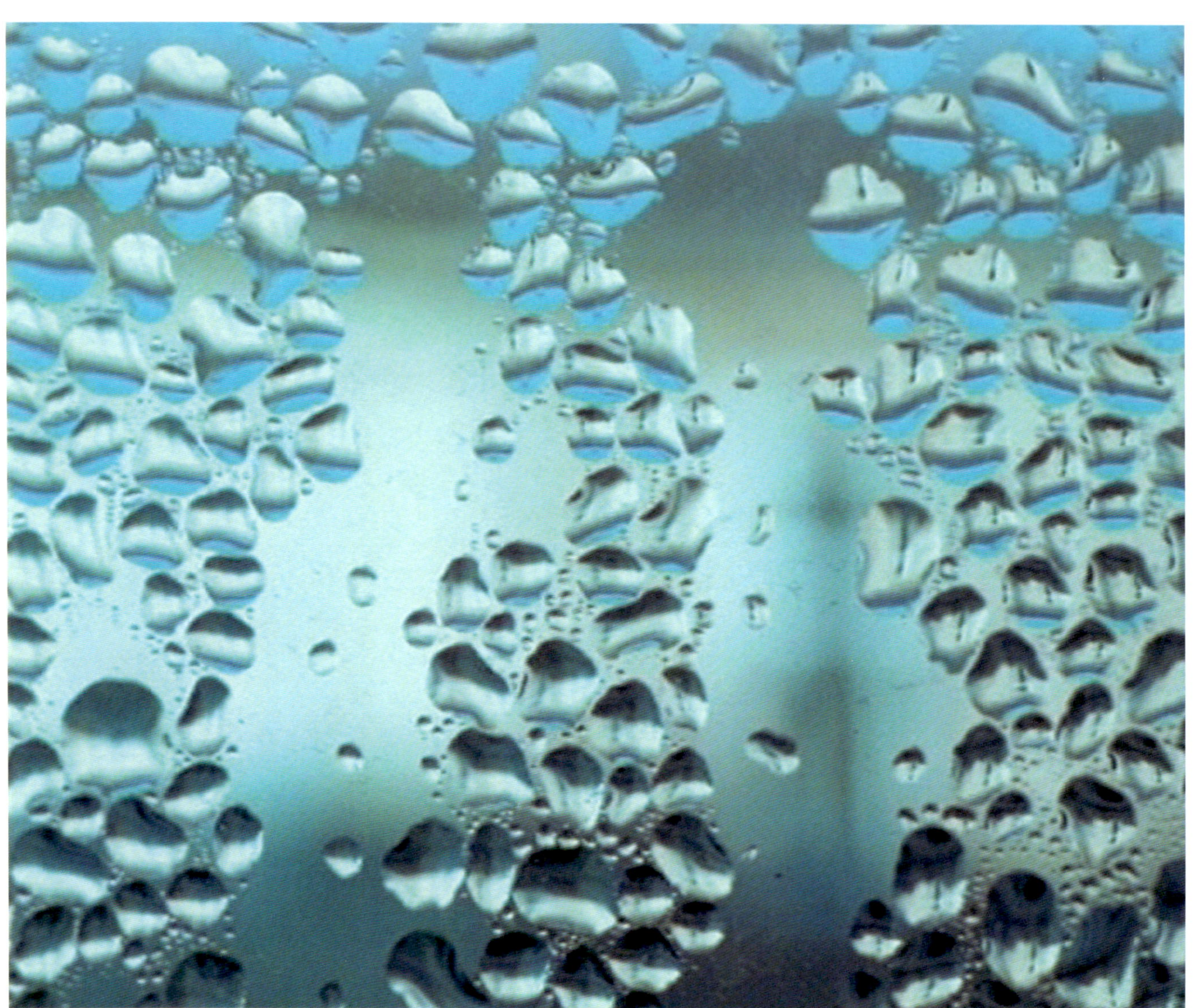

Filmografie

Wenn nicht anders vermerkt: Produktion, Regie, Kamera, Schnitt und Ton von Luke Fowler.

What You See Is Where You're At, 2001

DVD, Farbe und s/w, Ton
24 Min.
Produktion: Dundee Contemporary Arts, Dundee
Schnittassistent: Torsten Lauschmann
Ton: Rob Kennedy
Musik: Hassle Hound
Interview: Dr. Leon Redler und Luke Fowler
Archiv: Dr. Leon Redler, Richard Adams, Estate of Ronald D. Laing, Oddvar Foss

Ausstellungen (Auswahl)
2008
Kunsthalle Zürich, Zürich
2007
Widening Horizon, Pleasure Dome, Toronto
2005
Beck's Futures, ICA – Institute of Contemporary Arts, London; CCA – The Centre for Contemporary Arts, Glasgow
2004
Anti-Psychiatry Film Festival, Nova Cinema, Brüssel
2003
What You See Is Where You're At, Spacex, Exeter
Art/34/Basel, Basel
Electric Earth (British Council Wanderausstellung), State Russian Museum, St. Petersburg; Radio Laboratory Museum, Nizhni Novgorod; Yaroslavl Museum of Fine Art, Yaroslav; Na Solyanke Gallery, Moscow u. a.
2001
Beyond, Dundee Contemporary Arts, Dundee

Luke Fowlers Film *What You See Is Where You're At* wurde von der Pionierarbeit des Psychiaters, Psychoanalysten und Schriftstellers Ronald D. Laing inspiriert, der eine experimentelle Wohngemeinschaft in der Kingsley Hall ins Leben gerufen hatte. Diese Gemeinschaft begründete eine gewagte und innovative Zugangsweise und den Versuch einer Klärung zum Verständnis von „Wahnsinn": Ein Zusammenbruch – vielleicht in dem Sinne, dass das eigene Sein nicht mehr länger haltbar ist, vielleicht ein Zusammenbruch in dem Sinne, nicht mehr man selbst zu sein – wurde als möglicher Anfang zum Durchbruch in der Heilung von Fragmentierungen und Störungen des Gedächtnisses, des Körpers, der Seele und des Geistes verstanden. Konventionelle psychiatrische Diagnosen (die selten das „Hindurch Sehen" darstellen, die das Wort in seiner Etymologie andeutet), die komplexe Erfahrungen in spezifischen sozialen Kontexten zu Krankheitskategorien reduzierten, wurden der Komplexität und Tiefe der Erfahrungen vieler Personen mit mentalen Leiden nicht gerecht. Obwohl konventionelle Behandlungen oftmals dramatische „Erfolge" bei Menschen erzielten, die verstört waren und/oder verstörend auf andere wirkten, wurden dringende, schmerzliche und verblüffend emotionale, spirituelle und ethische Probleme zu oft verdrängt, getrübt oder gar hinausgeschoben. In Kingsley Hall konnten die Bewohner ihren eigenen Weg finden – auf ihre Weise, in ihrer eigenen Geschwindigkeit, allein oder in einem Umfeld, das sie frei wählten.

War die Kingsley-Hall-Erfahrung ein Erfolg? Sie war es und sie war es nicht; abhängig davon, wer man war, wo man war und was man als „Erfolg" erachtete. Sie war ein Erfolg, weil Fragen gestellt wurden, die sich jede Generation stellen muss: Was bedeuten „Gesundheit" und „Wahnsinn"? Auf welcher Grundlage, unter Einbezug von was und wessen Interessen wird die Unterscheidung gemacht? Was steht auf dem Spiel, je nach dem wie solche Fragen gestellt und beantwortet werden; von jedem Einzelnen von uns und von denen, die die Macht haben, sich über diese Angelegenheit zu äussern und entsprechend zu handeln? Sie war insofern ein Erfolg, als dass das Experiment denjenigen Raum und Respekt gab, die darauf bestanden zu fragen, wer wir wirklich sind und welche Wege vielleicht die besseren sein könnten für das Miteinander-auf-der-Welt-Sein, vor allem in tiefem Leid oder auf schwierigen „Reisen". Ein solcher Geist widersteht und wehrt sich gegen die Zwänge der Konventionen und überwindet die Versuchung, seinen Schmerz und seine Angst ohne überdachte Abwägung zu dämpfen, er hält Lebenskraft und Verantwortung in der Balance, auf Kosten dieser Abstumpfung und mit Ausblick auf ein leidenschaftliches Leben mit grösserer Integrität.

Fowler war fasziniert vom Mut, Drama, Pathos, der Poesie und manchmal von so etwas ähnlichem wie Surrealismus, der sich zwischen den unterschiedlichen Charakteren in Kingsley Hall entfaltete: „Zuerst und vor allem war ich zum Kingsley-Hall-Experiment aufgrund persönlicher Umstände hingezogen, aufgrund meiner eigenen Erfahrung mit der zeitgenössischen Psychiatrie [...], desillusioniert über die Art und Weise, wie mein Vater vom System behandelt wurde und ausgestattet mit einer insgesamt gesunden, zynischen Attitüde gegenüber Institutionen." (Luke Fowler im Gespräch mit Dr. Leon Redler, 2000)

Fowler hat sich denen angeschlossen, die der pharmazeutischen Industrie und den Medikamentenkartellen – die einen enormen Einfluss auf die psychiatrische Ausbildung, die Praxis wie auch die Forschung haben – äusserst kritisch gegenüberstehen. Die schreckliche Allianz der Psychiatrien mit der Pharmaindustrie, die, ermutigt durch die Regierung, in zunehmendem Masse wie Konzernstaaten geführt werden, marginalisieren diejenigen, die vorherrschende materielle Werte infrage stellen und die nach Ursprüngen für geistige Leiden im Alltag und im Umgang miteinander suchen.
—Dr. Leon Redler

The Way Out, 2003
(mit Kosten Koper)

DVD, Farbe und s/w, Ton
33 Min.
Produktion: Cubitt Gallery (Emily Pethick), London; Zenomap; The Modern Institute/Toby Webster Ltd, Glasgow
Kamera: Luke Fowler, Kosten Koper, Will Hunt
Schnittassistent: Duncan Campell
Musik: Die Trip Computer Die, The Homosexuals, Harmon E. Phraisyer, Xentos Jones, Milk From Cheltenham, L Voag, Leonard und Rodger, Comrad O'leau
Erzähler: Danny Saunders
Besetzung: Bing Selfish, Ed Baxter, Lepke B, Charlotte Prodger, Kosten Koper, Franz Ferdinand, Optimo
Archiv: Xentos „Fray Bentos", Lepke B

Ausstellungen (Auswahl)
2009
Serpentine Gallery, London
2008
Kunsthalle Zürich, Zürich
2007
Widening Horizon, Pleasure Dome, Toronto
Whenever It Starts It Is The Right Time, Frankfurter Kunstverein, Frankfurt am Main
2006
Adventures in Modern Music, The Gene Siskel Film Center, Chicago
2005
Beck's Futures, ICA – Institute of Contemporary Arts, London; CCA – The Centre for Contemporary Arts, Glasgow
2003
Jakob Kolding, Luke Fowler/Kosten Koper, Cubitt Gallery, London
ZENOMAP – New Works from Scotland for the Venice Biennale, 50. Biennale di Venezia, Venedig
Art/34/Basel, Basel

The Way Out porträtiert Xentos „Fray Bentos" Jones, ein Gründungsmitglied der Band The Homosexuals, die in Vergessenheit geriet, nachdem sie in der Post-Punk-Ära in Eigeninitiative eine Reihe wegweisender Schallplatten veröffentlicht hatte. Obwohl sich The Homosexuals auflösten, ohne je eine offizielle LP auf den Markt gebracht zu haben, veröffentlichte L Voag (alias Xentos) 1979 ein eigenes Soloprojekt *The Way Out*. *The Way Out* war ein cut-up Do-it-Yourself Konzeptalbum, das sich einen musikalischen

Kontext in einer verkehrten Parallelwelt vorstellt, wo Popmusik von Modernisten gemacht wird und das Komponieren serieller und avantgardistischer Musik den weniger akzeptierten Randfiguren überlassen wird. Im Laufe der 1980er Jahre produzierte Amos (aka Xentos) unter unzähligen verschiedenen Identitäten eine schier unermessliche Anzahl verschiedener Platten, die er über sein eigenes Label It's War Boys vertrieb, das die bekanntesten und unbekanntesten Genres unter sich vereinte. *The Way Out* verwebt neue Interviews, Drehbuchszenen, gefundenes und neues Filmmaterial sowie Super-8-Aufnahmen von Xentos selbst.

—Luke Fowler

Pilgrimage from Scattered Points, 2006

DVD, Farbe und s/w, Ton
45 Min.
Produktion: Dewar Arts Award, Kirkcudbright; The Modern Institute/ Toby Webster Ltd, Glasgow
Kamera: Luke Fowler, Guy Corbishley, Lucile Desamoray, Alasdair Willis
Musik: Cornelius Cardew und The Scratch Orchestra, Michael Chant und Hugh Shrapnell, Thurston Moore, John Tilbury, Michael Chant, Richard Ascough, Chris May, Christian Wolff, David Jackman
Besetzung: Cornelius Cardew (Archivmaterial), John Tilbury, David Sladen, Bryn Harris, Christopher Hobbs, Edwin Prevost, Richard Ascough, Laurie Baker, Stella Cardew, Psi Ellison, Hugh Shrapnell, Carole Finer, Michael Parsons, Dave Smith
Archiv: Cardew Estate, Hanne Boenisch, Arts Council England, BBC, Werner Bethsold, Michael Chant, Richard Ascough, Psi Ellison, Carole Finer, Alec Hill, Bryn Harris, David Jackman, Hugh Shrapnell, Dave Smith, Victor Schoenfield, John Tilbury

Ausstellungen (Auswahl)
2009
The Now now festival, Sydney
Serpentine Gallery, London
The Associates, DCA – Dundee Contemporary Arts, Dundee
2008
Milton Keynes Gallery, Milton Keynes
Sónar 2008, Barcelona
CPH:DOX International Documentary Film Festival, Kopenhagen
Hot Docs, Austin
Courtisane Film Festival, Arts Centre Vooruit & Sphinx Cinema, Ghent
KVIFF – Karlovy Vary International Film Festival, Prague International Film Festival, Prag
OFF: Other Film Festival, Brisbane
Artists's Films, Camden Arts Centre, London
The New Museum, New York
2007
Widening Horizon, Pleasure Dome, Toronto
You Have Not Been Honest, Museo d'Arte Contemporanea Donnaregina, Neapel
Never Still. MAP Magazine presents new artists' film, CCA – The Centre for Contemporary Arts, Glasgow
Twighlight Adventures in Music, Whitechapel Art Gallery, London
Kraak Festival, Hasselt
2006
White Columns, New York
The Modern Institute/Toby Webster Ltd, Glasgow
Tate Triennial. New British Art, Tate Britain, London
State of Innocence. International Film Festival Rotterdam, Rotterdam
Adventures in Modern Music, The Gene Siskel Film Center, Chicago
Normalisering, Rooseum Centre for Contemporary Art, Malmö
Avanto Festival, Muu Galleria, Helsinki

Pilgrimage from Scattered Points ist ein Film über den englischen Komponisten Cornelius Cardew (1936–1981) und das Scratch Orchestra (1968–1973). Cardew gründete The Scratch Orchestra 1968 zusammen mit Michael Parsons und Howard Skempton. Im Juni 1969 veröffentlichten sie den Entwurf seiner Statuten in *The Musical Times*. Hier wurden die Rahmenbedingungen festgelegt, die die musikalische Arbeit des Orchesters für die erste Hälfte seines Bestehens prägte: Vorgeschlagen war eine offene Gemeinschaft, in der Studenten, Büroangestellte, Amateurmusiker und einige professionelle Komponisten für gemeinsame Auftritte zusammen kommen, um Musik zu machen und produktive Zeit zu verbringen.

Die einzige vollständig existierende Aufnahme des Scratch Orchestra ist eine Performance von Cardews *The Great Learning* (1968–1970) – ein sechsstündiger Choral, der für das Orchester auf der Grundlage konfuzianischer Schriften geschrieben wurde. Das Werk benötigt eine grosse Anzahl an geschulten und ungeschulten Musikern, die singen, sprechen, trommeln, Aktionen und Gebärden ausführen, gewöhnliche und unkonventionelle Tonquellen benützen und mit diesen improvisieren.

Die Konzerte des Scratch Orchestra bestanden oftmals aus den folgenden Elementen: „Scratch Music", die anstelle von traditionellen Partituren auf grafischen oder verbalen Instruktionen beruhte; „Popular Classics", dem Persiflieren berühmter Werke, hauptsächlich aus dem klassischen Kanon; „Improvisation Rites", einem gemeinschaftlichen Ausgangspunkt für semi-strukturierte und freie Improvisationen; „Research Projects", Reisen, die in viele Dimensionen unternommen wurden – zeitlich, räumlich, intellektuell, spirituell und emotional. In Ablehnung des Musikestablishments suchte das Orchester nach neuen Örtlichkeiten und einem neuen Publikum für ihre Musik. Konzerte konnten in Rathäusern, Bahnhöfen, Einkaufszentren, im Yachthafen, an Hochzeiten oder in entfernten Dorfsälen stattfinden.

Nach zwei Jahren setzte dieses musikalische und soziale Experiment eine strenge Selbstkritik in Gang, mit Debatten über die Funktion ihrer Kunst und wem sie diente. Um diese Kritik öffentlich bekannt zu machen, wurden Treffen veranstaltet und eine „Akte der Unzufriedenheit" aufgesetzt. Dies spaltete das Orchester in zwei gegnerische Lager: Das erste Lager, die „ID Gruppe", glaubte an das maoistische Diktum, dass Musik dem Kampf der breiten Masse nutzen sollte. Das zweite, die „bourgeoisen Idealisten", kämpften für eine autonome Kunst, die in erster Linie formalen und musikalischen Experimenten und der Selbstdarstellung dient.

Pilgrimage from Scattered Points geht den internen Widersprüchen und Wirrungen des Scratch Orchestra in Interviews nach, unter Verwendung von neuem und archiviertem Filmmaterial, hauptsächlich aber von unveröffentlichten Musikaufnahmen.

—Luke Fowler

The Nine Monads of David Bell, 2006–2007

Super-8-Film, s/w, und Archivmaterial, Installation mit Ton
50 Min.
Produktion: The Modern Institute/Toby Webster Ltd, Glasgow; Dr. Leon Redler
Musik: Stuart MacRae
Besetzung: Stephan Bach, Ursel und Felix Gumbsch, Ulrich Bohnefeld, Bambam (Film), David Bell, Leon Redler (Ton)

Ausstellungen
2009
Serpentine Gallery, London
2007
Extra City – centrum voor hedendaagse kunst, Antwerpen
2006
Villa Concordia, Bamberg

Die Installation *The Nine Monads of David Bell* besteht aus neuen Arbeiten, die ihren Ausgangspunkt in Luke Fowlers früherem Film *What You See Is Where You're At* (2001) nehmen. Dieser ist ein Porträt über die Kingsley-Hall-Gemeinschaft (1965–1969), die vom abtrünnigen Psychiater Ronald D. Laing und der Philadelphia Association gegründet wurde, um denjenigen einen Ort des Rückzugs zu bieten, die verstört, gestresst oder mental erkrankt waren.

The Nine Monads of David Bell erforscht die Welt des David Bell, einem der poetischsten und wortreichsten Bewohner von Kingsley Hall. Bell war ein Mathematiker, der in den 1950ern nach London zog, um dort als Programmierer zu arbeiten. Nachdem ihn seine Freundin verlassen hatte, wurde Bell stark verhaltensauffällig und schliesslich eingewiesen. Er zog nach Kingsley Hall und freundete sich mit Dr. Leon Redler an, einem jungen amerikanischen Psychiater, der nach London gekommen war, um mit Laing zu arbeiten. Obwohl die lokalen Psychiatrien Bells Sprache als rein „schizophren" bewerteten, wurden seine Worte in Kingsley Hall geschätzt und aufgezeichnet. Weitere Dokumente von Bell, der in den 1990er Jahren verstarb, sind von Redler aufbewahrt worden – auf ihnen basiert die Installation von Fowler.

Die zentrale Komponente der Arbeit ist eine Toninstallation mit einer Länge von 50 Minuten. Das Material stammt von Kassetten, die zwischen 1965 und 1976 in Kingsley Hall und später in Redlers privater Praxis aufgenommen wurden. Durch eine lineare Darstellung arbeitet Fowler die verschiedenen Zustände von Bell heraus. Während der erste Teil Bells soziales Leben in und um Kingsley Hall beschreibt, konzentriert sich der zweite Teil auf den inneren Kampf seiner drei verschiedenen Persönlichkeiten „er", „sie" und „Junge". Der letzte Teil bildet einen starken Kontrast zu den beiden vorangegangenen: Man bekommt Einblick wie Bell, der unter dem starken Einfluss von Medikamenten steht, mit Redler sehr klar, jedoch stumpf und emotionslos über sein Verhalten der letzten Jahre spricht.

Der auf einem Monitor gezeigte Film, ursprünglich auf Super-8-Material gedreht, zeigt Amateurschauspieler, die die auf Kassetten archivierten Träume von Bell nachstellen. Fowler erarbeitet vier Traumsequenzen.

Die fotografische Dokumentation ist in drei Serien angelegt: Die erste zeigt Seiten von Zeitungen, die Bell als Schreibpapier benutzte – die Seiten sind eine Verbindung von Artikeln, Werbung und Bells eigenen Notizen. Die zweite beinhaltet Auszüge aus Bells Notizbüchern. Die letzte Folge schliesslich sind Fotografien, die in der Archways Gemeinschaft aufgenommen wurden, einem Nachfolgeprojekt von Kingsley Hall der Philadelphia Association. Die Bilder zeigen Bell und andere Bewohner in unterschiedlichen sozialen Situationen, aufgenommen von Mike Yokum, einem Bewohner und Pfleger der Archway Gemeinschaft. Des Weiteren sind zwei handschriftliche Karten und ein von Bell verunstalteter Pass zu sehen.
—Anselm Franke und Dr. Leon Redler

Bogman Palmjaguar, 2007

16mm-Film und Super-8-Film übertragen auf Video, Farbe, Ton
30 Min.
Produktion: Arts Council England; EASTInternational, Norwich
Ton: Lee Patterson
Besetzung: Bogman Bluequartz Palmjaguar, Dr. Leon Redler, Lee Patterson

Ausstellungen
2008
Kunsthalle Zürich, Zürich
International Film Festival Rotterdam, Rotterdam
Transmission Gallery, Glasgow

Scottish Shorts Showcase, Edinburgh Film Festival, Edinburgh
2007
EASTInternational 2007, Norwich

Bogman Palmjaguar ist das Porträt eines Mannes, der nach einer Serie von Schicksalsschlägen seinen Mitmenschen gegenüber misstrauisch geworden ist und sich in die Natur zurückgezogen hat. Bogman beschreibt sich selbst als „versteckte Katze" und „verfremdeten Wilden im Paradies" und kämpft gegen eine Diagnose, die ihn als „paranoiden Schizophreniker" bezeichnet. Seine frühen Lebensjahre und diese Diagnose wirkten sich auf seine sozialen Kontakte aus – sowohl innerhalb wie ausserhalb von medizinischen Einrichtungen. Der Entschluss, sich mit legalen Mitteln dieser gesellschaftlichen Stigmatisierung zu entledigen, ist für Bogman von lebenswichtiger Bedeutung – dabei ist er sowohl auf der Suche nach Gerechtigkeit wie auch nach den Gründen, die dazu führten, dass sein Leben in den vergangenen drei Jahrzehnten diesen Verlauf genommen hat.

Der Film entstand anlässlich von zwei Besuchen in Bogmans Haus in einem abgeschiedenen Dorf im Norden Schottlands. Der erste Besuch erfolgte, nachdem Bogmans Anwalt einen unabhängigen Krankheitsbericht durch Dr. Leon Redler (einem Kollegen von Ronald D. Laing) angefordert hatte, in dem dieser beurteilen sollte, ob die Diagnose „Paranoide Schizophrenie" gerechtfertigt war. Der zweite Besuch fand im Beisein des Tonkünstlers Lee Patterson statt und dokumentiert die Umgebung, die Bogman während seiner Zeit als Naturschützer zu bewahren versuchte: Bogman war fasziniert vom bedrohten Lebensraum in Schottlands Flow Country, einer verwilderten Landschaft mit Sümpfen und Torfmooren, die eine einzigartige Vielfalt an wilden Tieren beherbergte. Zugleich wurden die Torfmoore für ihn zu einem Versteck, in das er vor den eingrenzenden Versuchen der Behörden entfloh. Der Film ist eine Versöhnung des jungen Umweltschützers mit seinem älteren Selbst, das isoliert und zurückgezogen von der Gesellschaft lebt.
—Luke Fowler

Achterhaven Splinters, 2007
(mit Barry Burns und Mark Vernon)

16-mm-Film übertragen auf DVD, s/w, Ton
6 Min.
Produktion: Worm Filmwerkplaats, Rotterdam

Achterhaven Splinters ist ein fragmenthaftes Porträt von Achterhaven, einem Arbeiterklasse-Vorort von Rotterdam. Über einen Zeitraum von 24 Stunden gefilmt, werden flüchtige Momente des Alltagslebens unter

die Lupe genommen, um dann im Prozess der manuellen Entwicklung gesprengt zu werden: Die dokumentarischen Sequenzen verändern sich in ihrer Bedeutung, sobald sie physikalisch mit Hilfe von Licht, Chemie und anderen Materialien manipuliert werden. Der Ton wurde vor Ort aufgezeichnet und nachträglich den Bildern unterlegt. Die dynamische Textur des Soundtracks spiegelt die Bilder in ihrer Flüchtigkeit zwischen Realität und Abstraktion wider.
—Luke Fowler

The Harbour Doubts, 2007

16-mm-Film übertragen auf DVD, Farbe, Ton
6 Min.
Produktion: Worm Filmwerkplaats, Rotterdam

Ausstellungen
2007
The Harbour Doubts, Bad Bad Boys Club, Dundee
2008
Esther Schipper REC Projektraum, Berlin

The Harbour Doubts ist der erste 16-mm-Film von Luke Fowler. Es ist ein Werk, das die andere Seite von Fowlers Schaffen dokumentiert – die Klangwelten. Seit über zehn Jahren ist Fowler in Bands und elektronische Musik involviert; seit 1999 führt er das Label SHADAZZ. In den Gruppen Rude Pravo und Lied Music arbeitete er hauptsächlich mit der Technologie des Tonbands und selbst erfundenen Instrumenten, teils inspiriert von den Werken der wegbereitenden, britischen Improvisationskünstler der 1960er Jahre Hugh Davies und Keith Rowe (Gründungsmitglied von AMM).

In den letzten Jahren hat sich Fowler vor allem auf Kompositionen konzentriert, die auf Feldaufnahmen basieren. In *The Harbour Doubts* geht er dem Wunsch nach, die Musik mit seiner filmischen Arbeit zu kombinieren. Initiiert vom Programmierer Peter Taylor, wurde Fowler eingeladen, die 16-mm-Anlagen des Worm Studios in Rotterdam für seinen Film zu nutzen.

Film und Ton wurden während eines einwöchigen Atelieraufenthalts in Rotterdam im April 2007 von Fowler aufgenommen, geschnitten und komponiert. Die Aufnahmen untersuchen, wie sich vibrierende Oberflächen von Alltagssituationen in der Stadt in akustische Tonwellen übertragen lassen. Die Aufnahmen wurden mit Kontaktmikrophonen, selbstgemachten Hydrophonen und Miniatur-Kondensern gemacht. Der Film dokumentiert einfach die Örtlichkeiten, wo die Geräusche aufgenommen wurden. Er wurde unabhängig vom Ton geschnitten und zusammengestellt, um einen asynchronen Dialog zwischen Ton und Bild zu kreieren.
—Robert Meijer

George, 2008

16-mm-Film übertragen auf DVD,
Farbe, Ton
4 Min.

Ausstellungen
2008
a passable door for a movable passer,
Buccleuch Street, Glasgow
Aurora Film Festival, Norwich

George war ein Versuch, die Grundelemente meiner Annäherung an das Filmemachen zu überdenken und sie auf die wesentlichen Elemente zu reduzieren. War im vergangenen dokumentarischen Schaffen der Akt des Schauens implizit, wird er in dieser Studie zum Mittelpunkt. Der Ausgangspunkt des Films war die Gegend, in der ich geboren wurde und noch immer lebe – das Westend von Glasgow – sowie die Verbindung mit dem Ort, wo der Film zum ersten Mal gezeigt wurde – einer Wohnung in Garnethill. Der Fussweg zwischen den beiden Orten führt durch die Gegend von St. George X. Sie steht im Zentrum des Films. Der Film handelt von der Beziehung zwischen Ton und Bild, akustischen Phänomenen und architektonischen Details.
—Luke Fowler

An Abbeyview Film, 2008

16-mm-Film, Farbe, ohne Ton
11 Min.
Produktion: Nicola Atkinson Davidson,
Abbeyview Regeneration Office,
Communities Scotland, Fife Council

Ausstellungen
2008
Permanent vs. Temporary, Abbeyview
Community Centre, Dunfermline
Kunsthalle Zürich, Zürich

An Abbeyview Film entstand im Auftrag des Abbeyview Artist in Residence Programms Nicola Atkinson Davidson (2007–2008), als Teil des Sanierungsprogramms für eine Wohnsiedlung sozial benachteiligter Menschen im schottischen Dumfermline.
Statt zu seinem Thema einen klaren Standpunkt zu beziehen, liess sich Fowler vom Zufall leiten und liefert einen poetischen „Schnappschuss" vom Leben einer Gemeinschaft in einem sozialen Brennpunkt. Der Film ist keine Dokumentation von Wohnanlagen in der herkömmlichen Weise, sondern zeigt eine Ästhetik im Zwiespalt zwischen Trostlosigkeit und Hoffnung.
—Barry Burns

Another Day of Gravity, 2008
(mit Richard Youngs)

16-mm-Film übertragen auf DVD,
Farbe, Ton
4 Min.
Produktion: Arika, Edinburgh
Musik: Richard Youngs

Ausstellung
2008
Instal 2008, The Arches, Glasgow

Der Film *Another Day of Gravity* entstand für *Instal 08* im Auftrag von Arika. Grundlage sind Acapella-Verse des englischen Musikers Richard Youngs, dessen Aufnahmen dafür bekannt sind, die Liedform mit „minimalistischer" und improvisierter Musik weiterzuentwickeln. Der Film wurde im Verlauf eines Tages in Youngs Wohnung gedreht. Für jede neue Liedzeile ändert sich der Aufnahmewinkel der Kamera; mit jeder neuen Strophe wechselt der Film in den nachfolgenden Raum.
Der Film feierte mit einer Live-Begleitung von Youngs und Teilnahmemöglichkeiten des Publikums an der *Instal 08* in The Arches seine Premiere.
—Luke Fowler

Paddington Collaboration, 2008
(mit Anna McLauchlan)

16-mm-Film übertragen auf DVD,
Farbe, Ton
2 Min. 45 Sek.

Paddington Collaboration ist eine Zusammenarbeit mit der in Glasgow lebenden Künstlerin und Schriftstellerin Anna McLauchlan. Er wurde sowohl in der Wohnung ihrer Schwester wie auch in deren Umgebung in Paddington (London) am Morgen des 26. Dezembers 2007 gedreht. Der Inhalt des Films ist die Präsentation einer durchdachten Entschuldigung, um familiären Verpflichtungen zu entfliehen; er ist aber auch ein Versuch, McLauchlan wieder mit dem Medium vertraut zu machen, von welchem sie sich für viele Jahre zurückgezogen hatte. Der Film wurde mit einer einzigen Filmrolle gedreht, in der Kamera editiert und ist in zwei Teile geteilt: Der erste ist meine Idee und der zweite Teil die von McLauchlan.
—Luke Fowler

**B8016: Draw a Straight Line
and Follow It, 2008** (mit Lee Patterson)

16-mm-Film, Farbe, Ton
25 Min.
Produktion: Alice Koegel (für Tate
Modern, London)

Ausstellungen
2008
Kunsthalle Zürich, Zürich
The Long Weekend, Tate Modern, London

Für den Film *B8016: Draw a Straight Line and Follow It* wurden wir von La Monte Youngs Textpartitur *composition no. 10, draw a straight line and follow it* aus dem Jahr 1960 inspiriert. Unsere Reaktion auf die Partitur war, eine gerade Strasse zu finden, ihr zu folgen und die Erfahrungen in Film und Ton zu dokumentieren, während wir Material – menschliche Hinterlassenschaften und Naturalien – entlang des Weges sammelten. Das versteckte Potenzial dieser Objekte als „Ton-Objekte" wird in der Live Performance erfahrbar – sie bringen den Aspekt der Improvisation in die sonst statische Erfahrung des Sehens/Projizierens von Film.
Für unseren Fussmarsch wählten wir die Strasse B8016 auf der Insel Islay, Teil der Inneren Hebriden in Schottland. Diese Strasse zwischen Port Ellen und Bridgend wurde nicht nur aufgrund ihrer Länge und ihres geraden Verlaufs ausgesucht, sondern auch, weil sie durch unterschiedliche Geländetypen führt, einschliesslich Gegenden mit bebauter und ursprünglicher Natur. Für uns beide war es das erste Mal, dass wir diesen Weg gegangen sind. Die Arbeit vereint Anliegen, die Kernstücke unserer jeweiligen künstlerischen Praxis sind: die Kunst der Beobachtung, das heisst unter die Oberfläche zu schauen, und die Kunst des Sammelns, die ein Wiedergewinnen des Unerwünschten und Übersehenen ist.
—Luke Fowler und Lee Patterson

**Northwest from Chesterhill: Draw
a Straight Line and Follow It, 2008**
(mit Lee Patterson)

Live-Performance mit 16-mm-Film,
Farbe, Ton
Produktion: Arika, Edinburgh

Ausstellungen
2008
KYTN, DCA – Dundee Contemporary
Arts, Dundee

Northwest from Chesterhill: Draw a Straight Line and Follow It ist die zweite Arbeit meines fortlaufenden Projekts mit Lee Patterson. Als Ausgangspunkt des Spaziergangs wählten wir dieses Mal die Gefilde von Chester Hill, überquerten die Tay Bridge bis ins Stadtzentrum von Dundee. Ausgehend von einer durchgehend geraden Strasse, wie wir es in *B8016: Draw a Straight Line and Follow It* getan hatten, zogen wir nun eine gerade Linie auf einer Karte vom Zentrum der Stadt Dundee, wobei die Tay Bridge den zentralen Punkt bildete. Der Spaziergang fand in zwei Teilstrecken statt und endete mit der Ankunft in Dundees Law Hill.
—Luke Fowler

Composition for Flutter Screen, 2008
(mit Toshiya Tsunoda)

Installation mit 16-mm-Farbfilm und Projektor, handgemachter Leinwand, Timer, Kabel, Ventilatoren, Licht
Produktion: Yokohama Triennale, Yokohama

Ausstellungen
2009
Serpentine Gallery, London
2008
Yokohama Triennale 2008, Yokohama

Die Filminstallation ist das Ergebnis einer Zusammenarbeit mit Toshiya Tsunoda und wurde in Yokohama für die dortige Triennale 2008 erdacht und gedreht. Der Film zeigt eine Reihe von Objekten (Kerze, Karte, Kabel etc.), die an Örtlichkeiten platziert wurden, wo Tsunoda viel Arbeitszeit für seine Tonaufnahmen verbringt. Man sieht die Objekte in dem Moment, als sie die „Gegebenheiten" des Ortes erfassen, an dem sie gefilmt werden: örtliche Begebenheiten wie Vibrationen, Licht, Wind werden sichtbar durch die Bewegung der Flammen von zwei kleinen Kerzen, die Oberflächenspannung des Wassers in einem Glas am Punkt ihres Brechens, das Licht in einer Hafenanlage, das unterschiedliche Schatten auf eine Geländekarte zeichnet… Die Bilder benutzen auch illusionistische Techniken (Tiefenschärfe, Makro, 3D-Darstellung einer Bergkette), sodass sie den Betrachter über die Authentizität der Bilder zweifeln lassen.

Weitere Eingriffe wie die Verwendung eines Timers, tonverstärkte Kabel, Ventilatoren, Lichter und eine dünne Leinwand sind in die Installation integriert. Sie wirken als Störfaktoren einer traditionellen Kinoerfahrung.
—Luke Fowler

The Room, 2008ff.
(mit Keith Rowe und Peter Todd)

Live-Performance mit 16-mm-Farbfilmen und Ton
Produktion (zum Zeitpunkt der Drucklegung): Tate Modern, London; CAC Brétigny – Centre d'art contemporain de Brétigny, Brétigny-sur-Orge
Kamera: Luke Fowler, Peter Todd
Ton: Keith Rowe

Ausstellung
2008
Expanded Cinema for Rothko, Tate Modern, London

The Room ist der erste Teil in einer fortlaufenden Serie der Zusammenarbeit von drei Künstlern: 16-mm-Filme von Luke Fowler und Peter Todd verflechten sich mit einer Live-Gitarren-Improvisation von Keith Rowe. Wir arbeiten unabhängig voneinander, filmen in unterschiedlichen Räumen und bringen die Filme für jede der Performances zusammen.

Die erste Installation wurde in der Tate Modern am 28. November 2008 präsentiert. *The Room* ist ein wachsendes Werk, da mit jeder folgenden Performance zwei weitere Filme hinzugefügt werden. Die in den Filmen erkundeten Räume sind unbelebt, dennoch beherbergen sie Spuren menschlicher Aktivität, Beweise vergangener und momentaner Ereignisse, von persönlichen Einwirkungen und Zufälligem. Die jeweiligen Installationsräume sind einzigartig – in akustischer wie auch in visueller Hinsicht. Verborgene Frequenzen werden ausgehoben und hörbar gemacht; Radiosendungen und zufällige Sendungen werden eingespielt; flüchtige Lichtbewegungen eingefangen.
—Luke Fowler und Peter Todd

Advance the Unknown, 2008–2009

16-mm-Film, Farbe, ohne Ton
18 Min.
Produktion: CCA – The Centre for Contemporary Arts, Glasgow

Ausstellung
2008
Open Field, CCA – The Centre for Contemporary Arts, Glasgow

Ich führte im Vorfeld und während der Ausstellung *Open Field* ein filmisches Tagebuch. Die eiligen filmischen Einträge wurden unbearbeitet gezeigt und wechselten alle zwei Wochen. Während dieses aussergewöhnlich strahlenden und kalten Winters zog ich zwei Mal um, besuchte Freunde in Berlin, nahm Musik auf, reiste mit dem Zug etc.
—Luke Fowler

Tenement Films, 2009

16-mm-Film, Farbe, Ton
4 x 3 Min.
Derek Jarman Award, *3 Minute Wonder* für Channel 4
Erstausstrahlung: April 2009
Produktion: Film London, London; Channel 4; Derek Jarman Award
Musik: Lee Patterson, Toshiya Tsunoda, Taku Unami, Charles Curtis

Ausstellung
2009
Serpentine Gallery, London

Die für das Fernsehen produzierte Serie porträtiert vier Individuen, die im gleichen Haus zusammen wohnen.

Diese Kurzfilme entstanden im Miethaus, in dem ich acht Jahre lang lebte: Der erste wurde in meinem Schlafzimmer gefilmt, das meine damalige Freundin ebenfalls als Büro nutzte. Die anderen drei wurden in architektonisch identischen Räumen gedreht, die von meinen damaligen Nachbarn bewohnt wurden.

Gleichzeitig mit einer 16-mm-Bolex-Kamera aufgezeichnet und geschnitten, unter Verwendung der vorhandenen Lichtquellen, denken die Filme über die vier Protagonisten nach, wie sie die Räume bewohnen und zu einander stehen. Das ohne Unterlass schwenkende und aufspürende Kameraauge fängt unzählige Spuren ein, sodass in allen Filmen nicht fassbare Geschichten herumspuken.

Der erste Film, *Anna*, zeigt meine damalige Partnerin und flüchtige Spiegelbilder von mir, während ich die Kamera um sie herum und um architektonische Details des Raums kreisen lasse. Der Soundtrack in *Anna* ist eine Komposition von Lee Patterson. Grundlage bilden Aufnahmen vor Ort, die durch das Anbringen von Kontaktmikrofonen an Objekte und Gegenständen des Raumes entstanden sind.

Der zweite Film porträtiert Helen in einem markant dekorierten, goldenen Raum. Der Film schweift durch die schnellen Schnitte der Kamera zwischen einem grossen Spiegel und Erkerfenstern, Mehrfachbelichtungen und unvermittelten Kamerabewegungen in eine weitere Dimension des Selbst-Porträts. Er spinnt ein straffes Netz an Assoziationen zwischen persönlichen Ephemera, einem Gemälde, Objekten, Möbeln und der Aussenwelt. Der Soundtrack wurde von Toshiya Tsunoda komponiert und enthält Aufnahmen einer vorangegangenen Installation (*Composition for Flutter Screen*) und bereits existierende Gitarren- und Feldaufnahmen.

Ein Stockwerk höher im Mietshaus ist David der Protagonist des nächsten Films. Im Gegensatz zu den anderen Filmen ist Davids Einrichtung spärlich und einfach. Die Zeitstruktur des Filmes wird auf den Abend ausgedehnt – der Zuschauer kann Szenen vor Davids Fenster mitverfolgen: Autos, das Kommen und Gehen von Fussgängern, während das Tageslicht zur Dämmerung und dann zur tiefen Nacht wechselt. Der Soundtrack für diese Arbeit besteht aus Sinuswellen und diversem Händeklatschen in arrhythmischer Art und Weise und ist von Taku Unami komponiert.

Der letzte Film, *Lester*, der wohl am weichsten fliessende Film des Quartetts, zeichnet sich durch eine warme, schnörkelhafte Solo-Partitur für Cello und Sinuswelle aus, die von Charles Curtis interpretiert und komponiert wurde. Der Film suggeriert die Zusammenführung vorangegangener Experimente im Sinne der Erstellung eines Lexikons für Kameratechniken, die eingesetzt werden können, um diese persönlichen Räume zu benennen und auszukundschaften.
—Luke Fowler

Vorwort

Luke Fowlers Filme erkunden die Grenzen und Konventionen dokumentarischen Filmschaffens und setzen sich kritisch mit der Vorstellung auseinander, die Form biete dem Betrachter eine einzige objektive Wahrheit. Auf innovative Weise verbindet Fowler eigene Filmaufnahmen, Archivmaterial, Interviews und Fotografien mit dicht verwobenem Sound zu impressionistischen Porträts avantgardistischer Denker und Vertreter der Gegenkultur und gibt uns damit Gelegenheit, unsere Beziehung zur Geschichte und zu den grundlegenden Möglichkeiten von Film zu überdenken.

Diese in hohem Mass konstruierten, doch improvisiert wirkenden Collagen, brechen mit den traditionellen Methoden des Genres der Filmbiografie. Sie verwandeln das Filmmaterial in mehrdimensionale Porträts und fördern auf diesem Wege vergessene und verborgene Geschichten zutage. Fowlers akribisch recherchierte Projekte haben Protagonisten, die soziokulturelle Normen in Frage stellen, darunter den radikalen Komponisten Cornelius Cardew, den unkonventionelle Wege gehenden Psychiater Ronald D. Laing, den Post-Punk-Musiker Xentos „Fray Bentos" Jones und den Aussenseiter und Naturschützer Bogman Palmjaguar. Fowler spiegelt die Logik, Ästhetik und politische Einstellung seiner Protagonisten in der Form seines Films, den er über sie macht. Er schafft ein Mosaik atmosphärischer Geschichten, in denen sich die Kraft und Lebendigkeit der von ihm studierten Menschen reflektiert. Durch die Verquickung von Film, Fotografie und Archivdokumenten nimmt er uns mit auf eine Reise, auf der es keine festgelegte, allein gültige Wahrheit gibt und die unsere Beziehung zur Vergangenheit und unsere Erinnerungen an sie in Frage stellt.

Kollaborationen mit anderen Künstlern nehmen in Fowlers Schaffen eine Schlüsselfunktion ein, und er wechselt mühelos zwischen seinen Rollen als Künstler, Kurator, Historiker, Filmemacher und Musiker: Er ist aktives Mitglied der experimentellen Musikszene, gehört verschiedenen Bands an und unterhält die Multimediaplattform SHADAZZ, die in erster Linie LPs in Zusammenarbeit mit anderen Musikern und Künstlern produziert. Diese Projekte überlappen sich häufig mit seiner filmischen Arbeit, da Klang und Musik einen wesentlichen Teil seiner Filme und Installationen ausmachen, in deren Mittelpunkt oft Musiker stehen.

Die Arbeiten in den Ausstellungen *Luke Fowler* in der Kunsthalle Zürich und in der Londoner Serpentine Gallery wurden so ausgewählt, dass sie einen repräsentativen Überblick über das Schaffen des Künstlers, seine Filme, Musik, Fotografien und Installationen geben. Seine Schau in der Kunsthalle Zürich (30. August bis 2. November 2008) war die bisher erste umfassende institutionelle Ausstellung von Luke Fowlers Œuvre und innerhalb der Ausstellungen im Parallelraum der Kunsthalle eine wichtige Präsentation eines Künstlers am Beginn seiner Karriere. Parallel dazu lief die Ausstellung *Derek Jarman: Brutal Beauty*, kuratiert von Isaac Julien, ein weiteres Gemeinschaftsprojekt der beiden Institutionen. In der Serpentine Gallery ist die Ausstellung *Luke Fowler* vom 7. Mai bis 14. Juni 2009 zu sehen. Sie setzt mit dieser sowohl die Tradition, das Werk von Künstlern zu zeigen, die sich noch am Anfang ihres Schaffens befinden, als auch die Reihe der Ausstellungen, die dem Film der Avantgarde gewidmet sind, fort. Diese Schau ist die erste Einzelausstellung von Fowlers Werk in einer öffentlichen Institution in Grossbritannien.

Viele Einzelpersonen und Organisationen haben entscheidend dazu beigetragen, dass diese Ausstellungen realisiert werden konnten. Zuallererst möchten wir Luke Fowler dafür danken, dass er unsere Einladung, seine Arbeiten in Zürich und London zu zeigen, angenommen und beide Ausstellungen sowie den Katalog, auf den sich die Zusammenarbeit zwischen der Kunsthalle Zürich und der Serpentine Gallery konzentriert, aufmerksam und engagiert begleitet hat. Beide Institutionen sind ihm sehr dankbar, dass er eine limitierte Edition zur Verfügung gestellt hat, deren Verkaufserlös ihnen zugute kommt. Dank schulden wir auch dem Künstler Toshiya Tsunoda, der seine Zeit und Kompetenz der Film- und Klanginstallation in der Serpentine Gallery gewidmet hat.

Unseren herzlichen Dank für ihre grosszügigen Zuwendungen sprechen wir den Freunden der Kunsthalle Zürich und der Serpentine Gallery aus. Die LUMA Stiftung hat die Ausstellung in der Kunsthalle Zürich im Rahmen ihres Programms zur Förderung junger Künstler grosszügig unterstützt. Wir danken auch dem Council der Serpentine Gallery, einem ausgezeichneten Team, dessen Engagement von unschätzbarem Wert ist.

Wir freuen uns sehr, dass wir in diese Publikation einen Text von Will Bradley sowie ein Gespräch zwischen dem Künstler und Stuart Comer aufnehmen können, und danken beiden für ihre bereichernden Beiträge. Der Katalog entstand in fruchtbarer Zusammenarbeit zwischen der Kunsthalle Zürich und der Serpentine Gallery, und Rahel Blättler danken wir für die Betreuung des Buches bis zum Druck.

Wir danken auch Toby Webster und Kitty Anderson von The Modern Institute, das den Künstler in Glasgow repräsentiert, für ihre Unterstützung bei der Realisierung der Ausstellungen.

Die Teams der Kunsthalle Zürich (darunter Rahel Blättler und Katharina Pilz, kuratorische Assistenz und Führungen, Susanne Stortz, Presse, Mitglieder und Sponsoren, Alfonso Negri, Webseite, IT und Grafik, und Sylvie Ledermann, Direktionsassistenz) und der Serpentine Gallery (darunter Sophie O'Brien, Ausstellungskuratorin, Mike Gaughan, Galerieleiter, zusammen mit Sally Tallant, Programmleiterin, und Leila Hasham, Ausstellungsassistentin) haben diese Ausstellungen mit grossem Einsatz vorbereitet. Wir möchten auch diesen Teams danken, deren Engagement und Enthusiasmus wesentlich dazu beitragen, dass Projekte wie diese realisiert werden können.

Julia Peyton-Jones
Direktorin, Serpentine Gallery, und
Kodirektorin, Ausstellungen & Programme

Hans Ulrich Obrist
Kodirektor, Serpentine Gallery, Ausstellungen
& Programme, und Direktor, Internationale
Projekte

Beatrix Ruf
Direktorin und Kuratorin, Kunsthalle Zürich

„Diese Haltung schliesst einen Glauben an die Freiheit ein"[1]?

Will Bradley

Wenn die Schlussfolgerungen der Kritischen Theorie direktere Auswirkungen auf die Verfassung der Welt gehabt hätten, wäre das Genre des Dokumentarfilms vielleicht schon in den 1970er Jahren ausgestorben. Die Erkenntnis, dass es sich vom filmischen Standpunkt aus betrachtet bei der Wahrheit um einen zu konstruierenden Parameter und nicht um eine zu vermittelnde blosse Ansammlung von Fakten handelt, musste, so sollte man glauben, den fundamentalen Anspruch des Dokumentarischen unwiderruflich in Misskredit bringen. Tatsächlich aber erlebte man in den 1970er Jahren einen plötzlichen Boom auf dem Gebiet des Dokumentarfilms, welcher sich der Entwicklung preiswerter Handkameras, der Möglichkeiten des Direkttons, neuartigen tragbaren Videokameras und einer Post-68er-Begeisterung dafür verdankte, bislang ungehörte Stimmen und unterrepräsentierte Perspektiven einem Massenpublikum näher zu bringen. Wahrheit im Film war fortan nicht mehr ein angestrebtes Ideal, sondern ein Schlachtfeld, ein polemischer Ort, an dem selbst die radikalen Strategien von Selbstreflexion und Selbstentblössung bald nur noch als zweckmässige rhetorische Mittel fungierten.

Luke Fowlers filmische Praxis beginnt, wo diese Fragestellungen enden, das heisst, er erkennt die offensichtlichen Schlussfolgerungen an, schlägt aber eine kritische Antwort vor. Der Psychiater Roland D. Laing glaubte, die wichtigste Beziehung innerhalb der menschlichen Gesellschaft sei die zwischen dem Ich des Individuums und der Art und Weise, wie es von anderen Individuen verstanden und dargestellt werde. Diese Beziehung wiederum sei notwendiger- und problematischerweise durch die eigene Wahrnehmung vermittelt. Laings These bildet sowohl den Gegenstand wie auch die Grundlage für einen wesentlichen Teil von Fowlers Arbeiten, deren zentrale Frage möglicherweise der Art und Weise gilt, wie das Individuum mit den Mitteln des Films dargestellt wird.

Laings Theorien wurden zeitweilig von einer kurzlebigen, in der Londoner Kingsley Hall gegründeten Therapiegruppe umgesetzt, in der schizophrene Patienten in einer Wohngemeinschaft mit jenen radikalen Therapeuten zusammenlebten, die einen Kontext suchten,

der allen Neuankömmlingen ohne die Verordnung von Psychopharmaka oder anderen Zwangsmassnahmen gerecht wurde. Fowlers Filme *What You See Is Where You're At* (2001) und *Bogman Palmjaguar* (2007) sowie seine Installation *The Nine Monads of David Bell* (2006–2007) sind aus einer unmittelbaren Auseinandersetzung mit der Geschichte des Kingsley-Hall-Experiments entstanden, während sowohl *The Way Out* (2003) als auch *Pilgrimage from Scattered Points* (2006) direkt von Laings Denken geprägt sind. Was Fowler von Laing übernimmt, ist jedoch nicht dessen populärpsychiatrische Theorie – anders als zum Beispiel David Lamelas, der einige Passagen aus Laings Bestseller *Knots* (1967) für seinen Film *Reading Film from Knots* (1970) verwendete –, sondern der gesellschaftliche Radikalismus von Kingsley Hall. Von der etablierten Psychiatrie wurden Laings Thesen weitgehend abgelehnt, und ihre Wirksamkeit im Sinne einer Behandlung ist sowohl umstritten als auch schwer zu beurteilen im Rahmen einer Gesellschaftsordnung, die von Laing selbst als schädlich bezeichnet wurde. Das ihnen zugrunde liegende Prinzip jedoch ist moralischer Natur und umfasst eindeutig politische Konsequenzen. Einfach ausgedrückt, besagen sie, dass Menschen, die unter von der Gesellschaft heute als Psychosen bezeichneten Phänomenen leiden, dennoch Menschen sind, denen dieselben Rechte gewährt werden müssen wie allen anderen. Das bedeutet nicht, dass psychisch Kranke keine Hilfe benötigen, sondern eher das Gegenteil: dass sie nämlich, sofern sie Hilfe brauchen, moralisch dazu berechtigt sind, diese in einer Weise zu erhalten, die sie nicht aus der Gesellschaft ausgrenzt. Laing hat in seinem Werk nicht nur diese politische Frage angesprochen, sondern auch die Frage hinsichtlich des Funktionierens der Gesellschaft, das heisst die Frage danach, auf welcher Grundlage die Gesellschaft einen Menschen als zur Teilhabe an ihr tauglich definiert.

Fowler setzt sich bei seiner Beschäftigung mit Film ausserdem mit wesentlichen Aspekten einer Kritik des Dokumentarfilms auseinander. Anstelle eines Wahrheitsanspruchs kritisiert Fowler in seinen Arbeiten die Vorstellung, dass durch den Vorgang des Filmemachens möglicherweise eine einzelne

1 Lindsay Anderson, „The Free Cinema Manifesto, 5th February 1956", in: Paul Ryan (Hg.), *Never Apologise: The Collected Writings*, London 2004.

2   *The Room*, Tate Modern, London,
    28. November 2008.
3   Luke Fowler, „Expanded Cinema:
    Time/Space/Structure", in: *Map
    Magazine*, Dundee, Nr. 9, Frühjahr
    2007, S. 4–6.
4   Ebd., S. 6.
5   Anderson, „The Free Cinema
    Manifesto".
6   Alexander Trocchi, „A Revolutionary
    Proposal. Invisible Insurrection
    of a Million Minds", ursprünglich
    veröffentlicht unter dem Titel
    „Technique du coupe du monde",
    in: *Internationale Situationniste*,
    Nr. 8, Januar 1963.

Wahrheit ans Licht treten könnte. Seine Filme handeln vom politischen Kampf um die Idee der Wahrheit und davon, wie das Subjekt sich gegen seine Kategorisierung, seine Verwandlung in ein einfaches Bild wehren kann, das sich erfassen, verorten und von den herrschenden gesellschaftlichen Kräften manipulieren lässt, aber auch davon, wie beim Filmemachen das wechselseitige Verhältnis zwischen unserer Wahrnehmung anderer und deren Bild unserer Wahrnehmung kurzgeschlossen werden kann.

Abgesehen von Laing zählen zu Fowlers zugestandenen Einflüssen der sozialdemokratische Radikalismus im Nachkriegs-Grossbritannien, die Ideen des strukturalistischen Films, die Situationisten und die freie Improvisation, wobei man sich als Symbol für Fowlers herausragendste Vorläufer ein zugegebenermassen unwahrscheinliches Quartett bestehend aus Hollis Frampton, Lindsay Anderson, Alexander Trocchi und Cornelius Cardew vorstellen müsste.

Fowler hat wiederholt auf seine Affinität zum strukturalistischen Film hingewiesen, und zwar nicht nur bei seiner jüngsten Zusammenarbeit mit Peter Todd und Keith Rowe[2], sondern auch in seinem Aufsatz „Expanded Cinema: Time/Space/Structure"[3]. Fowler formuliert seinen Text unweigerlich als „Ansichten eines Aussenseiters" angesichts der Zeit, die seit der Blüte des strukturalistischen Films in den 1970er Jahren und der Entstehung seines Artikels im Jahr 2007 vergangen ist. Dennoch deutet er an, dass die Expanded-Cinema-Bewegung die zeitgenössische Videokunst vorweggenommen habe, und fährt fort, ihre Vertreter beabsichtigten eine „vollständige Kontrolle über die Produktions-, Präsentations- und Vertriebsmittel"[4]. Anders ausgedrückt, er stimmt mit jener Denkrichtung überein, die das Expanded Cinema als politisierten filmischen Ansatz begreift, der einen Kampf um die Darstellungs- und Produktionsmittel führte.

Diese Fragen hinsichtlich der politischen Bedingungen des Filmemachens standen auch im Zentrum der Free-Cinema-Bewegung im Grossbritannien der späten 1950er Jahre, an deren Entwicklung der Regisseur Lindsay Anderson wesentlichen Anteil hatte. Das Free Cinema markierte den Beginn des politisch engagierten Films in Grossbritannien, der mit den Anfängen der französischen Nouvelle Vague zusammenfiel und zum Teil von denselben technischen Entwicklungen profitierte – leise Handkameras und lichtempfindliches Filmmaterial, mit dem bei vorhandenen Beleuchtungsverhältnissen mit Direktton gedreht werden konnte und ein unauffällig beobachtender „Fly on the Wall"-Dokumentarstil möglich wurde. Die Grundsätze des New Cinema lauteten: „Kein Film kann zu persönlich sein. Das Bild spricht. Ton verstärkt und kommentiert. Die Grösse ist unerheblich. Perfektion ist kein Ziel. Eine Haltung bedeutet einen Stil. Ein Stil bedeutet eine Haltung."[5] Diese Maximen standen im Mittelpunkt einer Bewegung, die sich deutlich im Einklang mit den Veränderungen innerhalb der britischen Gesellschaft befand, welche von den sozialdemokratischen Bestimmungen der Nachkriegszeit geprägt waren. Eine neue Generation von Dramatikern, Dichtern, Romanautoren, Drehbuchautoren, Fernsehproduzenten, Journalisten und Künstlern aus der Arbeiterklasse bestätigte nicht nur die Effizienz freier Hochschulbildung zur Förderung sozialer Mobilität, sondern betrachtete sich selbst als Teil einer Revolution massgeblicher gesellschaftlicher Werte. Dem lag vielleicht die unausgesprochene Vermutung zugrunde, dass es sich bei diesem Wandel der institutionellen Repräsentationsbedingungen um mehr handeln könnte als ein blosses Symptom eines keynesianischen Wirtschaftskompromisses, und dass daraus ein sich selbst verstärkendes System entstehen könnte, das letztlich, zumindest im Medienbereich, die vorherrschenden Mythen des britischen Kapitalismus zu überwinden helfen würde.

Fowler übernahm den Titel von Alexander Trocchis Aufsatz „The Invisible Insurrection of a Million Minds"[6] (1963) für eine Kompilation mit grösstenteils in Glasgow entstandener elektronischer Musik, die er 2001 unter seinem Label SHADAZZ veröffentlichte. Man sollte Trocchis Einfluss auf Fowlers Arbeit nicht zu hoch einschätzen, doch es existieren bedeutsame, wenn auch flüchtige Verbindungen zwischen „The Invisible Insurrection of a Million Minds" und dem Milieu des British Free Cinema. An einer Stelle seines Aufsatzes zitiert Trocchi den walisischen marxistischen

Literaturkritiker Raymond Williams mit dem Satz: „Die Frage ist nicht, wer die Künste fördern wird, sondern welche Formen möglich sind, bei denen Künstler die Kontrolle über ihre eigenen Ausdrucksmittel besitzen, und zwar dergestalt, dass sie in einer Beziehung zu einer Gesellschaft und nicht zu einem Markt oder einem Förderer stehen."[7]

Eine zweite ins Auge fallende Anregung für Fowlers Filme ist die Idee der freien Improvisation, welche Fowler in seinem Film über Cornelius Cardew und The Scratch Orchestra, *Pilgrimage from Scattered Points* sowohl würdigt als auch in Frage stellt. In keinem seiner bislang entstandenen Filme kommt Fowler den Konventionen des Dokumentargenres einerseits so nahe, um sich andererseits so weit vom Einflussbereich Laings zu entfernen. Es wird hier die Geschichte des von Cornelius Cardew, Michael Parsons und Howard Skempton im Jahr 1969 gegründeten Musikensembles The Scratch Orchestra nacherzählt (der Titel des Films verdankt sich ihrem Stück *Pilgrimage from Scattered Points on the Surface of the Body to the Brain, the Inner Ear, the Heart and the Stomach* von 1970), wobei der Film teilweise eine Überarbeitung von Hanne Boenischs Film über das Orchester, *Journey to the North Pole* (1971), darstellt. In *Pilgrimage from Scattered Points* wechseln sich Archivaufnahmen mit einander widersprechenden aktuellen Interviews ab, sodass sich eine Erzählung um die schliessliche Auflösung des Scratch Orchestra entspinnt, bei der insbesondere ideologische Fragen innerhalb individueller Wechselwirkungen in den Blickpunkt gerückt werden.

Das Scratch Orchestra wurde – mit dem Abdruck einer „Draft Constitution" in *The Musical Times* – im Juni 1969 als konsequent utopische Gruppe gegründet, in der sich Musiker und Nichtmusiker zusammenfanden, um angesichts der avantgardistischen Auflösung der Ästhetik in der Politik miteinander Musik zu machen. Das Orchester definierte sich als „eine Vielzahl von Enthusiasten, die ihre (nicht in erster Linie materiellen) Ressourcen bündeln und gemeinsame Aktionen (Musik, Auftritte, Bildung) durchführen"[8]. Diese ohnehin allgemeinen Begriffe wurden noch mehr durch die Anmerkung erweitert, dass „das Wort Musik und seine Ableitungen an dieser Stelle nicht als lediglich auf Töne sich beziehend zu verstehen sind [...]. Vielmehr verweisen sie auf etwas Flexibles, das ausschliesslich von den Mitgliedern des Scratch Orchestra abhängt. Das Scratch Orchestra soll in der Öffentlichkeit wirken"[9].

Am Anfang stand eher eine Frage als eine Antwort, allerdings eine konkrete Frage. Beabsichtigt war nicht die Umsetzung eines bestimmten Ergebnisses, sondern die Untersuchung eines besonderen Verhältnisses zwischen Individuum und Kollektiv. Das Resultat dieser Untersuchung sollten „Musik, Auftritte, Bildung"[10] sein, aber ebenso das Scratch Orchestra selbst.

Während der Film *Journey to the North Pole* dieses Ergebnis festhält, konzentriert sich Fowler in seinem Film auf die gestellte Frage. Dabei wird das Scratch Orchestra nicht lediglich als Performance-Truppe betrachtet, sondern als mikrokosmische Gesellschaft, deren Mitglieder in politische Machtverhältnisse und verborgene Hierarchien verstrickt sind. Obwohl viele Beteiligte es als befreiend empfanden, Teil des Orchesters zu sein, wurde die von ihnen entdeckte Freiheit letztlich als unzureichend erkannt. Das, was den authentischen individuellen Ausdruck begründete, wurde zum Streitpunkt, wobei die individuelle Freiheit des Ausdrucks stets nur auf dem begrenzten Gebiet der Performance verwirklicht wurde; die allgemeinere Frage nach der Struktur, Leitung und Bedeutung des Projektes bleibt entschieden und zwangsläufig politisch.

Erschwert wurde die Situation im Jahr 1971, als Cardew und andere Mitglieder des Orchesters sich eine explizit maoistische Perspektive hinsichtlich des Verhältnisses von Kultur und Klassenkampf zu eigen machten. Indem sie sich gegen einen nach ihrer Ansicht bürgerlichen Individualismus wandte, versuchte die maoistische Fraktion des Scratch Orchestra, die Gruppe im Sinne einer aktivistischen Propagandaeinheit neu zu organisieren, die bei ihren Auftritten volkstümliche Formen zur Erziehung des Publikums nutzen sollte. So kam es zu unerträglichen Spannungen zwischen den neu definierten Maoisten und den inzwischen als bürgerliche Individualisten Gescholtenen,

7   Ebd.
8   Cornelius Cardew, „A Scratch Orchestra: Draft Constitution", in: Michael Parsons (Hg.), *Twenty Five Years from Scratch*, London 1994, S. 20.
9   Ebd.
10 Ebd.

11   Clancy Sigal, Aaron Esterson,
Joan Cunnold, David Cooper und
Sid Briskin.

die nach wie vor an Cardews ursprünglichen Idealen festhielten. Die angestrebte Verwandlung der Gruppe von einem isolierten Utopiemodell in einen aktivistischen Kader führte zu einer Phase unproduktiver Stagnation, bis Cardew im Jahr 1973 mit anderen schliesslich ein neues Kollektiv namens People's Liberation Music gründete.

In Fowlers Darstellung spiegelt Cardews Experiment insofern Kingsley Hall wider, als auch hier versucht wurde, eine gesellschaftliche Grenze zu überwinden beziehungsweise ihre Aufhebung zu untersuchen. Ebenso wie die Philadelphia Association (jene psychiatrische Stiftung, die von Laing und anderen[11] ins Leben gerufen wurde, die später Kingsley Hall gründeten) von der radikalen These ausging, dass die Stimmen der als schizophren Diagnostizierten Gehör verdienten, setzte Cardew voraus, dass die Musik, die von Menschen gemacht wurde, welche von der Gesellschaft als Nichtmusiker „diagnostiziert" wurden, ebenfalls wertvoll sei. Und in derselben Weise, wie in Kingsley Hall eine Gesellschaft entstand, in der sich (zuvor ausgeschlossene) Geisteskranke und Gesunde einen produktiven Austausch erhofften, sassen innerhalb des Scratch Orchestra klassisch ausgebildete Virtuosen neben unmusikalischen Anfängern und verliehen damit ihrer politischen Überzeugung Nachdruck, dass hierbei dennoch Musik entstehe. Ausserdem bedurfte es zur Legitimation in beiden Fällen der Intervention eines gesellschaftlich anerkannten Fachmanns (Laing als ausgewiesener Psychoanalytiker und Cardew als ehemaliger Student der Royal Academy of Music).

Fowlers zuvor (in Zusammenarbeit mit Kosten Koper) entstandener Film *The Way Out* kreiste um eine Figur, die sich den Filmemachern gegenüber konsequent jeder offenen oder unmittelbaren Aussage verweigert hatte. Dieses Antiporträt eines Vermissten wurde zum grössten Teil aus privaten Filmaufnahmen, Archivmaterial und Interviews zusammenmontiert und mit Filmfragmenten aus eigens zu diesem Zweck improvisierten Szenen ergänzt. Vielleicht existiert tatsächlich irgendwo jener Mensch aus Fleisch und Blut, der seit den späten 1970er Jahren bis heute unter so unterschiedlichen Namen wie Jim Welton, L Voag, Amos, Xentos Bentos,

Xentos Jones und so weiter die verschiedenen Musikaufnahmen – Bassläufe, Gesang, Keyboard, Gitarre – auf Kassetten oder Platten einspielte, die von mehr oder weniger undergroundmässigen Bands auf unabhängigen Vertriebswegen dem Publikum zugänglich gemacht wurden. Doch der Film scheitert bewusst bei dem Versuch, durch die Montage von Tonaufnahmen, selbstgedrehten Super-8-Filmen, gespielten Erinnerungen und Aufrufen ein zusammenhängendes Bild von Xentos zu zeichnen. Stattdessen wird der Film zum Kollaborateur von Xentos' eigenem Projekt und unterstreicht so die gebrochene, flüchtige und dennoch wechselseitige Natur der Beziehungen zwischen den Vorgängen innerhalb des Lebens eines Individuums und deren gesellschaftlicher Wahrnehmung. Unter dem Aspekt einer konventionellen Dokumentation wird die eigentliche Suche nach dem Ursprung, nach der verbindenden Wahrheit hinter all diesen verschiedenen Masken zu einem Film darüber, warum diese Suche zum Scheitern verurteilt ist. *The Way Out* behauptet nicht, dass der echte Xentos in irgendeiner Weise durch das Netz des Dokumentarischen geschlüpft ist, sondern dass diese „reale" Person nicht das Thema war und nie das Thema sein könnte. Die Tatsache, dass schliesslich ein Kritiker die Frage stellte, ob Xentos überhaupt „real existierte" oder in Wirklichkeit vielleicht eine Erfindung der beiden Filmemacher sei, liegt sicher nicht am fehlenden kritischen Verständnis dieses Journalisten, sondern an der Weigerung von *The Way Out*, sich an allgemein anerkannte Beurteilungskriterien zu halten.

Fowler ist freilich selbst innerhalb dieses Systems gefangen, in dem Autoren nach ihren erfolgreichen Werken und Werke nach ihren erfolgreichen Autoren beurteilt werden, in dem aus kultureller Aufmerksamkeit kulturelles Kapital entsteht und Assoziationsketten und kulturelle Verknüpfungen verfolgt werden, nur um zeitweilig an Punkten zur Ruhe zu kommen, an denen diese Verknüpfungen einem markttauglichen Mythos entsprechen. Durch Fowlers Interesse für das Scratch Orchestra rückte Cardews Werk wieder in den Blickpunkt der Kunstwelt, wobei das daraus resultierende Feedback zweifellos das Ansehen des Filmemachers per Assoziation auch bei denjenigen erhöht, die *Pilgrimage from Scattered Points* nie gesehen haben.

Daher war es von wesentlicher Bedeutung, dass Fowler sich für seinen nächsten längeren Film *Bogman Palmjaguar* von dieser Methode distanzierte. Bogman Palmjaguar ist kein typischer gegenkultureller Held – er ist ein offensichtlich gestörter Mann mittleren Alters, der zurückgezogen in Nordschottland lebt und sich in einem hartnäckigen Streit mit niedrigen Staatsbeamten befindet –, wobei das eigentliche Streitthema unfilmbar ist: Palmjaguars Rechtsstatus, seine amtliche Freiheit. Fowlers Film beabsichtigt weniger, die staatliche Diagnose von Palmjaguars Schizophrenie zu diskutieren – diese Aufgabe kommt Dr. Leon Redler zu, einem früheren Kollegen Laings, der Palmjaguar in Rechtstreitigkeiten unterstützt und ebenfalls im Film auftritt – oder „seine Geschichte zu erzählen", um an das aktivistische Mitgefühl des Zuschauers zu appellieren. Vielmehr formuliert er eine verhaltene, poetische Polemik zugunsten der Vorstellung, dass individuelles Verhalten in höchstem Masse von der jeweiligen Situation und Umwelt abhängig ist.

In Fowlers zuvor entstandenen Filmen wurden zu einem grossen Teil Archivaufnahmen genutzt. *Bogman Palmjaguar* hingegen basiert erstmals primär auf eigenem Filmmaterial, das von Lee Pattersons Tonaufzeichnungen ergänzt wird. Die Perversität des Gedankens, einen Film über einen Menschen zu drehen, der jeden zwischenmenschlichen Kontakt meidet und sich weigert, sein Gesicht der Kamera preiszugeben, passt durchaus zu Fowlers bisherigem paradoxem Umgang mit dem Filmmedium zur Offenlegung der Unzuverlässigkeit und Kontingenz, durch die sich jeder Versuch auszeichnet, eine Persönlichkeit als Bild und nicht als gesellschaftlichen Prozess darzustellen.

Dennoch balanciert der Film auf dem schmalen Grad zwischen einer unkritischen Präsentation und Affirmation seines Gegenstandes und der Reproduktion eines Stereotyps des schizophrenen Anderen. Diesem Problem – ein unausweichliches Darstellungsproblem, das sich den herrschenden gesellschaftlichen Kategorien verdankt – stellt sich Fowler, indem er die filmische Darstellung in drei verschiedene Modi aufspaltet. Im ersten sieht der Zuschauer die Landschaft und hört dazu die Umgebungsgeräusche mit eingestreuten Gedanken Palmjaguars zu dieser Landschaft und seiner Beziehung zu ihr. Im zweiten Modus sieht man, wie Palmjaguar vor der Kamera flüchtet und sein Gesicht hinter einer Federmaske zu verstecken versucht. Im dritten sind aus dem Off mit ihm geführte Interviews über den Rechtsstreit zu hören, den er führt, um als zurechnungsfähig anerkannt zu werden, das heisst um in einem einvernehmlichen Verhältnis zur normalen Gesellschaft leben und sämtliche damit verbundenen Grundrechte geniessen zu können. Dieser dreifache Ansatz entspricht einer Analyse von Bogman Palmjaguar selbst im Sinne eines politischen Subjektes beziehungsweise einer Analyse der Prozesse, die ihn im Sinne eines politischen Subjektes konstruieren. Diese Analyse jedoch, dieses Aufgliedern des Untersuchungsgegenstandes, vollzieht sich in keiner Weise offensiv, sondern im Sinne einer Analyse, die im Gegensatz zu jener einfachen Kategorisierung Palmjaguars steht, wie sie von den Ämtern vorgenommen wird, denen er rechtlich ausgeliefert ist.

Wenn Palmjaguar vom Flow Country spricht, jenem eigenartigen, unerschlossenen Teil der schottischen Landschaft, in dem er sich niedergelassen hat, werden seine Worte zur Beschwörungsformel, in der sich bürokratische Legitimationsmassnahmen, Tourismus-Slogans und amtliche Fakten mit persönlichen Beobachtungen und Betrachtungen sowie Bekräftigungen hinsichtlich therapeutischer Veränderungen mischen, wodurch sich die verborgene biosphärische Bedeutung der Landschaft und Palmjaguars Glück, in ihr seinen Platz gefunden zu haben, zu einem Ganzen vereinigen. In diesen Monologen liegt eine offensichtliche Überidentifikation vor, aber auch das klare und freudige Erkennen eines funktionierenden Kontextes für eine besondere Persönlichkeit. Tatsächlich scheint eine enge Verwandtschaft zwischen Palmjaguars Betrachtungen und Henry David Thoreaus berühmten Beschreibungen seines abgeschiedenen Lebens am Walden Pond zu bestehen, wo „sich die süsseste und zarteste, die argloseste und erbaulichste Gesellschaft in jedem natürlichen Gegenstand finden lässt, selbst für

12   Henry David Thoreau, *Walden, or Life in the Woods*, Raleigh NC 1975, S. 88.

den armseligen Misanthrop und den melancholischsten Menschen"[12].

Palmjaguar ist gleichermassen in der Lage, ja begierig darauf, sich selbst darzustellen, und trotz seines Widerwillens, sein Gesicht zu zeigen, findet sich eine Möglichkeit der Zusammenarbeit mit dem Filmteam. Im dritten Modus stellt der Film erstmals wirkliche Fragen, wobei Fowler diese Fragen in nützlicher Weise mit den ersten beiden Herangehensweisen im Hinblick auf Palmjaguars Leben in Verbindung setzt. Auch wenn sich die Mehrzahl von Palmjaguars Symptomen plausibel als gesellschaftlich sanktionierte – und unbestreitbar exzentrische – Haltungen in Bezug auf die Rolle des Individuums innerhalb der gesellschaftlichen/natürlichen Ordnung beschreiben lässt, bleibt hier lediglich Palmjaguars oppositionelles Verhältnis zu den normierenden gesellschaftlichen Institutionen übrig. Anders ausgedrückt, Fowler deutet an, dass Palmjaguars Konflikt mit der Gesellschaft sich nicht einer speziellen a-sozialen Überschreitung verdankt, sondern dass seine Art zu leben und zu denken, für die er auf andere, friedliche Weise einen Platz fand, partout nicht anerkannt wird.

Palmjaguar hat sich keines Verbrechens schuldig gemacht, wird allerdings praktisch kriminalisiert, da er paranoid geworden ist. Aus tief verwurzelten gesellschaftlichen und persönlichen Gründen fühlt er sich verfolgt, daher wehrt er sich mit den ihm zur Verfügung stehenden begrenzten Mitteln, worauf die Institutionen wiederum mit dem Versuch reagieren, ihn zu zügeln. Dies schliesslich bildet für ihn die legitime Grundlage seiner Paranoia und verstrickt ihn in ein nicht zu gewinnendes Spiel mit den psychiatrischen Behörden.

Fowler behauptet in seinem Film nicht, eine Antwort auf Palmjaguars Situation zu liefern. Allerdings formuliert er dessen Situation häufig als Frage, jedoch nicht im strengen Sinne polemisch, sondern aufgrund überprüfter Fakten der filmischen Beobachtung und beigesteuerten Liveaufnahmen. Diese Frage kreist eher um eine reale Situation als um ein imaginiertes Individuum und bleibt auch noch nach Ende des Films im Raum stehen.

Luke Fowler stellt in seinen Arbeiten die Konventionen des Dokumentarischen auf den Kopf, dies jedoch auf unerwartete und produktive Weise. Er kehrt die inzwischen zur Banalität gewordene Frage nach der Wahrhaftigkeit der Bilder, der Glaubwürdigkeit des Schnitts um. Dabei nutzt er häufig vordigitale Techniken, welche eine Echtheit der Aufnahme versprechen, um die Wahrnehmung der sie erzeugenden gesellschaftlichen Wechselwirkungen in Frage zu stellen. Montagetechniken kommen bei Fowler nicht zum Einsatz, um eine scheinbar nahtlose Darstellung zu konstruieren oder um sie zu verfremden beziehungsweise zu problematisieren, sondern vielmehr als Mittel der argumentativen Auseinandersetzung. Seine Filme sind auf schamlose Weise polemisch, die Polemik jedoch steht im Dienst der Behauptung, dass dieselben Brüche, Paradoxe und Pannen innerhalb der Kommunikation, um die es im Kino geht, auch im un-vermittelten Leben herrschen. Fowlers Arbeiten scheinen anzudeuten, dass die zusammenhangslose, subjektive, lückenhafte Konstruktion, die sich im Film findet, die tatsächlich wirksamen Vorgänge besser zu reflektieren vermag. Das heisst nicht, dass Fowlers Filme eine authentischere Darstellung der Welt liefern als andere, sondern dass sie aus dem wahren Drang nach Authentizität entstehen, die im Rahmen einer öffentlichen Auseinandersetzung nur in ausgesprochener Weise provisorisch, einseitig und persönlich sein kann.

Luke Fowler im Gespräch
mit Stuart Comer

sc – Deine Arbeiten sind aus kollektiven Aktivitäten hervorgegangen, sie schöpfen aus verschiedenen Subkulturen, in denen sich die Grenzen zwischen Musik und Kunst verwischen, und präsentieren eine Bricolage aus Dokumenten, Filmaufnahmen und musikalischen Auftritten. Obwohl in jüngsten Projekten wie deiner Arbeit mit Toshiya Tsunoda in Yokohama und mit Keith Rowe und Peter Todd in London immer noch ein Interesse von dir zu spüren ist, mit anderen Künstlern zusammenzuarbeiten und Hierarchien zu unterwandern, bist du allmählich dazu übergegangen, diese Annäherung aus unterschiedlichen Richtungen zu persönlichen 16-mm-Film-„Porträts" zu verdichten. Was glaubst du, welche Möglichkeiten bietet dir ein veraltetes Medium wie der 16-mm-Film im Gegensatz zu anderen Plattformen wie Musik oder Internet?

LF – Das 16-mm-Format reizte mich, als ich in meine Filme Super-8-Aufnahmen einfügte und auf der Suche nach einem Medium war, das ich besser kontrollieren konnte und das letzten Endes eigenständig, d. h. direkt vom Film zu projizieren wäre und nicht auf Video überspielt werden müsste. 16-mm ist sehr viel flexibler als Super-8, obwohl ich an diesem Format noch immer die Robustheit schätze. Aber weil beide, wie du sagst, ziemlich veraltet sind, fällt der Preisunterschied zwischen beiden Verfahren nicht ins Gewicht.

Ich finde interessant, dass du eine Linie ziehst zwischen meiner Hinwendung zu unabhängigen und Künstlerfilmen auf 16-mm und meiner Abkehr von den facettenreichen Projekten der Vergangenheit. Es gibt verschiedene Gründe für diesen Schritt. Im Wesentlichen sehe ich das als Fortsetzung früherer Anliegen, aber mit grösserer Konzentration auf die ästhetischen Aspekte und den zeitlichen Rahmen bei der Frage, wie der Betrachter die Gedanken und zutage geförderten Informationen aufnimmt. Einen Film zu machen ist für mich immer noch in hohem Masse ein sozialer Prozess, der eine disziplinübergreifende Zusammenarbeit mit Musikern, Akademikern, anderen Künstlern usw. einschliesst. Mich interessieren einfach mehr die Abläufe und die Möglichkeiten, die mir der Film bietet, im Gegensatz zu Installationen oder kuratierten Projekten.

sc – Da deinen Arbeiten deutlich anzumerken ist, dass sie eine vielfältige „intermediale" Geschichte haben, könntest du ein wenig konkreter sagen, warum du ein so „romantisches" Format wie 16-mm verwendest? Wie lässt sich deiner Meinung nach eine „postmediale" Position mit deinem Interesse an einem materialbasierten Filmschaffen vereinbaren?

LF – Meines Erachtens haben sich Künstler doch schon immer für veraltete Medien interessiert. Ich meine, warum verwenden Künstler immer noch viktorianische Druckerpressen? Oder warum schneiden sie mit einer richtigen Schere Fotokopien auseinander, um daraus Collagen zu machen, wenn sie das mit Hilfe von Scanner und Photoshop erledigen könnten? Warum nehmen manche Musiker lieber mit analogen Bändern auf oder spielen analoge Synthesizer, wenn sie doch moderne digitale Alternativen nutzen könnten? Der Grund ist sicher, dass sie den individuellen Charakter ihres Mediums und seine besonderen Eigenschaften vorziehen und unzufrieden sind mit welchen anderen modernen Methoden auch immer, die es abgelöst haben.

Wir befinden uns an einem beispiellosen Zeitpunkt in der Geschichte, wo die vorhandene 16-mm-Technik von Fujifilm und Kodak immer noch weiterentwickelt wird und in Verbindung mit digitalen Bearbeitungstechniken benutzt werden kann, entweder als Abzug oder digitalisiert. Ich habe beides versucht und würde in den meisten Fällen lieber einen Film projizieren, anstatt Video zu verwenden – aber natürlich ist das teuer und in manchen Fällen unpraktisch.

16-mm, im Kontext von Ausstellungen eingesetzt, hat eine ganze Reihe unterschwelliger Bedeutungen; Künstler verwenden oft Filmprojektoren mit Loopern als skulpturartige Objekte oder als Rückgriff auf frühe konzeptuelle Arbeiten. Wenn ich die Wahl hätte, würde ich meine Filme viel lieber im Kino zeigen, wo nicht die Gefahr besteht, dass Vergleiche zu dergleichen Taktiken gezogen werden und die Leute den Inhalt wichtiger finden als die Art und Weise der Vorführung.

sc – Aus welchem Grund hast du begonnen, dich für die Geschichte des experimentellen und strukturalistischen Films zu interessieren und bestimmten radikalen kulturellen Figuren wie Cornelius Cardew und Ronald D. Laing nachzuspüren?

LF – Ernsthaft dafür interessiert, einige der etablierten experimentellen/strukturellen Filme ausfindig zu machen und mich näher mit ihnen zu befassen, habe ich mich ziemlich spät, eigentlich erst in den letzten Jahren. Auf der Kunsthochschule in Dundee war es sehr schwierig, überhaupt einen der klassischen (britischen oder anderen) Avantgardefilme zu sehen, da die Abteilung für zeitbezogene Medien, die von einem der frühen Pioniere der Videokunst in Grossbritannien, Stephen Partridge, aufgebaut worden war, Künstler förderte und protegierte, die mit neuen Medien arbeiteten (Bill Viola war ihr Gott). Damals, Ende der 1990er Jahre, hatte die Videokunst ihre richtig grosse Zeit. Gefragt waren monumentale Videospektakel, die den Zuschauer zu Zwergen schrumpfen liessen und eher unverbindlich wirkten.

Einem unserer Dozenten, Alan Woods, gelang es zum Glück irgendwie, eine Vorschaukopie von Johan Grimonprez' Videofilm *Dial H-I-S-T-O-R-Y* (1997) zu beschaffen, der in dem Jahr auf der *Documenta X* gezeigt wurde. Ein wenig später, auf der Hochschule, sah ich *Rock My Religion* (1982–1984) von Dan Graham und *London* (1994) von Patrick Keiller. Diese Arbeiten und andere klassische Dokumentarfilme haben einen tiefen Eindruck auf mich gemacht und waren wohl richtungsweisend für meinen eigenen Essayfilm *What You See Is Where You're At* (2001) über Ronald D. Laings Kingsley-Hall-Experiment. Mein erster Film war keineswegs so künstlerisch vollendet und sprachlich ausgefeilt wie diese Vorbilder, die mich beeinflusst haben, aber er bedeutete sowohl eine Zustimmung – zu einer forschungsorientiert Form – als auch eine Ablehnung der damals in der Videokunst herrschenden Strömungen: Spontanauftritte vor der Kamera und diese prachtvollen Loopingspektakel.

Mein Interesse an der Geschichte britischer und amerikanischer experimenteller/strukureller Arbeiten rührt vom Wunsch her, dass ich verstehen wollte, wie sich ein Bereich, mit dem ich immer öfter zu tun bekam, entwickelt hatte und was von ihm geblieben war. In gewisser Weise waren es die gleichen Beweggründe wie bei einer Pilgerfahrt, nur mit dem Unterschied, dass es hier um britische experimentelle und improvisierte Musik und konkret um die Entwicklung einer politisch engagierten Bewegung von Komponisten/Musikern ging.

Für Ronald D. Laing hatte ich mich schon viel früher zu interessieren begonnen, als ich noch die Hochschule besuchte. Für jemanden wie mich, der im intellektuellen Brennpunkt des Glasgower West End aufwuchs, war Laing eine Berühmtheit, auf die man stolz war. Ich erinnere mich, dass meine Schwester Meg damals, als sie ihre Doktorarbeit schrieb und ich auf der Kunsthochschule war, sein Buch *The Divided Self* (1960) in der Familie diskutierte. Ich hörte aufmerksam zu und muss mir wohl vorgenommen haben, selbst einen Blick hineinzuwerfen.

Im Jahr vor meinem Abschluss arbeitete ich dann an einer Reihe von Projekten, die soziologische und psychologische Experimente voraussetzten. Bei der Ausstellung *The Social Engineer* (1999) für die Transmission Gallery ging es darum, ein unglaublich aufwendiges Netz aus spontanen Begegnungen und Gesprächen aufzubauen, die ich zwischen politischen und sozialen Gegnern „eingefädelt" habe (der Direktor des Barlinnie-Gefängnisses spricht mit einem Body-Art-Künstler usw.). Um diese Zeit empfahl mir Meg, über Laings Kingsley-Hall-Experiment nachzulesen, denn ich hatte Recherchen über Persönlichkeiten wie Stanley Milgram oder Philip Zimbardos Experimente angestellt. Ich fand in der Biografie, die Adrian Laing über seinen Vater geschrieben hatte, einen faszinierenden Bericht über Kingsley Hall, der mir die Idee zu einem Filmprojekt gab.

SC – Psychische Störungen, vor allem Laings „geteiltes Selbst", sind in deinen Filmen ein häufig wiederkehrendes Thema, genau wie in den Arbeiten radikaler oder exzentrischer Figuren der Musik, zum Beispiel Cardew und Xentos Jones. Da scheint es eine Resonanz zu geben zwischen Laings Interesse an Gruppentherapie, bei dem er Begriffe im Umfeld der „Familie" hinterfragt, und Cardews People's Liberation Music und dessen Auffassung, der Akt des Improvisierens beinhalte eine gemeinsame Eigentümerschaft und Verantwortung. Wie wirkt sich ihre Arbeit auf dein eigenes Interesse an der Gemeinschaft, der Zusammenarbeit mit anderen Künstlern und den Synchronizitäten zwischen Klang und Bild aus?

LF – Was Laing betrifft, so war es zum Teil darauf zurückzuführen, dass er zum intellektuellen Erbe Glasgows gehört und ich mich zuvor mit sozialen Experimenten befasst hatte. Der andere entscheidende Faktor war der Versuch, für die verschiedenen Zusammenbrüche, die ich damals in meiner eigenen Familie erlebte, eine rationale Erklärung zu finden. Laing zu lesen und Leon Redler aufzusuchen war für mich sehr trostreich.

Dass ich eine Arbeit über Cardew und The Scratch Orchestra machen wollte, hatte damit zu tun, dass ich in Glasgow in die frei improvisierende Musikszene geriet und mit ihren historischen Wurzeln in Grossbritannien in Berührung kam. Wenn du dir die Mitgliederliste des Orchesters in seiner Blütezeit ansiehst, so liest sich das fast wie ein Who's Who der britischen Komposition und freien Improvisation: Gavin Bryars, Brian Eno, AMM, Michael Nyman, Howard Skempton, David Jackman, Michael Parsons, Christopher Hobbs – über hundert prominente Namen.

Auch einige der politischen Fragen, die Cardew und seine Leute aufwarfen, stimmten mit den grundlegenden politischen Fragen überein, mit denen sich die meisten Künstler auseinandersetzen: Wem dient deine Kunst? Welche Funktion hat die Kunst? Kann Kunst eine politische oder revolutionäre Rolle übernehmen? Geht diese soziale und politische Funktion immer auf Kosten künstlerischer Neuerung?

Mein Interesse an der Frage, wie mit diesen beiden grossen Persönlichkeiten umzugehen wäre, würde immer davon abhängig sein, auf welche Weise ihre Arbeit eine Gemeinschaft unterstützte, in der die herrschenden Normen in Frage gestellt und eine wirkliche Alternative zu ihnen geboten wurde. Bei Laing ging es darum, wie unsere Gesellschaft mit psychisch Kranken verfährt; bei Cardew ging es eher darum, einem Elitedenken in der Avantgardemusik entgegenzuwirken, was letzten Endes auf die Frage hinauslief, ob die Avantgarde als solche in einem politischen Umfeld überhaupt von Belang war oder ob es wirkungsvollere Methoden des Engagements gab. Es war immer meine Absicht, zu begreifen, wie

diese „charismatischen Führer" ihre eigenen Gemeinschaften angelegt und definiert haben und wie sich ihr Konzept auf der menschlichen Ebene ausgewirkt hat.

In formaler Hinsicht war mir daran gelegen, Klangschichten und Bildsequenzen übereinander zu lagern, die sich sehr häufig in Spannung zueinander befinden und auseinanderdriften. Stimme und Musik mussten nicht unbedingt synchron verlaufen und die Bildspur stützen. Das ist vielleicht einer der Bereiche, wo meine Arbeit sich am weitesten vom Grierson'schen Dokumentarfilm entfernt, der eine bestimmte Interpretation und damit Bedeutung festlegen will. Natürlich gibt es eine kleine, aber reiche Tradition an Essay- oder Anti-Dokumentarfilmen (z. B. Dsiga Wertow, Guy Debord, Chris Marker, Jean-Marie Straub & Danièle Huillet, Harun Farocki, Peter Watson, Berwick Street Film Collective, Black Audio Film Collective), wo dieser Bruch zwischen Illusionismus und festgelegter Bedeutung zu erwarten ist. Dass sie in jüngerer Zeit wieder in museale Kontexte zurückgeholt werden, ist für die wachsende Bedeutung bezeichnend, die ihnen auf der Suche nach Vorläufern der aktuellen Generation zukommt. Meiner Ansicht nach kennzeichnet das den allgemeinen Zusammenbruch der alten Trennung zwischen unabhängigen Filmemachern, die ihre Arbeit in Kinos zeigen, und visuellen Künstlern, die dafür eine Institution in Anspruch nehmen. In gewisser Hinsicht erhöht das den Wert von Künstlern in Bezug auf ihr kritisches Engagement in Verbindung mit einem hohen Mass an formaler Vollendung.

SC – Das wirft die Frage auf nach einem Phänomen, das Peter Wollen Mitte der 1970er Jahre „die beiden Avantgarden" nannte. Die erste Gruppe, die Wollen beschrieb, war im weitesten Sinne mit der Co-op-Bewegung gleichzusetzen, und zu ihr gehörten viele Vertreter des strukturalistischen Films, auf die du dich in deiner jüngsten Arbeit berufst, so wie Peter Gidal, Malcolm Le Grice und Gregory Markopoulos. Zur zweiten Gruppe gehörten die Filmemacher, die du erwähnst, wie Marker, Jean-Luc Godard, Straub & Huillet, Farocki und andere, die diskursive Essayfilme gemacht haben.

Die von Okwui Enwezor 2002 kuratierte *Documenta 11* trug dazu bei, dass sich die Tendenz festigte, dokumentarisch orientierte

1   Peter Wollen, „The Two Avant-
     gardes", in: *Studio International*,
     London, Nr. 190, November–
     Dezember 1975, S. 171–175.

Filme und Videopraktiken im Ausstellungskontext zu zeigen. Viele dieser Arbeiten sind generell einem Erbe verpflichtet, das eher von Wertow und Sergei Eisenstein herrührt als von der formbetonten Optik der Co-op. Während es daran anschliessend durchaus ein neu erwachtes Interesse gab, dokumentarische Praktiken zu hinterfragen, ist in der Kunstwelt, wie du angedeutet hast, auch eine beachtliche Popularität des 16-mm-Films zu beobachten, bei Künstlern wie Tacita Dean, Mark Leckey und Daria Martin, die alle grossangelegte, auf mehrere Flächen verteilte Videoinstallationen meiden und stattdessen eher eigenständige 16-mm-Filme zeigen.

Deine Arbeiten sind, was Wollen ein „multiples System" nennen würde; sie scheinen einen Raum zwischen diesen verschiedenen Positionen einzunehmen. Sie sind in gleicher Weise dem Dokumentarfilm, dem Essayfilm wie dem formalistischen und persönlichen Filmschaffen verpflichtet. Wollen behauptete: „Obwohl sich eine einfache Konvergenz kaum erreichen lässt, ist von entscheidender Bedeutung, dass die beiden Avantgarden einander gegenüber und nebeneinander gestellt werden."[1] Hast du das Bedürfnis, diese verschiedenen Systeme und geschichtlichen Entwicklungen aufzulösen oder einen Raum für Dialektik und Diskussion zu schaffen? Auf welche Weise würde eine solche Art der Annäherung dir erlauben, dich mit Avantgardefiguren der Vergangenheit auseinanderzusetzen und dir Möglichkeiten geben, die Radikalität ihrer Beiträge in vollem Umfang darzustellen?

LF – Ich glaube, Wollens Postulat in Bezug auf die Konfrontation beider Avantgarden ist inzwischen – obwohl zu ihrer Zeit eine kritische Analyse – in der postmedialen Praxis ganz und gar untergegangen. Es sieht nicht mehr danach aus, dass es zwei einander bekriegende Lager gibt – oder dass narrative und didaktische Interessen der Position eines unabhängigen Kunstfilmers zuwiderlaufen. Daher nein, ich habe nicht das Bedürfnis, diese geschichtlichen Entwicklungen aufzulösen; ich befasse mich damit, dieser reichen Geschichte nachzuspüren, sie mir anzusehen, und ich respektiere sie als das, was sie ist. Jetzt, da sich die Torhüter der Avantgarde allmählich vom Platz zurückziehen, können wir vielleicht

damit anfangen, Filme, Kino, Fernsehdokumentationen usw. nach ihrem eigenen Wert zu bemessen, statt sie nur als Schachfiguren auf einem ideologischen Schlachtfeld zu sehen.

Einer der Gründe, warum die Avantgarde zusammengebrochen ist, hat vielleicht mit dem Verlust an Gemeinschaft zu tun, der sich durch die Staffelung der Produktions- und Vertriebsnetze ereignet hat (diese Spaltung begann, als London Video Arts Ende der 1970er Jahre gegründet wurde). Ob man das für eine gute Sache hält oder nicht, es gibt kein zentrales Komitee mehr wie die London Filmmakers' Co-op, das zusammenkam, um zu produzieren, Theorie und Praxis auszutauschen und zu verbreiten. Das bedeutet, der zentrale, entscheidende Kern dessen, was eine Avantgarde wäre, ist weggefallen, und an seiner statt entstand eine atomisierte Ansammlung von Filmemachern und Künstlern, deren Arbeiten durch öffentliche und private Institutionen verbreitet werden, in Kinos und in der Kunstwelt.

SC – Könntest du dein Interesse an bestimmten Filmemachern wie Markopoulos, der Free-Cinema-Bewegung usw. näher erläutern? Deine Arbeiten scheinen sich allmählich zu einer eher historisch ausgerichteten Praxis entwickelt zu haben. Auf welche Weise, glaubst du, schwingt die Vergangenheit in deinen Arbeiten mit, und inwieweit macht dein Interesse an Live-Auftritten die Sache komplizierter?

LF – Ich finde die Arbeiten von Robert Beavers und Hollis Frampton aussergewöhnlich. Frampton behauptet, der Film sei innerhalb der Gattungen in eine Falle geraten, er müsse neu angelegt werden und habe alles einzuschliessen, von den Komplexitäten der natürlichen Welt bis hin zum menschlichen Bewusstsein. In Beavers' Arbeiten finde ich auch dieses Abrücken von der verbalen Sprache in Richtung eines unerforschten Geländes im Film; er schafft faszinierende Beziehungen zwischen Ort, Klang, Bild und dem Ich und liefert komplexe Geflechte aus Bildern und Klängen, die den Verstand ebenso wie die Sinne ansprechen.

Ich habe manche strukturelle Arbeiten gern gesehen, aber sie erwecken sehr deutlich den Eindruck, als hätten sie mit einer Reihe von Belangen und Polemiken zu tun, die zu einer bestimmten Zeit aktuell waren. Ich bin mir nicht sicher, wie sie ausserhalb dieser Zeitgebundenheit wirken. Nathaniel Dorsky, der grosse amerikanische Filmkünstler, sagte sehr schön, einen Film zu machen sei wie eine innige Zwiesprache mit einem Freund – man sollte immer versuchen, ein guter Gesprächspartner zu sein und mit dem Herzen wie mit dem Verstand sprechen. Seiner Meinung nach sind Künstler zu häufig schlechte Kommunikationspartner: Sie bevormunden, belehren, wiederholen sich und langweilen. Ihr Ziel, so scheint es oft, sei einzig und allein, das Publikum zu quälen.

Was den Nachhall der Vergangenheit betrifft, ich weiss nicht – es käme darauf an, welche Vergangenheit du meinst. Natürlich schwingt in den Filmen meine eigene persönliche Vergangenheit mit, und auf jeden Fall befassen sich viele von ihnen mit historischen Wendepunkten – Kingsley Hall, The Scratch Orchestra, Punk. Ich hoffe, dass dieses Engagement Fragen aufwirft und wieder aktiv werden lässt, statt nur alte Klischees aufzuwärmen.

sc – Was deine eigene Vergangenheit betrifft, so haben deine frühen Arbeiten, wie das SHADAZZ-Projekt, ihre Wurzeln in der Glasgower Musikszene. Musik- und Klanguntersuchungen spielen noch immer eine sehr wichtige Rolle in deinen Filmen, zum Beispiel in der jüngsten Arbeit zusammen mit Toshiya. In welche Beziehung würdest du das zu früheren Projekten setzen?

lf – Eigentlich sehe ich sie als völlig verschiedene Dinge. SHADAZZ ist ein Vehikel, um meine und die Musik meiner Freunde publik zu machen – es hat keine andere Aufgabe, als Sachen herauszubringen, die ich gerne höre und unterstütze. Es ist ein sehr kleiner, sporadischer Liebesdienst.

Das erste Musikprojekt, mit dem ich zu tun hatte, entstand, als ich vierzehn oder fünfzehn Jahre alt war, zusammen mit einem Freund, Luke Arnold, der den Bass spielte. Ich besass ein vierspuriges Tonbandgerät, und er hatte so eine Nachäffmaschine (ein frühes Bandecho) von einem Musiker bekommen, der mit seinen Eltern befreundet war. Uns gingen ständig die leeren Bänder aus, daher überspielten wir die Interviewbänder meiner Mutter; sehr häufig sickerte im Mix die Stimme durch wie ein Geist oder kam an anderer Stelle zwischen den Spuren zum Vorschein. Später auf der Kunsthochschule, bei den inszenierten Interviews für das Projekt *The Social Engineer*, von dem ich sprach, habe ich sie dann als Ausgangsmaterial für Kompositionen verwendet. Das war ausschlaggebend für meine Vorliebe, die Stimme einzubinden, manchmal nur als Textur, und gegen dissonantere Klänge und Musik abzusetzen. So sahen die verschiedenen Medien aus, die ich zusammenzubringen versuchte, als ich auf den Film kam. Ich finde, die Entwicklung in den neuen Arbeiten ist darauf zurückzuführen, dass ich etwas schaffen wollte, was mir Anregungen gibt, was die Möglichkeit bietet, mit anderen zusammenzuarbeiten und Gedanken, Argumente, Menschen und Orte in neuen Konstellationen zu erkunden. Vergangene Arbeiten sind insofern an diesem Prozess beteiligt, als ich versuche, ein beachtliches Stück weiterzukommen, manchmal sogar entgegen meiner eigenen methodischen Prinzipien.

Die Zusammenarbeit mit Toshiya ist der Einladung zu verdanken, an der Triennale in Yokohama teilzunehmen, und ausserdem interessierte ich mich sehr für seine Klangarbeiten. Ich hatte ihn im Jahr zuvor kennengelernt, als ich von Arika eingeladen wurde, für ein Projekt in Argyll unter dem Titel *Half Life* Klanginstallationen zu machen. Ich arbeitete damals gerade an einem Film mit Lee Patterson, und so fungierte ich bei ihren Feldexpeditionen als Chauffeur und Dokumentarfilmer gleichzeitig. Toshiya und ich führten in dieser Zeit ein paar interessante Diskussionen. Sein Interesse, sagte er, gelte nicht den eigentlichen Feldaufnahmen. Er gehe nicht einfach hinaus mit seiner Ausrüstung und sammle oder erjage Klänge; es habe eher eine philosophische Grundlage. Wenn er versuche, die wechselnden Gegebenheiten von Objekten oder Merkmale vertrauter Orte aufzunehmen, bemühe er sich, zum „vollkommenen Kreis" des Konstrukteurs ein klangliches Äquivalent zu schaffen, ungewöhnliche Klangphänomene (zum Beispiel Vibrationen der Luft oder fester Körper) zu dokumentieren, die überall vorhanden, vom Ohr jedoch nicht wahrzunehmen seien. In vielerlei Hinsicht ist das eine sehr strukturelle Annäherung an den Klang. Die Arbeit erhebt weder einen Anspruch darauf, als Musik zu gelten, noch will sie eine pseudowissenschaftliche Forschung sein.

Es sind Aufnahmen, die ein hervorragender Beobachter gemacht hat. Ihr Wert liegt in den wesenhaften Eigenschaften der Klänge selbst und in den subtilen Unterschieden, die Toshiya zu Tage fördert, wenn er mehrere Ausprägungen dieser unter unterschiedlichen Bedingungen zusammengetragenen Phänomene zeigt. Ich war der Meinung, es müsste ein faszinierendes Erlebnis sein, mit ihm zusammen an einem Film zu arbeiten. Und so machte ich ihm den Vorschlag, für Yokohama eine Gemeinschaftsarbeit zu machen.

Toshiya schickte mir diese wunderbare Erklärung, in der er die Absicht äussert, einfache Kunstwerke zu schaffen, denen eine Bedeutung oder umfangreichere bedeutungsvolle Strategien fehlen. Er wollte wissen, wie Kunstwerke aussehen, wenn sie so weit wie möglich von künstlerischen Intentionen befreit wären. Vielleicht schildert er in gewisser Weise eine Situation, die den Phänomenen ähnelt, die er aufzunehmen versucht. Die Vibrationen haben keine narrative oder konzeptuelle Bedeutung; sie sind einfach Nebenprodukte materieller Beziehungen zwischen einem Objekt und seiner Umgebung.

Toshiyas Interesse richtete sich sofort auf einen Komplex von Bedingungen, die für ihn völlig neu waren – die Filmprojektion. Wenn wir die recht theaterhaften Requisiten (Ventilator, Beleuchtung, Kabel) in die Filminstallation einbezogen, so verfolgten wir damit das Ziel, den illusionären Charakter der Bilder in Frage zu stellen und ein Hindernis aufzubauen, das den Betrachter nicht unmittelbar in sie eintauchen lässt. Die Bilder in unserem Film sind so gewählt, dass sie die Einfühlung in den jeweiligen Ansatz des anderen wie auch unsere ungleich verlaufene Entwicklung und die unterschiedlichen Arbeitsweisen erkennen lassen, wobei wir eine kompromittierende Lösung strikt vermieden haben.

sc – Du hast in jüngerer Zeit mit Keith Rowe zusammengearbeitet, einem Gründungsmitglied von AMM und einer Schlüsselfigur der Klangimprovisation. Wie war es, mit ihm zu arbeiten, nachdem du einen Film über Cornelius Cardew gemacht hattest?

LF – Ich lernte Keith kennen, als er mit John Tilbury in Glasgow spielte. Da Tilbury die Biografie über Cornelius schrieb, schien es mir passender, mit ihm über dieses Projekt zu reden, statt mit Keith. Als ich die Interviews machte, schrieb ich auch an Keith, der in Frankreich lebt, erhielt aber nichts zurück, und so machte ich einfach weiter ohne seinen Beitrag und dachte immer, es sei schade, denn es wäre wichtig gewesen, auch seine Meinung über die Dinge dabeizuhaben. Sagt nicht ein altes Sprichwort, Abwesende hätten immer Unrecht? Nach einer Bemerkung zu urteilen, die er in dem Archivmaterial und einem Interview mit John macht, schien Keith in irgendeiner Weise für die maoistische Agitation verantwortlich gewesen zu sein, die zu Splittergruppen innerhalb des Orchesters führte. Es wäre gut gewesen, doch noch seine Seite der Geschichte zu erfahren. Keith stand Cardew und dessen Politik sehr nahe; er engagierte sich recht uneigennützig für die Kampagnen des linken Flügels (gegen Imperialismus, Rassismus, „die Umstände"), spielte eine sehr traditionelle Gitarre in dem, was im Grunde genommen die Agitprop- und Marschkapellenfraktion der People's Liberation Music war. Zum Schluss wandte er sich wieder den abstrakteren Belangen von AMM zu.

Mit Keith und dem Filmemacher Peter Todd zu arbeiten, war wirklich grossartig, weil jeder dem anderen völlig zu vertrauen und dessen Fähigkeiten zu respektieren schien. Ich glaube, es herrscht eine Menge Verwirrung, was Keiths Methoden als Improvisator betrifft; verschiedene Leute haben sich darüber aufgeregt, dass Keith wohl nicht auf das reagiert, was seine Partner machen. Na ja, wenn das so ist, dann macht ihn das meiner Ansicht nach nicht zu einem schlechten Improvisator; es wirft die Frage auf, warum sich Improvisatoren offenbar stillschweigend auf vereinbarte Verhaltensweisen und Interaktionen verlassen. Warum sollte es nicht zulässig sein, mit den Bedingungen eines Raums oder den zufälligen Vorgängen, die ein willkürlich eingestelltes Radio auslöst, zu improvisieren? Ich meine, es ist eine recht grosszügige Leistung, wenn für die anderen eine allgemeine, grundlegende Farbe geschaffen wird, in die sie hineinschneiden und die sie formen können. In dieser Hinsicht, glaube ich, ist Keith ein sehr enthusiastischer, innovativer und toleranter Improvisator.

sc – Ich würde gern wissen, wie sich dein Interesse an gemeinschaftlicher Arbeit über künstlerische Generationen hinweg auf deine „Porträt"-Filme ausdehnt oder ausdehnen könnte. In welcher Weise, glaubst du, befreit deine Arbeitsweise bei Dokumentationen die Protagonisten deiner Filme von reiner Biografie? Werden die Protagonisten deiner Filme zu Metafiguren für ein breiteres Interesse, das du offenbar an radikaler Politik hast?

LF – Erstens wäre es, wo auch immer meine Sympathien liegen mögen, unaufrichtig, wenn ich mich einen Aktivisten nennen würde oder durchblicken liesse, dass ich mich für irgendwelche radikale Gruppen besonders stark engagierte. Ich versuche persönliche Filme zu machen, die neue Formen finden und Fragen stellen.

Bogman Palmjaguar (2007) ist ein Film, der Fragen aufwirft über die Kohärenz und narrative Anlage von Dokumentation und Biografie. Berichte über psychische Krankheiten verschleiern oft die zugrunde liegenden sozialen Bedingungen und Konflikte, die in der Beziehung des betreffenden Menschen zu anderen Personen Zorn und Argwohn schaffen können. In meinem Film skizziere ich zunächst einige Erlebnisse aus Bogmans Leben als Naturschützer; diese entflechten sich allmählich zu schmerzlichen Schilderungen von Kränkung und Verrat. Über den Titel des Films gewinnt man eine Vorstellung davon, wie Bogman durch eine Reihe vielschichtiger sozialer Prozesse geformt wurde. Nur durch unsere persönlichen Erfahrungen können wir zu einer Reaktion auf diese Prozesse gelangen, die uns entweder die Möglichkeit geben, uns in seine Lage zu versetzen, oder die unser Misstrauen erregen.

Wenn über den Verlauf einer psychischen Krankheit berichtet wird, ist es die Norm, den betreffenden Menschen isoliert zu betrachten – als Fall –, anstatt zu versuchen, die komplexen sozialen Prozesse zu ergründen, die sein „störendes" Verhalten verursacht haben. Cinéma vérité oder jüngere Formen des „Reality TV" bemühen sich, mit dem Begriff der Persona als Hülle des Ichs zu brechen. Sie unternehmen den trügerischen Versuch, den „Menschen hinter der Maske" zum Vorschein kommen zu lassen. Damit wird nicht anerkannt, dass dieser Mensch in ihrer eigenen Selbstdarstellung häufig eine bewusste Rolle spielt.

Ich glaube, der Dokumentarfilm gerät oft in die Falle, durch die Begriffe „Realität" und „Unvoreingenommenheit" eingeschränkt zu werden, da er nicht eindeutig an objektiven Realitäten festgemacht werden kann. Umgekehrt bemühe ich mich, einen Komplex aus Erlebnissen, Ansichten oder Fragmenten zu vermitteln, die sich nicht automatisch zu einem sauberen Bündel an Erfahrungen zusammenfügen, sondern stattdessen die vielfältigen und widersprüchlichen Berichte, die „kollektive Darstellungen" ausmachen, in Frage stellen und auf diese Weise das Potenzial des Films zu erkennen geben, den komplexen Zusammenhängen und Widersprüchen gelebter Erfahrung und (mit-)geteilter Geschichte(n) gerecht zu werden.

Als Künstler habe ich den Entschluss gefasst, diese Fragen nicht einfach so zu stellen, wie es ein Historiker oder Biograf tun würde, sondern indem ich eine ästhetische Sprache benutze. Letztendlich lässt sich der Wert meiner Arbeiten nur durch die Gesetze von Bildern beurteilen und wie dauerhaft diese Bilder sind.

Interview vom 28.–29. Februar 2009.

Biography/
Biografie

Born 1978 in Glasgow, Scotland
Lives and works in Glasgow, Scotland

Education
1996–2000
BA (Hons) Fine Art Duncan of
Jordanstone College of Art, Dundee

Selected Solo Exhibitions
2009
Serpentine Gallery, London
2008
Kunsthalle Zürich, Zurich
2007
Extra City – centrum voor hedendaagse
kunst, Antwerp
Esther Schipper REC Projektraum, Berlin
2006
The Nine Monads of David Bell, Villa
Concordia, Bamberg
Pilgrimage from Scattered Points,
White Columns, New York
Pilgrimage from Scattered Points,
The Modern Institute/Toby Webster Ltd,
Glasgow
2004
Fowler/Koper, Supportico Lopez, Naples
Video and Sound Works, TART, San
Francisco
2003
*Jakob Kolding, Luke Fowler/Kosten
Koper*, Cubitt Gallery, London
What You See Is Where You're At,
Spacex, Exeter
2001
UTO: The Technology of Tears, Casco
Project Space, Utrecht
2000
How Did You Get This Number?,
Generator Projects, Dundee
The Social Engineer, Transmission
Gallery, Glasgow

**Selected Group Exhibitions
and Screenings**
2009
Younger than Jesus, New Museum,
New York
The Associates, DCA – Dundee
Contemporary Arts, Dundee
Cornelius Cardew, CAC Brétigny –
Centre d'art contemporain de Brétigny,
Brétigny-sur-Orge
2008
Open Field, CCA – The Centre for
Contemporary Arts, Glasgow
Expanded Cinema for Rothko,
Tate Modern, London
Charles H. Scott Gallery, Emily Carr
University, Vancouver
KYTN, DCA – Dundee Contemporary
Arts, Dundee
Yokohama Triennale 2008, Yokohama
Scottish Shorts Showcase, Edinburgh
Film Festival, Edinburgh
*KVIFF – Karlovy Vary International Film
Festival*, Prague International
Film Festival, Prague

Pilgrimage from Scattered Points,
Milton Keynes Gallery, Milton Keynes
Three Blows, St Celia Hall, Edinburgh
Sónar 2008, Barcelona
The Long Weekend, Tate Modern, London
The Harbour Doubts, Bad Bad Boys
Club, Dundee
*Now Showing. New Film and Video
from The Arts Council Collection*, Hove
Museum and Art Gallery, Hove
Present, H.P. Garcia Gallery, New York
Courtisane Festival, Arts Centre Vooruit
& Sphinx Cinema, Ghent
Pop! goes the weasel, Badischer
Kunstverein, Karlsruhe
International Film Festival Rotterdam,
Rotterdam
Permanent vs. Temporary, Abbeyview
Community Centre, Dunfermline
Bogman Palmjaguar, Transmission
Gallery, Glasgow
2007
a passable door for a movable passer,
52 Buccleuch Street, Glasgow
Videomedeja 2007, Museum of Voivodina,
Novi Sad
EASTinternational 2007, Norwich
Gallery, Norwich School of Art & Design,
Norwich
REC.OLLECTION, Esther Schipper, Berlin
Organizing Chaos, P.S.1 Contemporary
Art Center, Long Island
You Have Not Been Honest, Museo
d'Arte Contemporanea Donnaregina,
Naples
Prague Biennale 3, Prague
Lost & Found, Shedhalle, Zurich
Harry Smith Anthology Remixed, Alt.
Gallery, Newcastle
Saturn Falling, Corridor Gallery,
Reykjavik
Whenever It Starts It Is The Right Time,
Frankfurter Kunstverein, Frankfurt
am Main
*Fantastic Politics. Art in Time of
Political Crisis*, Museum of
Contemporary Art, Oslo
Widening Horizon, Pleasure Dome,
Toronto
*Never Still. Map Magazine presents
new artists' film*, CCA – The Centre
for Contemporary Arts, Glasgow
Twilight Adventures in Music,
Whitechapel Art Gallery, London
2006
Normalisering, Rooseum Centre
for Contemporary Art, Malmö
Tate Triennial. New British Art,
Tate Britain, London
*Huddersfield Contemporary Music
Festival*, Huddersfield
Avanto Festival, Muu Galleria, Helsinki
Adventures in Modern Music, The
Gene Siskel Film Center, Chicago
*State of Innocence. International Film
Festival Rotterdam*, Rotterdam
2005
Beck's Futures (nominee), ICA –
Institute of Contemporary Arts, London;
CCA – The Centre for Contemporary
Arts, Glasgow
Anti-Literature, Barcelona
Re-Escape, Hamburg
2004
Moderna by night, Moderna Museet,
Stockholm
Past Imperfect, Casco Projects, Utrecht
Vis-onic, Belfast/Derry International
A/V festival, Belfast
Anti-Psychiatry Film Festival, Nova
Cinema, Brussels

2003
Be Dear Crazy Loud (Performance
by Fowler, P6, Sue Tompkins), Flourish
Nights, Glasgow
The Moment of Fiction, Cooper Gallery,
Dundee
Attachments, Bootlab, Berlin
*ZENOMAP – New Works from Scotland
for the Venice Biennale*, 50. Biennale
di Venezia, Venice
Electric Earth (British Council touring
exhibition), State Russian Museum,
St Petersburg; Radio Laboratory
Museum, Nizhni Novgorod; Yaroslavl
Museum of Fine Art, Yaroslav; Na
Solyanke Gallery, Moscow et al.
Hard to Touch the Real, Kunstverein
München, Munich
Art Remixing Culture, Govett-Brewster
Gallery, New Plymouth
*It doesn't matter what you know
because this is real life*, Gavin Brown's
enterprise, New York
Art/34/Basel, Basel
2002
Art is like Rock'n'Roll…, Kent Institute
of Art & Design, Rochester
40 Jahre: Fluxus und die Folgen.
Internationales Netzwerk, Wiesbaden
Manifesta 4, Frankfurt am Main
FAIR, Royal College of Art, London
2000
Cinilingus, Catalyst Arts, Belfast
Rencontres Video, Annecy
Beyond, Main Gallery, DCA – Dundee
Contemporary Arts, Dundee
Me We, Project Space, Athens

Curated Projects
2007
I Seek You, S1 Artspace, Sheffield
2005
Le Weekend Festival (with Rude Pravo),
Stirling
L'ombre Hyperbole, Project Rooms,
Glasgow
2003
Outsider Documentary (curated with
D. Campbell), Frankfurter Kunstverein,
Frankfurt am Main
2002
METALLIC KO, NIFCA – Nordic Institute
for Contemporary Art, Helsinki
2001
Electric City, The Lighthouse, Glasgow
2000
Lecture and performance by Scanner,
Transmission, 13th Note Club, Glasgow
1999
Accelerated Learning, Duncan of
Jordanstone College of Art, Dundee

Publications, Editions, Recordings
2005
*SHADAZZ 06 – Danny Saunders,
Gold* (7" Vinyl)
*SHADAZZ 05 – Rude Pravo, The Dust
is Flying* (7" Vinyl)
Remixed Water (CD, with Daniel Padden),
Lawrence Weiner Bookworks project
2004
*Shorn off his nipples he dances like
a King* (CD, with Ergo Phizmiz; Alex
Neilson)
2002
Gemeinschaften (with Finger),
Newsletter for Contemporary Cultural
Phenomena
SHADAZZ 04 – Evil Eye Is Source (VHS,
compilation with artists and bands)

2001
SHADAZZ 03 – Insert for Casco Issues,
Holland (artists' project and CD)
*SHADAZZ 02 – The Invisible Insurrection
of a Million Minds* (CD)
2000
*SHADAZZ 01 – The Scottish Demo
Collective* (fanzine and CD)

Residencies
2008
Grierson Archive, Stirling
2006–2007
Internationales Künstlerhaus Villa
Concordia, Bamberg
2005
Kenchington/Gilbert Scott, Balfron
2002
NIFCA – Nordic Institute for
Contemporary Art, Helsinki
1999
Hogschule fur de Kunst, Utrecht

Awards
2008
Derek Jarman Award, London
2004
Deward Arts Awards, Kirkcudbright

Colophon/ Impressum

This publication is released on the occasion of the exhibitions
Luke Fowler, Kunsthalle Zürich, 30 August–2 November 2008
Luke Fowler, Serpentine Gallery, 7 May–14 June 2009

Exhibitions

Kunsthalle Zürich
Limmatstrasse 270
CH–8005 Zürich
T +41 (0)44 272 15 15
F +41 (0)44 272 18 88
www.kunsthallezurich.ch

Beatrix Ruf: Director and Curator
Sylvie Ledermann: Personal Assistant/ Secretariat
Rahel Blättler: Assistant Curator/ Guided Tours
Katharina Pilz: Assistant Curator/ Guided Tours
Susanne Stortz: Press/Members/ Sponsors
Alfonso Negri: Website/IT/Graphics
Attila Panczel, Silvan Goette, Rachel Honsinger, Hans Heinrich Schwendener, Oliver Stäudlin, Julia Weber, Nina Weber: Technical Team
Alexandra Hermann, Nadine Hofer, Joya Indermühle, Konstantinos Manolakis, Siri Peyer, Isabelle Zürcher: Cashiers
Marina Bräm, Nadja Crola, Evelyne Derron, Livia Di Giovanna, Christoph Eisenring, Alessandro Ganser, Ruedi Lüthi, Rahel Neuenschwander, Raphael Zürcher: Supervisory Staff

Serpentine Gallery
Kensington Gardens
UK–London W2 3XA
T +44 (0)20 7402 6075
F +44 (0)20 7402 4103
www.serpentinegallery.com

Julia Peyton-Jones: Director, Serpentine Gallery, and Co-Director, Exhibitions & Programmes
Hans Ulrich Obrist: Co-Director of Exhibitions & Programmes and Director, International Projects
Cherie Fullerton: Personal Assistant to Julia Peyton-Jones
Alexandra Henderson: Personal Assistant
Lorraine Two: Personal Assistant to Hans Ulrich Obrist

Kathryn Rattee: Exhibition Curator
Sophie O'Brien: Exhibition Curator
Mike Gaughan: Gallery Manager
Leila Hasham: Exhibitions Assistant

Sally Tallant: Head of Programmes
Nicola Lees: Public Programmes Curator
Janna Graham: Education Project Organiser
Eleanor Farrington: Education Organiser

Rose Dempsey: Head of Press
Fleur Treglown: Senior Press Manager
Varind Ramful: Press Assistant

Louise McKinney: Head of Development
Alexandra Bitterlin: Head of Individual Giving
Darryl de Prez: Head of Grants
Naomi Waite: Head of Corporate Development
Kate Davey: Events Manager
Jo Langer: Events Administrator
Ricki Worth: Development Co-ordinator
Rachel Stephens: Membership Secretary
Deborah Bullen: Prints Manager
Matt Johnstone: Prints Assistant

Julie Winfield: Head of Buildings
Sarah Carroll: Duty Manager
Mark Songui: Duty Manager
Richard Kendall-Tobias: Designated Premises Supervisor
John Stokes: Facilities Assistant

Julie Burnell: Head of Projects

Louise Robson: Head of Finance
Julie Fitzjohn: Financial Controller
Nina Yao: Senior Finance Officer
Unnati Patel: Finance Officer

Rachel Seghers: HR Manager
Elizabeth Clayton: HR Administrator

Victoria Burns, Joshua Dowson, Victoria Grosch, Jack Hardwick, Susan Holtham, Rob Nicol, Anne Parkes, Rajesh Punj, Hannah Rowe, Hannah Rumball, Rene Songui, Mary Toal, Gemma Walker, George Williams, Duncan Wooldridge: Gallery Assistants

Publication

Editors: Beatrix Ruf, Julia Peyton-Jones, Hans Ulrich Obrist
Editorial Coordination: Rahel Blättler, Salome Schnetz
Copyediting: Rahel Blättler, Melissa Larner, Sophie O'Brien
Proofreading: Rahel Blättler, Sophie O'Brien, Katharina Pilz, Salome Schnetz
Translations (English–German):
Gudrun Meier (Introduction, Interview), Ralf Schauff (Will Bradley), Kunsthalle Zürich (Filmography)
Graphic Design: Gavillet & Rust/Eigenheer, Geneva
Colour separation and Print: Musumeci S.p.A., Quart (Aosta)

Dustjacket: Luke Fowler and Tsunoda Toshiya, *Composition for Flutter Screen*, 2008, Film strip

Flyleaves: *The Nine Monads of David Bell*, 2007, Archived Newspaper, 37 × 55 cm, Courtesy The Modern Institute/ Toby Webster Ltd and Dr Leon Redler

All works courtesy the artist and The Modern Institute/Toby Webster Ltd

Photo Credits:
Alan Dimmick (p. 67, 96); Carsten Eisfeld (p. 49); Robert Johnston (cover, p. 40–43, 45–47, 50–55, 58–61, 64–65); Donald Nisbet (flyleaves); Kathy Nobie (p. 66); Veno Norihiro (p. 62–63); Mike Sperlinger, LUX (p. 35–39); all other photos by Luke Fowler.

Acknowledgments

Richard Adams, Kitty Anderson, Arika (Barry + Bryony), Nicola Atkinson Davidson, Ute Aurand, Lepke B, Ed Baxter, Robert Beavers, Boris Belay, Rahel Blättler, Hanne Boenisch, Lionel Bovier, Will Bradley, Katrina Brown, Barry Burns, Steven Cairns, Duncan Campbell, Cardew Estate, Edwin Carels, Channel 4, Stuart Comer, Charles Curtis, Rhodri Davies, Lucile Desamoray & Nicholas Bussmann, Derek Jarman Award, Dewer Award, Alan Dimmick, Diskono, Katy Dove, Film London, Fowler Family, Dan Fox, Anselme Franke, Mike Gaughan, Silvan Goette, Leila Hasham, Daniel Henry, Alexandra Hermann, Mathew Higgs, Alec Hill, Nadine Hofer, Rachel Honsinger, Kevin Hutcheson, Joya Indermühle, Robert Johnson, Stephen Jones & Jill Wilson, Xentos Jones, Isaac Julien, Rob Kennedy, Toshiyuki Kobayashi, Alice Koegel, Jakob Kolding, Kosten Koper, Tomas Korber, Adrian Laing, Sylvie Ledermann, London Musicians Collective, Sarah Lowndes, Kirsteen MacDonald, Stuart MacGregor, Stuart MacRae, Gregor Marks, Duncan Marquiss, Chus Martinez, Konstantinos Manolakis, Neil McDonald, Russell McEwan, Francis McKee, Anna McLauchlan, Kenny McLeod, Robert Meijer, Metamkine, Donald MNS, Stéphanie Moisdon, Dylan Morrissey, Scott Myles, Alfonso Negri, No.w.here lab, Sophie O'Brien, Daniel Padden, Bogman Bluequartz Palmjaguar, Attila Panczel, John Pattenden-Fail, Lee Patterson, Emily Pethick, Siri Peyer, Katharina Pilz, William Raban, Leon Redler, Kath Roper-Caldbeck, Keith Rowe, Jim Rusk, Sarah and Bel, Danny Saunders, Salome Schnetz, Hans Heinrich Schwendener, Ben Scott, Scottish Arts Council, Dave and Laura Sherry, Lisette Smits, Oliver Stäudlin, Polly Staple, Katherine Stewart, Susanne Stortz, Zoe Strachan, Superflex, Stephen Sutcliffe, Corin Sworn, Peter Taylor, The Lux - Ben Cook & Mike Sperlinger, The Modern Institute/Toby Webster Ltd, Len Thornton, John Tilbury, Peter Todd, Torsten and Cathy, Transmission Gallery, Toshiya Tsunoda, Ultra Eczema, Taku Unami, Mark Vernon, Vitamin B12, Andrew Wake, Mark Webber, Toby Webster, Louise Welsh, Ian White, Worm Filmwerkplaats, Jan Younghusband, Richard Youngs, Isabelle Zürcher, Michael Zyrd

Kunsthalle Zürich would like to thank for their continuous support:

Präsidialdepartement der Stadt Zürich
Swiss Re

Special thanks to
LUMA Foundation for generous support of the exhibition and catalogue.

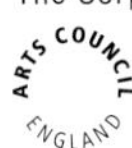

The Serpentine Gallery is supported by

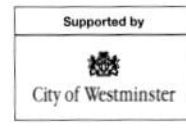

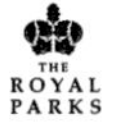

And a very special thanks to Luke Fowler.

Published by:
JRP|Ringier
Letzigraben 134
CH–8047 Zurich
T +41 (0) 43 311 27 50
F +41 (0) 43 311 27 51
E info@jrp-ringier.com
www.jrp-ringier.com

ISBN 978-3-03764-046-3

JRP|Ringier books are available internationally at selected bookstores and from the following distribution partners:

Switzerland
Buch 2000, AVA Verlagsauslieferung AG, Centralweg 16, CH–8910 Affoltern a.A., buch2000@ava.ch, www.ava.ch

France
Les Presses du réel, 35 rue Colson, F–21000 Dijon, info@lespressesdureel.com, www.lespressesdureel.com

Germany and Austria
Vice Versa Vertrieb, Immanuelkirchstrasse 12, D–10405 Berlin, info@vice-versa-vertrieb.de, www.vice-versa-vertrieb.de

UK and other European countries
Cornerhouse Publications, 70 Oxford Street, UK–Manchester M1 5NH, publications@cornerhouse.org, www.cornerhouse.org/books

USA, Canada, Asia, and Australia
D.A.P./Distributed Art Publishers, 155 Sixth Avenue, 2nd Floor, USA–New York, NY 10013, dap@dapinc.com, www.artbook.com

For a list of our partner bookshops or for any general questions, please contact JRP|Ringier directly at info@jrp-ringier.com, or visit our homepage www.jrp-ringier.com for further information about our program.

Jack Kirkland
Marina Kissam
Katherine Knox and James Harvey
Niels Kroner
Alexa Jeanne Kusber
Georgina and Alastair Laing
Mans Larsson
Mr Edouard Lecieux
Jason Lee
Arianne Levene
James Lindon
Angus Maguire
Marina Marini
Jose Mazoy
Anne Mellentin
Fernando J. Moncho Lobo
Sheryl Needham
Isabelle Nowak and Torsten Winkler
David Olsson
Karim Palmieri
Samira Parkinson-Smith
Julia Pincus
Andrew Pirrie
Harry Plotnick
Robert Ramsauer
Laurent Rappaport
Piotr Rejmer
Rebecca Richwhite
David Risley
Nick Rose
Christophe Rust
Melanie Salmon
Xandi Schemann
Lea and Peter Schwartz
Alyssa Sherman
Sudhanshu Swaroop
Mieka Sywak
Christopher Thomsen
Jérémie Vaislic
Sam Waley-Cohen
Lauren Weinberg
Hailey Widrig-Ritcheson
Lucy Wood
Edward Wyckoff Williams
Nabil N. Zaouk
Fabrizio D. Zappaterra

Benefactors
Shane Akeroyd
Max Alexander and Anna Bateson
Mr Niklas Antman and Miss Lisa Almen
Paul and Kia Armstrong
Jane Attias
Laurie Benson
Anne Best and Roddy Kinkead-Weekes
Roger and Beverley Bevan
David and Janice Blackburn
Anthony and Gisela Bloom
Mr and Mrs John Botts
Marcus Boyle
Vanessa Branson
Michael and Pauline Brennan
Nick and Paulette Brittain
Benjamin Brown
Ossi and Paul Burger
Lavinia Calza Beveridge
Jonathan and Vanessa Cameron
Andrew Cecil
Azia Chatila
Sadie Coles
Carole and Neville Conrad
Matthew Conrad
Alexander Corcoran
Gul Coskun
Yasmine Datnow
Helen and Colin David
Christopher and Caroline Didizian
Robin and Noelle Doumar
Jessica Dunne and Brian Reshefsky
Mike Fairbrass
David Fawkes

Mr and Mrs Mark Fenwick
John Ferreira
Ruth Finch
David and Jane Fletcher
Eric and Louise Franck
Honor Fraser
Zak and Candida Gertler
Leonardo and Alessia Giangreco
Hugh Gibson
David Gill
Barbara Gladstone
Rami Goldstein
Dimitri J. Goulandris
Richard and Judith Greer
Linda and Richard Grosse
Ellie Guy
Louise Hallett
Caroline Hansberry
Susan Harris
Timothy and Daška Hatton
Maria and Stratis Hatzistefanis
Alison Henry
Michael and Sarah Hewett
Mrs Samantha Heyworth
Mrs Martha Hummer-Bradley
Diane Ipkendanz
Iraj and Eva Ispahani
Mrs Christine Johnston
Jennifer Kersis
Malcolm King
Mickey and Jean Klein
Herbert and Sybil Kretzmer
Mr and Mrs Lahoud
Barbara Lloyd and Judy Collins
George and Angie Loudon
Sotiris T.F. Lyritzis
Mr Otto Julius Maier and Mrs Michèle
Claudel-Maier
Cary J. Martin
Cat Martin
Mr and Mrs Stephen Mather
Guy and Ruth Maxted
Viviane and James Mayor
Warren and Victoria Miro
Gillian Mosely
Dr Maigaello Moulene
Angela Nikolakopoulou
Georgia Oetker
Tamiko Onozawa
Desmond Page and Asun Gelardin
Maureen Paley
Dominic Palfreyman
Midge and Simon Palley
Andrew and Jane Partridge
George and Carolyn Pincus
Jonathan Pascoe Pratt
Julia Peyton-Jones OBE
Lauren Papadopoulos Prakke
Victoria Preston
Sophie Price
Mathew Prichard
Mrs Janaki Prosdocimi
Ashraf Qizilbash
Stephan C. Reinke
Bruce and Shadi Ritchie
Kasia Robinski
Kimberley Robson-Ortiz Foundation
Jacqueline and Nicholas Roe
Victoria, Lady de Rothschild
James Roundell and Bona Montagu
Michael and Julia Samuel
Ronnie and Vidal Sassoon
Joana and Henrik Schliemann
Mr and Mrs Mark Shanker
Nick Simou and Julie Gatland
Mr and Mrs Jean-Marc Spitalier
J. Sucharewicz
Simone and Robert Suss
Emma Tennant and Tim Owens
The Thames Wharf Charity
Britt Tidelius

Gretchen and Jus Trusted
Emily Tsingou
J.P. Ujobai
Ashley and Lisa Unwin
Hako and Dorte Graf von Finckenstein
Bina and Philippe von Stauffenberg
Christian and Sarah von Thun-
Hohenstein
Audrey Wallrock
Offer Waterman
Daniel and Cecilia Weiner
Laura Weinstock
Lady Corrine Wellesley
Alannah Weston
Helen Ytuarte White
Dr Yvonne Winkler
Mr Ulf Wissen
Mr and Mrs M. Wolridge
Henry and Rachel Wyndham
Mr and Mrs Nabil Zaouk
Andrzej and Jill Zarzycki

And Patrons, Future Contemporaries
and Benefactors who wish to remain
anonymous

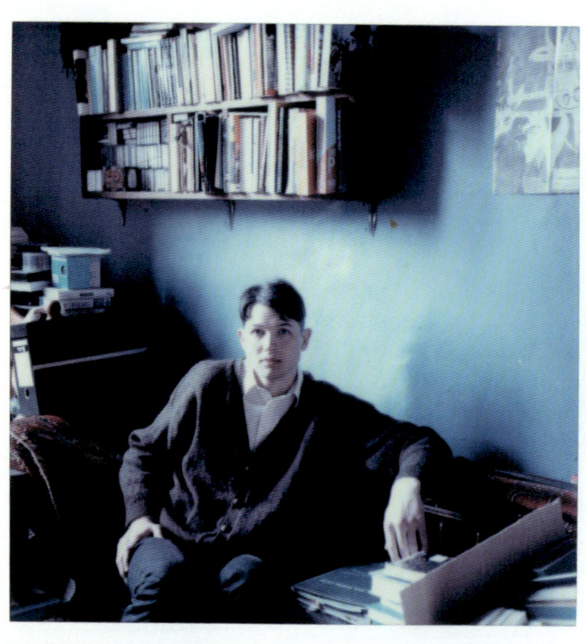

London schools' banding system may be illegal

By ALISON TRUEFITT

FEARS that London's system of selecting children for grammar and other secondary schools may have to be dropped because it could be illegal, are being urgently discussed by officials of the Inner London Education Authority.

After taking legal advice, they are worried that the new Bill, introduced by Education Secretary of State, Mr. Edward Short, to end "the selection of pupils for admission to secondary schools by reference to ability or aptitude," may mean that the elaborate system of "banding" used in London since 1965 may have to be dropped.

A letter is in the post today from London's Chief Education Officer, Sir William Houghton, asking for clarification on the wording of the Bill from the Department of Education's Permanent Secretary, Sir Herbert Andrew.

But until the Bill becomes law —in May, if the Secretary of State has his way—officials at the Department are saying they cannot give a final answer on its implications for London.

Graded

At present the 33,500 11-year-olds who transfer each year from primary to secondary school are graded according to a seven-point scale.

Head teachers can estimate a child's level without a test, but most prefer to use a specially prepared verbal reasoning test like the old IQ test. The children also take tests in English and arithmetic.

About 17 per cent of the children are chosen for grammar schools—of which there are 65 out of a total of 223 secondary schools in the Inner London area.

Children who don't get grammar school places are then allocated to other schools so that each school has a fair spread of bright, average and slow children.

Although this sometimes means that the school parents have given as their first choice has no more vacancies in the ability "band" of their child, 87 per cent of parents do get the school of their first choice.

If this system had to be dropped it is hard to see how the ILEA could find a way of selecting the top 17 per cent of bright children for its grammar schools which would be legal.

Reputation

Another area of London which could also be affected by the new law is Haringey—where the proposal to introduce a form of banding led to accusations of racism and riots in the council chamber.

The Haringey system—now approved by the council—is for children to be allocated to the borough's 12 comprehensive schools according to the reputation of their primary schools.

Tests on pupils who left the previous year will be used to show the "usual" range of ability in each primary school.

"We just will not know until the Bill becomes an Act whether or not/our scheme is legal," said Mr. Gerald Murphy, chairman of Haringey Education Committee.

It is understood that the Bill, which had its second reading last Thursday, was not specifically designed to outlaw the London banding systems. But they are nevertheless outside the spirit of comprehensive education as understood by Government leaders, and revisions of the Bill at the committee stage may make more explicit rulings against banding.

Mass teachers' strike begins

BIRMINGHAM'S 500 State schools will be paralysed today when nearly 5000 members of the National Union of Teachers go on strike indefinitely in support of the teachers' pay claim.

More than 300 schools will definitely be closed and it is expected that many more will be forced to take the same decision when headteachers assess the staff position. The strike is expected to affect more than 150,000 children.

Indefinite strikes will start in two London areas next week —at Waltham Forest on Monday and at Southwark next Wednesday.

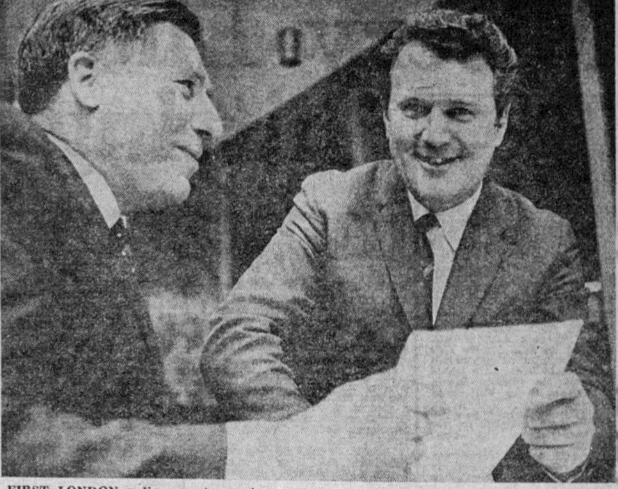

FIRST LONDON policeman to receive a Bar to his British Empire Medal is Det.-sgt. Patrick Gibbins (right), 39, of Upminster, Essex. Here he receives his award from Commander Roy Yorke, Co-ordinator of the Regional Crime Squad at New Scotland Yard.

Sergeant Gibbins, married with an 11-year-old son, received the BEM for his single-handed arrest in 1965 of escaped prisoner Walter "Angel Face" Probyn, who fired three shots at him.

The Bar comes for his cornering of two armed men who struck him with an iron bar. He led the chase for them in spite of his injuries.

Super-rats are now on the march!

By MICHAEL JEFFRIES

WATCH OUT! Super-rats and super-mice—normal-sized rodents resistant to poisons — are on the march.

A Ministry of Agriculture expert warned a meeting of the Royal Society of Health in London today that new and effective poisons were needed urgently to control them.

Dr. E. W. Bentley, of the Ministry's Infestation Control Laboratory, said that rats and mice in Britain were now becoming resistant to present control compounds, particularly Warfarin.

Resistance to compounds of this type had spread across the country at the rate of three miles a year since first reported 10 years ago.

Dr. Bentley said the main areas of resistant rats were in Montgomeryshire, Shropshire, a small part of Radnorshire, and was roughly centred on Welshpool.

The battle was now on to keep one jump ahead of the animals by finding new rodent poisons, he said.

But we must also find out why they were harder to kill and how the resistance spread in Britain.

Four years ago the spread had been stemmed with an intensive control plan and new methods. But although it slowed up their march towards urban areas of the West Midlands it was now losing its effectiveness.

Interruption of the plan by the last foot-and-mouth epidemic, and lack of co-operation from farmers who were over-using Warfarin, might have caused this, he said.

Mr. A. C. Saword, chief public health inspector at Hull, alerted the meeting to the dangers of bad workmanship in house drainage.

He said that, if a careless joint was made between house soil pipe and drain, rats could find their way into cavity walls, under bedroom floors and in the roof spaces of homes.

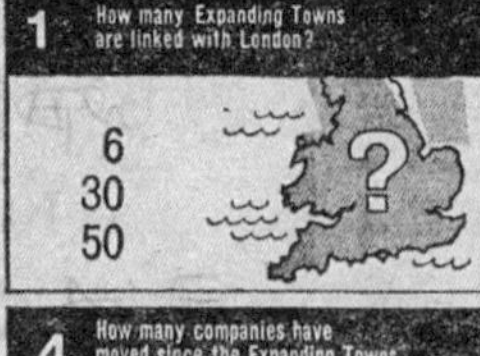

Join the INSTANT TEACH-IN on Expanding Towns

How much do you know?

1 How many Expanding Towns are linked with London?
6
30
50

2 Factory floor rents in the Expanding Towns start at around
7/3
9/9
14/6 per sq. ft.

3 Most Expanding Towns are within
50 miles
100 miles
200 miles
of London

4 How many companies have moved since the Expanding Towns scheme started? Over
40
250
500

5 When a company decides to move to an Expanding Town, how many of its workers move with it?
20%
40%
60%

6 Most Expanding Towns are well served by transport facilities
True
False

7 How many London families want homes or jobs in an Expanding Town?
3,000 20,000
50,000

8 Homes for workers moved to Expanding Towns are normally ready for occupation:
a. After a period of a year.
b. After a period depending on the local lists.
c. Immediately.

9 The lowest rent of an acre of land for industrial development in the Expanding Towns is roughly
£ 360
£ 760
£1300 p.a.

10 Which of these 3 things will you get through the Industrial Centre
a. A site.
b. Homes for your staff.
c. Help in finding additional staff.

Answers

1. There are 30 Expanding Towns linked with London.
2. Floor rents start at 7/3 per sq. ft.
3. Most of the Expanding Towns are within 100 miles of London.
4. To date, 512 companies have moved out of London.
5. On average 40% of a firm's labour force tends to move with it to an Expanding Town.
6. True.
7. Over 50,000 families have asked to move out of London.
8. Homes for workers moving to the Expanding Towns are usually available immediately.
9. Land rents in the Expanding Towns start at around £360 per acre, per year.
10. You'll get practical help for all these problems by contacting the Industrial Centre.

If you'd like to find out more about the Expanding Towns and what they can do for your business, just fill in the coupon and post it off to:

The Industrial Centre, County Hall, London, S.E.1, or phone: 01-633 5000 Extension 749. or 7595 in strict confidence.

Name ....
Position ....
Company Name ....
Company Address ....
ES12

Expanding Towns

GREATER LONDON COUNCIL